FORM C
EIGHTH EDITION

The Least You

Should Know about

English

Writing Skills

Paige Wilson

Pasadena City College

Teresa Ferster Glazier

THOMSON

WADSWORTH

Australia   Canada   Mexico   Singapore   Spain   United Kingdom   United States

THOMSON
™
WADSWORTH

The Least You Should Know about English, Form C, Eighth Edition
Writing Skills
Paige Wilson and Theresa Ferster Glazier

Publisher: *Michael Rosenberg*
Acquisitions Editor: *Stephen Dalphin*
Associate Production Project Manager:
  Karen Stocz
Marketing Manager: *Carrie Brandon*

Associate Marketing Manager: *Joe Piazza*
Senior Print Buyer: *Mary Beth Hennebury*
Compositor/Project Manager: *Argosy Publishing*
Cover Designer: *Dutton and Sherman Design*
Printer: *Phoenix Color Corp.*

Printed in the United States of America
2 3 4 5 6 7 8 9 10   09 08 07 06 05 04

For more information contact Thomson Wadsworth, 25 Thomson Place, Boston, MA 02210 USA,
or you can visit our Internet site at http://www.wadsworth.com

Library of Congress Control Number: 2004104215
ISBN: 1-4130-0253-6

This book is for students who need to review basic English skills and who may profit from a simplified "least you should know" approach. Parts 1 to 3 cover the essentials of word choice and spelling, sentence structure, punctuation, and capitalization. Part 4 on writing teaches students the basic structures of the paragraph and the essay, along with the writing skills necessary to produce them.

Throughout the book, we try to avoid the use of linguistic terminology whenever possible. Students work with words they know instead of learning a vocabulary they may never use again.

There are abundant exercises, including practice with writing sentences and proofreading paragraphs—enough so that students learn to use the rules automatically and *thus carry their new skills over into their writing.* Exercises consist of sets of ten thematically related, informative sentences on such subjects as the first cloned horse, hairless bears, and superstitions about brooms. Such exercises reinforce the need for coherence and details in student writing. With answers provided at the back of the book, students can correct their own work and progress at their own pace.

For the eighth edition, we have added a section on parts of speech to Part 1 and have continued to enhance Part 4 on writing. Part 4 introduces students to the writing process and stresses the development of the student's written "voice." Writing assignments follow each discussion, and there are samples by both student and professional writers. Part 4 ends with a section designed to help students with writing assignments based on readings. It includes articles to read, react to, and summarize. Students improve their reading by learning to spot main ideas and their writing by learning to write meaningful reactions and concise summaries.

The Least You Should Know about English functions equally well in the classroom and at home as a self-tutoring text. The simple explanations, ample exercises, and answers at the back of the book provide students with everything they need to progress on their own. Students who have previously been overwhelmed by the complexities of English should, through mastering simple rules and through writing and rewriting simple papers, gain enough competence to succeed in further composition courses.

For their thoughtful commentary on the book, we would like to thank the following reviewers: Brenda Freaney, *Bakersfield College*; Ann George, *Northwestern Michigan College*; Bronwyn Jones, *Northwestern Michigan College*; Kaye Kolkmann, *Modesto Junior College*; Rosella Miller, *North Idaho College*; Carol Miter, *Riverside Community College*; Brigid Murphy, *Pima Community College*; Barbara Perry, *Northwest Indian College*; and Jane Wilson, *Modesto Junior College*.

For their specific contributions to Form C, we extend our gratitude to the following student writers: Brett Atkins, Eric Coffey, Amanda K. Gomez, Linda Lam, and Sherika McPeters.

In addition, we would like to thank our publishing team for their expertise and hard work: Stephen Dalphin, Acquisitions Editor; Karen Stocz, Associate Production Project Manager; and Kevin Sullivan, Project Manager.

As always, we are indebted to Herb and Moss Rabbin, Kenneth Glazier, and the rest of our families and friends for their support and encouragement.

Paige Wilson and Teresa Ferster Glazier

As in all previous editions, **Form C** differs from **Forms A and B** in its exercises, writing samples, and assignments; however, the explanatory sections are the same.

A **Test Packet** with additional exercises and ready-to-photocopy tests accompanies this text and is available to instructors.

Contents

What Is the Least You Should Know?   1

What Is the Least You Should Know?

Most English textbooks try to teach you more than you need to know. This book will teach you the least you should know—and still help you learn to write clearly and acceptably. You won't have to deal with grammatical terms like *gerund, modal auxiliary verb,* or *demonstrative pronoun.* You can get along without knowing such technical labels if you learn a few key concepts. You *should* know about the parts of speech and how to use and spell common words; you *should* be able to recognize subjects and verbs; you *should* know the basics of sentence structure and punctuation— but rules, as such, will be kept to a minimum.

The English you'll learn in this book is sometimes called Standard Written English, and it may differ slightly or greatly from the spoken English you use. Standard Written English is the form of writing accepted in business and the professions. So no matter how you speak, you will communicate better in writing when you use Standard Written English. You might *say* something like "That's a whole nother problem," and everyone will understand, but you would probably want to *write,* "That's a completely different problem." Knowing the difference between spoken English and Standard Written English is essential in college, in business, and in life.

Until you learn the least you should know, you'll probably have difficulty communicating in writing. Take this sentence for example:

Since I easily past my driving test, I deserve a car of my own.

We assume that the writer used the *sound,* not the meaning, of the word *past* to choose it and in so doing used the wrong word. If the sentence had read

Since I easily *passed* my driving test, I deserve a car of my own.

then the writer would have communicated clearly. Or take this sentence:

The boss fired John and Jeanine and I got a promotion.

This sentence includes two statements and therefore needs punctuation, a comma in this case:

The boss fired John, and Jeanine and I got a promotion.

But perhaps the writer meant

The boss fired John and Jeanine, and I got a promotion.

Punctuation makes all the difference, especially for Jeanine. With the help of this text, we hope you'll learn to make your writing so clear that no one will misunderstand it.

As you make your way through the book, it's important to remember information after you learn it because many concepts and structures build upon others. For example, once you can identify subjects and verbs, you'll be able to recognize fragments, understand subject-verb agreement, and use correct punctuation. Explanations and examples are brief and clear, and it shouldn't be difficult to learn from them—*if you want to.* But you have to want to!

How to Learn the Least You Should Know

1. Read each explanatory section carefully (aloud, if possible).

2. Do the first exercise. Compare your answers with those at the back of the book. If they don't match, study the explanation again to find out why.

3. Do the second exercise and correct it. If you miss a single answer, go back once more to the explanation. You must have missed something. Be tough on yourself. Don't just think, "Maybe I'll get it right next time." Reread the examples, and *then* try the next exercise. It's important to correct each group of ten sentences before moving on so that you'll discover your mistakes early.

4. You may be tempted to quit after you do one or two exercises perfectly. Instead, make yourself finish another exercise. It's not enough to *understand* a concept or structure. You have to *practice* using it.

5. If you're positive, however, after doing several exercises, that you've learned a concept or structure, take the next exercise as a test. If you miss even one answer, you should do all the rest of the questions. Then move on to the proofreading and sentence-composing exercises so that your understanding carries over into your writing.

Learning the basics of word choice and spelling, sentence structure, and punctuation does take time. Generally, college students spend a couple of hours outside of class for each hour in class. You may need more. Undoubtedly, the more time you spend, the more your writing will improve.

PART 1

Word Choice and Spelling

Anyone can learn to use words more effectively and become a better speller. You can eliminate most of your word choice and spelling errors if you want to. It's just a matter of deciding you're going to do it. If you really intend to improve your word choice and spelling, study each of the following eight sections until you make no mistakes in the exercises.

Your Own List of Misspelled Words
Words Often Confused (Sets 1 and 2)
The Eight Parts of Speech
Contractions
Possessives
Words That Can Be Broken into Parts
Rule for Doubling a Final Letter
Using a Dictionary

Your Own List of Misspelled Words

On the inside cover of your English notebook or in some other obvious place, write correctly all the misspelled words from your previously graded papers. Review the correct spellings until you're sure of them, and edit your papers to find and correct repeated errors.

Words Often Confused (Set 1)

Learning the differences between these often-confused words will help you over-come many of your spelling problems. Study the words carefully, with their examples, before trying the exercises.

a, an

Use *an* before a word that begins with a vowel *sound* (*a, e, i,* and *o,* plus *u* when it sounds like *uh*) or silent *h*. Note that it's not the letter but the *sound* of the letter that matters.

an apple, *an* essay, *an* inch, *an* onion

an umpire, *an* ugly design (The *u*'s sound like *uh*.)

an hour, *an* honest person (The *h*'s are silent.)

Use *a* before a word that begins with a consonant sound (all the sounds except the vowels, plus *u* or *eu* when they sound like *you*).

a chart, *a* pie, *a* history book (The *h* is not silent in *history*.)

a union, *a* uniform, *a* unit (The *u*'s sound like *you*.)

a European vacation, *a* euphemism (*Eu* sounds like *you*.)

accept, except

Accept means "to receive willingly."

I *accept* your apology.

Except means "excluding" or "but."

Everyone arrived on time *except* him.

advise, advice

Advise is a verb. (The *s* sounds like a *z*.)

I *advise* you to take your time finding the right job.

Advice is a noun. (It rhymes with *rice*.)

My counselor gave me good *advice*.

affect, effect

Affect is a verb and means "to alter or influence."

All quizzes will *affect* the final grade.

The happy ending *affected* the mood of the audience.

Effect is most commonly used as a noun and means "a result." If *a, an,* or *the* is in front of the word, then you'll know it isn't a verb and will use *effect*.

The strong coffee had a powerful *effect* on me.

We studied the *effects* of sleep deprivation in my psychology class.

all ready,
already

If you can leave out the *all* and the sentence still makes sense, then *all ready* is the form to use. (In that form, *all* is a separate word and could be left out.)

We're *all ready* for our trip. (*We're ready for our trip* makes sense.)

The banquet is *all ready*. (*The banquet is ready* makes sense.)

But if you can't leave out the *all* and still have a sentence that makes sense, then use *already* (the form in which the *al* has to stay in the word).

They've *already* eaten. (*They've ready eaten* doesn't make sense.)

We have seen that movie *already*.

are, our

Are is a verb.

We *are* residents of Colorado Springs.

Our shows we possess something.

We painted *our* fence to match the house.

brake, break

Brake used as a verb means "to slow or stop motion." It's also the name of the device that slows or stops motion.

I *brake* to avoid squirrels.

Luckily I just had my *brakes* fixed.

Break used as a verb means "to shatter" or "to split." It's also the name of an interruption, as in "a coffee break."

She never thought she would *break* a world record.

I will enjoy my spring *break*.

choose, chose

The difference here is one of time. Use *choose* for present and future; use *chose* for past.

I will *choose* a new major this semester.

We *chose* the best time of year to get married.

clothes, cloths

Clothes are something you wear; *cloths* are pieces of material you might clean or polish something with.

I love the *clothes* that characters wear in movies.

The car wash workers use special *cloths* to dry the cars.

coarse, course   *Coarse* describes a rough texture.

I used *coarse* sandpaper to smooth the surface of the board.

Course is used for all other meanings.

Of *course* we saw the golf *course* when we went to Pebble Beach.

complement, compliment   The one spelled with an *e* means to complete something or bring it to perfection.

Use a color wheel to find a *complement* for purple.

Juliet's personality *complements* Romeo's; she is practical, and he is a dreamer.

The one spelled with an *i* has to do with praise. Remember "*I* like compl*i*ments," and you'll remember to use the *i* spelling when you mean praise.

My evaluation included a really nice *compliment* from my coworkers.

We *complimented* them on their new home.

conscious, conscience   *Conscious* means "aware."

They weren't *conscious* of any problems before the accident.

Conscience means that inner voice of right and wrong. The extra *n* in conscience should remind you of *No*, which is what your conscience often says to you.

My *conscience* told me not to keep the expensive watch I found.

dessert, desert   *Dessert* is the sweet one, the one you like two helpings of. So give it two helpings of *s*.

We had a whole chocolate cheesecake for *dessert*.

The other one, *desert*, is used for all other meanings and has two pronunciations.

I promise that I won't *desert* you at the party.

The snake slithered slowly across the *desert*.

do, due

Do is a verb, an action. You *do* something.

I always *do* my best work at night.

But a payment or an assignment is *due;* it is scheduled for a certain time.

Our first essay is *due* tomorrow.

Due can also be used before *to* in a phrase that means *because of.*

The outdoor concert was canceled *due to* rain.

feel, fill

Feel describes *feel*ings.

Whenever I stay up late, I *feel* sleepy in class.

Fill describes what you do to a cup or a gas tank.

Did they *fill* the pitcher to the top?

fourth, forth

The word *fourth* has four in it. (But note that *forty* does not. Remember the word *forty-fourth.*)

That was our *fourth* quiz in two weeks.

My grandparents celebrated their *forty-fourth* anniversary.

If you don't mean a number, use *forth.*

We wrote back and *forth* many times during my trip.

have, of

Have is a verb. Sometimes, in a contraction, it sounds like *of.* When you say *could've,* the *have* may sound like *of,* but it is not written that way. Always write *could have, would have, should have,* and *might have.*

We should *have* planned our vacation sooner.

Then we could *have* used our coupon for a free one-way ticket.

Use *of* only in a prepositional phrase (see p. 63).

She sent me a box *of* chocolates for my birthday.

hear, here

The last three letters of *hear* spell "ear." You *hear* with your ear.

When I listen to a seashell, I *hear* ocean sounds.

The other spelling *here* tells "where." Note that the three words indicating a place or pointing out something all have *here* in them: *here, there, where.*

I'll be *here* for three more weeks.

it's, its	*It's* is a contraction and means "it is" or "it has."
	It's hot. (*It is* hot.)
	It's been hot all week. (*It has* been hot all week.)
	Its is a possessive. (Words such as *its, yours, hers, ours, theirs,* and *whose* are already possessive forms and never need an apostrophe. See p. 38.)
	The jury had made *its* decision.
	The dog pulled at *its* leash.
knew, new	*Knew* has to do with knowledge (both start with *k*).
	New means "not old."
	They *knew* that she wanted a *new* bike.
know, no	*Know* has to do with knowledge (both start with *k*).
	By Friday, I must *know* all the state capitals.
	No means "not any" or the opposite of "yes."
	My boss has *no* patience. *No,* I need to work late.

EXERCISES

Underline the correct word. Don't guess! If you aren't sure, turn back to the explanatory pages. When you've finished ten sentences, compare your answers with those at the back of the book. Correct each set of ten sentences before continuing so you'll catch your mistakes early.

Exercise 1

1. Did you ever (<u>hear</u>, here) of "brain freeze"?
2. (<u>It's</u>, Its) the unpleasant sensation you may get when eating frozen (<u>desserts</u>, deserts), such as ice creams and sorbets.
3. Suddenly you (<u>feel</u>, fill) a sharp pain in your forehead or behind one of your eyes.
4. You can't (<u>do</u>, due) anything but wait for the pain to go away.
5. (<u>A</u>, An) young middle-school student recently discovered the reason for this "brain freeze" (affect, <u>effect</u>).

6. The renowned *British Medical Journal* (choose, chose) to publish the results of thirteen-year-old Maya Kaczorowski's experiment.

7. Kaczorowski (knew, new) that it wouldn't be difficult to get 150 of her fellow students to eat ice cream.

8. She asked half of her subjects to (feel, fill) their mouths with ice cream fast and the other half to spoon the ice cream in slowly.

9. Her experiment showed that "brain freeze" results when (a, an) icy substance quickly reaches the back of the mouth where certain nerves (are, our).

10. Kaczorowski gives the following (advise, advice) to avoid "brain freeze": eat your frozen (desserts, deserts) leisurely.

Source: Current Science, February 28, 2003

Exercise 2

1. (It's, Its) never too late to learn something (knew, new).

2. After living for nearly one hundred years without knowing how to read or write, George Dawson could (have, of) just (accepted, excepted) his life as it was.

3. But he never did (feel, fill) good about hiding his illiteracy from his children or signing his name with (a, an) X.

4. In 1996, George Dawson (choose, chose) to start school for the first time at the age of ninety-eight.

5. Dawson, who was (all ready, already) in his teens when the *Titanic* sank, worked all of his life to support his family and even outlived his (fourth, forth) wife.

6. He had enough memories to (feel, fill) a book, (accept, except) he wouldn't (have, of) been able to read it.

7. When a man in Seattle came to (hear, here) of Dawson's long life and strong desire for (a, an) education, he gave Dawson some (advise, advice)

8. Richard Glaubman, a teacher himself, suggested that Dawson share his experiences in a book; they (are, our) now coauthors of Dawson's auto-biography.

9. In the (coarse, course) of his life as an African-American man and the grandson of slaves, Dawson witnessed and felt the (affects, effects) of racism and oppression.

10. But Dawson always believed that the joyful moments in life more than (complemented, complimented) the painful ones, and he titled his book *Life Is So Good.*

Source: Jet, April 17, 2000

Exercise 3

1. If you wear any (clothes, cloths) made of polyester, you may be wearing what used to be (a, an) old movie print.

2. (Do, Due) to the huge numbers of reels of film needed to meet the demands of today's movie audiences, recycling is (a, an) necessary part of the motion picture industry.

3. Companies such as Warner Bros. and New Line Cinema (accept, except) the responsibility for film recycling.

4. Of (coarse, course), the best prints of movies are saved for the future, but there (are, our) usually thousands of leftover copies (all ready, already) to be turned into something else.

5. The recycling process begins by chopping the film into (course, coarse) pieces, then transforming the rubble into a (knew, new) substance, such as polyester fabric.

6. Movie distributors are ((conscious), conscience) that collectors and other interested parties would love to get their hands on these extra movie prints.

7. Therefore, security is (a, (an)) essential part of the movie-recycling process.

8. Someone trying to (brake, (break)) into a warehouse in search of last month's hottest release would ((feel) fill) very disappointed.

9. The five to six reels of each film would ((have) of) (all ready, (already)) been separated and mixed together with other films' reels.

10. ((It's) Its) (know, (no)) surprise that movie companies want to protect their interests.

Source: Los Angeles Times, February 17, 2003

Exercise 4

1. I've been out of high school for two years, and I (all ready, already) miss it.

2. While I was still in high school, my parents bought my (clothes, cloths) and took care of all my necessities.

3. When my car needed to have (it's, its) (brakes, breaks) fixed, they paid the repair bills.

4. Every time I had to (choose, chose) a new elective or a summer activity, my family gave me the best (advise, advice).

5. One summer, I spent a spectacular week in the (dessert, desert) with my school's geology club.

6. That firsthand experience with nature strongly (affected, effected) me, especially the sight of the brilliant blue sky and the feeling of the (coarse, course), rocky sand.

7. Now that I am (hear, here) at college, I am (conscious, conscience) of a change in my parents' attitude.

8. (It's, Its) as if they (feel, fill) that (are, our) lives should grow apart.

9. I didn't (know, no) that this change was coming, or I would (have, of) tried to prepare myself for it.

10. Now I go back and (fourth, forth) between wishing for the past and trying to (accept, except) the future.

Exercise 5

1. According to (a, an) recent study, the leading health problem for dogs in Britain is obesity.

2. The Chartered Society of Physiotherapy found that dogs' obesity problems (complement, compliment) those of their human companions.

3. People and dogs, it seems, continue to (feel, fill) up on treats and (desserts, deserts) even after they should (have, of) stopped.

4. The same dogs who eat too much (do, due) very little exercise.

5. The British study cited traffic injuries as the second major health threat to (it's, its) canines.

6. By the time drivers (brake, break) for an animal as small as a dog, (it's, its) often too late.

7. Back problems (affect, effect) so many dogs in Britain that they are the third most common ailment.

8. Obesity may even have a worsening (affect, effect) on back injuries.

9. British researchers stopped short of naming the (fourth, forth) highest danger for their dogs.

10. However, animal experts both (hear, here) and abroad (advise, advice) dog owners to keep their pets lean, fit, and on a leash.

Source: http://www.csp.org.uk

PROOFREADING EXERCISE

Find and correct the ten errors contained in the following student paragraph. All of the errors involve Words Often Confused (Set 1).

conscious

During my singing recital last semester, I suddenly became very self-conscience. My heart started beating faster, and I didn't ~~no~~ *knew* what to ~~due~~ *do*. I looked around to see if my show of nerves was having an ~~affect~~ *effect* on the audience. Of ~~coarse~~ *course*, they could ~~here~~ *hear* my voice shaking. I was the ~~forth~~ *fourth* singer in the program, and everyone else had done so well. I felt my face turn red and would ~~of~~ *have* run out the door if it had been closer. After my performance, people tried to give me compliments, but I ~~new~~ *knew* that they weren't sincere.

SENTENCE WRITING

The surest way to learn these Words Often Confused is to use them immediately in your own writing. Choose the five pairs of words that you most often confuse from Set 1. Then use each of them correctly in a new sentence. No answers are provided at the back of the book, but you can see if you are using the words correctly by comparing your sentences to the examples in the explanations.

Words Often Confused (Set 2)

Study this second set of words carefully, with their examples, before attempting the exercises. Knowing all of the word groups in these two sets will take care of many of your spelling problems.

lead, led

Lead is the metal that rhymes with *head.*

> Old paint is dangerous because it may contain *lead.*

The past form of the verb "to lead" is *led.*

> What factors *led* to your decision?
>
> I *led* our school's debating team to victory last year.

If you don't mean past time, use *lead*, which rhymes with *bead.*

> I will *lead* the debating team again this year.

loose, lose

Loose means "not tight." Note how *l o o s e* that word is. It has plenty of room for two *o*'s.

> My dog has a *loose* tooth.

Lose is the opposite of win.

> If we *lose* this game, we will be out for the season.

passed, past

The past form of the verb "to pass" is *passed.*

> She easily *passed* her math class.
>
> The runner *passed* the baton to her teammate.
>
> I *passed* your house on my way to the store.

Use *past* when it's not a verb.

> I drove *past* your house. (Meaning "I drove *by* your house.")
>
> I try to learn from *past* experiences.
>
> In the *past*, he worked for a small company.

personal, personnel

Pronounce these two correctly, and you won't confuse them—*pérsonal, personnél.*

> She shared her *personal* views as a parent.

Personnel means "a group of employees."

> I had an appointment in the *personnel* office.

piece, peace	Remember "piece of pie." The one meaning "a *piece* of something" always begins with *pie*.
	Many children asked for an extra *piece* of candy.
	The other one, *peace*, is the opposite of war.
	The two sides finally signed a *peace* treaty.
principal, principle	*Principal* means "main." Both words have *a* in them: princip*a*l, m*a*in.
	Their *principal* concern is safety. (main concern)
	He paid both *principal* and interest. (main amount of money)
	Also, think of a school's "princi*pal*" as your "*pal*."
	An elementary school *principal* must be kind. (main administrator)
	A *principle* is a "rule." Both words end in *le:* princip*le*, ru*le*.
	I am proud of my high *principles*. (rules of conduct)
	We value the *principle* of truth in advertising. (rule)
quiet, quite	Pronounce these two correctly, and you won't confuse them. *Quiet* means "free from noise" and rhymes with *diet*.
	Tennis players need *quiet* in order to concentrate.
	Quite means "very" and rhymes with *bite*.
	It was *quite* hot in the auditorium.
right, write	*Right* means "correct" or "proper."
	You will find your keys if you look in the *right* place.
	It also means in the exact location, position, or moment.
	Your keys are *right* where you left them.
	Let's go *right* now.
	Write means to compose sentences, poems, essays, and so forth.
	I asked my teacher to *write* a letter of recommendation for me.
than, then	*Than* compares two things.
	I am taller *than* my sister.

Then tells when (*then* and *when* rhyme, and both have *e* in them).

I always write a rough draft of a paper first; *then* I revise it.

their, there, they're

Their is a possessive, meaning belonging to them.

Their cars have always been red.

There points out something. (Remember that the three words indicating a place or pointing out something all have *here* in them: *here, there, where.*)

I know that I haven't been *there* before.

There was a rainbow in the sky.

They're is a contraction and means "they are."

They're living in Canada now. (*They are* living in Canada now.)

threw, through

Threw is the past form of "to throw."

We *threw* snowballs at each other.

I *threw* away my chance at a scholarship.

If you don't mean "to throw something," use *through.*

We could see our beautiful view *through* the new curtains.

They worked *through* their differences.

two, too, to

Two is a number.

We have written *two* papers so far in my English class.

Too means "extra" or "also," and so it has an extra *o.*

The movie was *too* long and *too* violent. (extra)

They are enrolled in that biology class *too.* (also)

Use *to* for all other meanings.

They like *to* ski. They're going *to* the mountains.

weather, whether

Weather refers to conditions of the atmosphere.

Snowy *weather* is too cold for me.

Whether means "if."

I don't know *whether* it is snowing there or not.

Whether I travel with you or not depends on the weather.

were, wear, where

These words are pronounced differently but are often confused in writing.

Were is the past form of the verb "to be."

We *were* interns at the time.

Wear means to have on, as in wearing clothes.

I always *wear* a scarf in winter.

Where refers to a place. (Remember that the three words indicating a place or pointing out something all have *here* in them: *here, there, where.*)

Where is the mailbox? There it is.

Where are the closing papers? Here they are.

who's, whose

Who's is a contraction and means "who is" or "who has."

Who's responsible for signing the checks? (*Who is* responsible?)

Who's been reading my journal? (*Who has* been reading my journal?)

Whose is a possessive. (Words such as *whose, its, yours, hers, ours,* and *theirs* are already possessive forms and don't need an apostrophe. See p. 38.)

Whose keys are these?

woman, women

The difference here is one of number: wo*man* refers to one adult female; wo*men* refers to two or more adult females.

I know a *woman* who won $8,000 on a single horse race.

I bowl with a group of *women* from my work.

you're, your

You're is a contraction and means "you are."

You're as smart as I am. (*You are* as smart as I am.)

Your is a possessive meaning "belonging to you."

I borrowed *your* lab book.

E X E R C I S E S

Underline the correct word. When you've finished ten sentences, compare your answers with those at the back of the book. Do only ten sentences at a time so that you will catch your mistakes early.

Exercise 1

1. Parents are gaining (piece, peace) of mind with the arrival of some new "kids" in (their, there, they're) neighborhoods.

2. Actually, (their, there, they're) 3-D plastic statues called "Kid Alert Visual Warning Systems."

3. What makes these warning devices so useful is (their, there, they're) unique combination of size, shape, and color.

4. (Their, There, They're) kid-sized, kid-shaped, and bright-yellow-colored.

5. The Kid Alert statues are designed to stop drivers from speeding carelessly (threw, through) neighborhoods where children play.

6. (Weather, Whether) placed at curbs or near driveways, these eye-catching statues seem to be working.

7. When cars drive (passed, past) them, drivers know instantly that children may be playing nearby.

8. The 3-D signs are definitely more noticeable (than, then) the traditional flat road signs.

9. (Their, There, They're) is no need to (right, write) "Children at play" on these 3-D markers.

10. However, many of them hold red flags, and some have the word "slow" written on them (two, too, to).

Source: Newsweek, July 28, 2003

Exercise 2

1. As a student on financial aid, I was advised to work on campus or (loose, lose) some of my benefits.

2. At first I didn't know (were, wear, where) to work.

3. It definitely needed to be a (quiet, quite) place so that I could study or (right, write) a paper in my free time.

4. I finally chose to take a job in the (personal, personnel) office.

5. Now that I have been working (their, there, they're) for (two, too, to) months, I know that I made the (right, write) decision.

6. My (principal, principle) duties include filing documents and stuffing envelopes.

7. However, when the receptionist takes a break, I am the one (who's, whose) at the front desk.

8. Once I was sitting up front when the (principal, principle) of my old high school came in to apply for a job at the college.

9. I didn't know (weather, whether) to show that I recognized her or to keep (quiet, quite) about the (passed, past).

10. As a student, I like working on campus for financial-aid benefits better (than, then) working off campus for a tiny paycheck.

Exercise 3

1. (You're, Your) not alone if you don't know (were, wear, where) to shop for pants anymore.

2. (Weather, Whether) (you're, your) a man or a (woman, women), it isn't easy to decide on the best pants to (were, wear, where).

3. The styles are often (two, too, to) (loose, lose) or (two, too, to) tight.

4. (Their, There, They're) never (quiet, quite) (right, write).

5. Anyone (who's, whose) tried to find the perfect pair of jeans, for instance, knows that the fabric is often more important (than, then) the fit.

6. Fabric choice can be a matter of (personal, personnel) taste.

7. You like (you're, your) jeans to be either light or dark, or (you're, your) the kind of person (who's, whose) able to (were, wear, where) both.

8. I have (passed, past) whole rows of dark-colored jeans on my quest for a lighter pair with just the (right, write) amount of fading.

9. I have a friend (who's, whose) wardrobe consists of nothing but vintage jeans and T-shirts.

10. She's a (woman, women) who dresses the same way in every kind of (weather, whether) and for every occasion.

Exercise 4

1. A (piece, peace) of toy history went up for auction in July 2003, but auction participants (were, wear, where) (quiet, quite) disappointed with the results.

2. Up for sale was the original, one-of-a-kind, handmade version of G.I. Joe, (who's, whose) popularity as a collectible was thought to be unlimited.

3. This G.I. Joe prototype became the (principal, principle) attraction of the Comic-Con convention held in San Diego, California.

4. Before the auction, the twelve-inch-tall prototype had been the (personal, personnel) property of the doll's creator, Don Levine.

5. Back in the mid-1960s, the Hasbro toy company introduced G.I. Joe (two, too, to) offer a male alternative to Barbie, (who's, whose) obviously a (woman, women).

6. The fun of owning Barbie and G.I. Joe was that both (were, wear, where) designed to (were, wear, where) different outfits and use different accessories depending on (their, there, they're) special models.

7. Designers at Hasbro thought that the market was ready for a masculine Barbie counterpart, and they (were, wear, where) (right, write).

8. Although the G.I. Joe prototype had hand-painted features and hand-sewn clothes and boots, Joe's design went (threw, through) few changes after his prototype was made.

9. Ironically, this first-ever "action figure" failed (two, too, to) fetch its anticipated selling price of just over half a million dollars.

10. In fact, the low number of bids (lead, led) auction officials to cut the doll's reserve price down to $250,000, but (their, there, they're) still (were, wear, where) no bidders at that level.

Source: Chicago Sun-Times, July 20, 2003, and www.heritagecomics.com

Exercise 5

1. On a beautiful morning in June, you may receive a phone call that changes (you're, your) life.

2. The caller will tell you that (you're, your) half a million dollars richer and that you don't have to do anything other (than, then) be yourself to deserve the money.

3. You might wonder (weather, whether) it is a real or a crank call.

4. Believe it or not, this wonderful (piece, peace) of news is delivered to between twenty and thirty special men and (woman, women) in America every year.

5. (Their, There, They're) unofficially called the "Genius Awards," but (their, there, they're) real title is the MacArthur Fellowships.

6. The MacArthur Foundation awards its fellowships each year based on the (principal, principle) that forward-thinking people deserve an opportunity to pursue their ideas freely and without obligation to anyone.

7. No application is necessary (two, too, to) receive the gift of $100,000 a year plus health insurance for five years, and no particular field of work receives more consideration (than, then) another.

8. The (principal, principle) characteristic that MacArthur Fellows share is (their, there, they're) creative potential—in any area.

9. Each year, the MacArthur Foundation sends about one hundred "scouts" across the country looking for people with untapped potential (two, too, to) nominate; (than, then) another anonymous group selects the year's recipients.

10. The nominees don't even know that (their, there, they're) going (threw, through) the process until the phone rings on that fateful morning in June.

PROOFREADING EXERCISE

See if you can correct the ten errors in this student paragraph. All errors involve Words Often Confused (Set 2).

Sometimes it's hard to find the ~~write~~ *right* place to study on campus. The library used ~~too~~ *to* be the ~~principle~~ *principal* location for students to do ~~they're~~ *their* difficult course work, ~~weather~~ *whether* it was preparing research papers or writing critical essays. But now most library resources are available online, ~~two~~ *too*. This change has ~~lead~~ *led* students to use campus computer labs and cafés as study halls. There, students can go online, get up-to-date sources, write their reports, and have peace and ~~quite~~ *quiet* without the stuffy atmosphere of the library. The only problem with doing research online is that it's easier to ~~loose~~ *lose* a piece of information on the computer ~~then~~ *than* it is to lose a hard copy in the library.

SENTENCE WRITING

Write several sentences using any words you missed in doing the exercises for Words Often Confused (Set 2).

Sentence writing is a good idea not only because it will help you remember these Words Often Confused but also because it will be a storehouse for ideas you can later use in writing papers. Here are some topics you might consider writing your sentences about:

—Friends from childhood

—Favorite actors/actresses

—A hobby or a collection

—Something you would like to accomplish this year

—Your favorite getaway spot

The Eight Parts of Speech

Choosing the right word is an important aspect of writing. Some words sound alike but are spelled differently and have different meanings (*past* and *passed,* for instance), and some words are spelled the same but sound different and mean different things (*lead,* for the action of "leading," and *lead,* for the stuff inside pencils).

One way to choose words more carefully is to understand the roles that words play in sentences. Just as one actor can play many different parts in movies (a hero, a villain, a humorous sidekick), single words can play different parts in sentences (a noun, a verb, an adjective). These are called the *eight parts of speech,* briefly defined with examples below.

1. **Nouns** name some*one, thing, place,* or *idea* and are used as subjects and objects in sentences.

   The **technician** fixed the **computers** in the **lab.**

2. **Pronouns** are special words that replace nouns to avoid repeating them.

   She (the technician) fixed **them** (the computers) in **it** (the lab).

3. **Adjectives** add description to nouns and pronouns—telling *which one, how many,* or *what kind, color,* or *shape* they are.

   The **new** technician fixed **thirty old** computers in the **writing** lab.

4. **Verbs** show action or state of being.

   The new technician **fixed** the old computers in the writing lab; Terri **is** the technician's name.

5. **Adverbs** add information—such as *when, where, why,* or *how*—to verbs, adjectives and other adverbs, or whole sentences.

    > **Yesterday** the new technician **quickly** fixed the **very** old computers in the writing lab.

6. **Prepositions** show position in *space* and *time* and are followed by nouns to form prepositional phrases.

    > The technician fixed the computers **in** the writing lab **at** noon.

7. **Conjunctions** are connecting words—such as *and, but,* and *or*—and words that begin dependent clauses—such as *because, since, when, while,* and *although.*

    > Students still visited the lab **and** the media center **while** the computers were broken.

8. **Interjections** interrupt a sentence to show surprise or other emotions and are rarely used in Standard Written English.

    > **Wow,** Terri is a valuable new employee.

To find out what parts of speech an individual word can play, look it up in a good dictionary (see p. 50). A list of definitions beginning with an abbreviated part of speech (*n, adj, prep,* and so on) will catalog its uses. However, seeing how a word is used in a particular sentence is the best way to identify its part of speech.

Look at these examples:

The **train** of a wedding gown flows elegantly behind it.

(*Train* is a noun in this sentence, naming the part of a gown we call a "*train.*")

Sammy and Helen **train** dolphins at SeaWorld.

(*Train* is a verb in this example, expressing the action of teaching skills we call "*training.*")

Doug's parents drove him to the **train** station.

(*Train* is an adjective here, adding description to the noun "station," telling what *kind* of station it is.)

All of the words in a sentence work together to create meaning, but each one serves its own purpose by playing a part of speech. Think about how each of the words in the following sentence plays the particular part of speech labeled:

adj   adj   n   v   prep   n conj pro   adv   v   n   prep n
Many college students work during the day, so they usually take classes at night.

Familiarizing yourself with the parts of speech will help you spell better now and understand phrases and clauses better later. Each of the eight parts of speech has characteristics that distinguish it from the other seven, but it takes practice to learn them.

EXERCISES

Label the parts of speech above all of the words in the following sentences using the abbreviations n, pro, adj, v, adv, prep, conj, and interj. For clarity's sake, the sentences here are very brief, and you may ignore the words *a, an,* and *the.* These words are actually special forms of adjectives (called articles), but they are so numerous that there's no need to mark them. Refer back to the definitions and examples of the parts of speech whenever necessary. When in doubt, leave a word unmarked until you check the answers at the back of the book after each set of ten sentences. You'll find that many of the ones you found difficult to label will be *adverbs,* the most versatile of the parts of speech.

Exercise 1

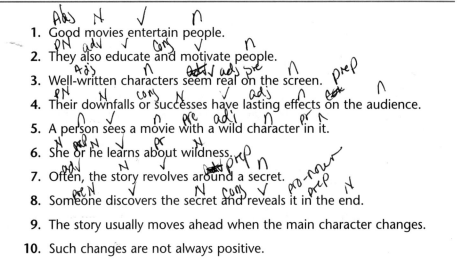

1. Good movies entertain people.
2. They also educate and motivate people.
3. Well-written characters seem real on the screen.
4. Their downfalls or successes have lasting effects on the audience.
5. A person sees a movie with a wild character in it.
6. She or he learns about wildness.
7. Often, the story revolves around a secret.
8. Someone discovers the secret and reveals it in the end.
9. The story usually moves ahead when the main character changes.
10. Such changes are not always positive.

Exercise 2

1. In 1992, a boatload of rubber ducks sailed from China to the West Coast of America.
2. Thousands of them washed overboard in the middle of the Pacific Ocean.
3. The ducks floated from sea to sea.
4. They traveled the same route that the infamous *Titanic* did at one point.
5. Ocean experts used the "duck-slick" as a study tool.

6. In 2003, the bleached bath toys finally arrived in America.

7. However, they landed on the Atlantic Coast.

8. The journey took a long time.

9. The rubber ducks floated for eleven years.

10. Some stray ducks landed on European and Hawaiian shores.

Source: The Guardian, July 12, 2003

Exercise 3

1. Wow, mechanical pencils are delicate instruments.
2. I see other students with them.
3. Then I buy one.
4. I open the package.
5. I load the pencil with the tiny shaft of lead.
6. As I put the pencil tip down on the paper, the lead snaps off.
7. Am I an unrefined clod?
8. I believe that I am.
9. Now I know my limitations.
10. Ballpoint pens and wooden pencils are the only writing tools for me.

Exercise 4

1. The following old sayings still have meaning today.
2. A penny saved is a penny earned.
3. A stitch in time saves nine.
4. Haste makes waste.
5. Love me, love my dog.
6. A picture is worth a thousand words.
7. He or she who hesitates is lost.
8. Time flies when you are having fun.

9. The grass is always greener on the other side of the fence.

10. The truth of many old sayings lies beneath their surfaces.

Exercise 5

1. Most children in schools take standardized tests.

2. The test results become part of the children's permanent records.

3. School districts want high scores from their students.

4. Parents and children hope for good scores from them, too.

5. Sugar may raise the children's test scores.

6. A researcher discovered a link between high calories and higher test scores.

7. Schools sometimes feed their students more calories during testing time.

8. Test results show increases of several percentage points.

9. Some parents know about this link now.

10. Cookies for breakfast on test days may be a good idea!

Source: Discover, August 2003

PARAGRAPH EXERCISE

Here is a brief excerpt from a vintage book called *838 Ways to Amuse a Child,* by June Johnson. This excerpt comes from the chapter entitled "Fun with Science." We have modified some of the phrasing in the excerpt for this exercise. Label the parts of speech above as many of the words as you can before checking your answers at the back of the book.

Some materials are excellent conductors of heat. Some are poor conductors. Each does a different job. Try this experiment: hold a match against low heat on the stove. The wood of the match remains cool even when the match ignites and burns toward the fingers because wood is a poor conductor of heat. Now place an empty pan on that low heat and hold a hand flat against the bottom for a moment. The metal pan, an excellent conductor, gets hot almost immediately. . . . This experiment indicates the reason for many of the common uses of wood and metal.

SENTENCE WRITING

Write ten sentences imitating those in Exercise 1. Instead of beginning with "Good movies entertain people," you may begin with "Old cars fascinate me" or "Yellow lights confuse drivers," then continue to imitate the rest of the sentences in Exercise 1. Label the parts of speech above the words in your imitation exercise.

The next two sections on contractions and possessives involve spelling words correctly through the use of apostrophes.

Contractions

When two words are shortened into one, the result is called a *contraction:*

is not	·······➤ isn't	you have	·······➤ you've

The letter or letters that are left out are replaced with an apostrophe. For example, if the two words *do not* are condensed into one, an apostrophe is put where the *o* is left out.

do not	don't

Note how the apostrophe goes in the exact place where the letter or letters are left out in these contractions:

I am	I'm
I have	I've
I shall, I will	I'll
I would	I'd
you are	you're
you have	you've
you will	you'll
she is, she has	she's
he is, he has	he's
it is, it has	it's
we are	we're
we have	we've
we will, we shall	we'll
they are	they're
they have	they've
are not	aren't
cannot	can't
do not	don't
does not	doesn't
have not	haven't
let us	let's
who is, who has	who's
where is	where's
were not	weren't
would not	wouldn't
could not	couldn't

should not	shouldn't
would have	would've
could have	could've
should have	should've
that is	that's
there is	there's
what is	what's

One contraction does not follow this rule: *will not* becomes *won't*.

In all other contractions that you're likely to use, the apostrophe goes exactly where the letter or letters are left out. Note especially *it's*, *they're*, *who's*, and *you're*. Use them when you mean two words. (See p. 38 for the possessive forms—*its*, *their*, *whose*, and *your*—which don't contain apostrophes.)

E X E R C I S E S

Put an apostrophe in each contraction. Then compare your answers with those at the back of the book. Be sure to correct each set of ten sentences before going on so you'll catch your mistakes early.

Exercise 1

1. I bet you've never heard of a "geep"; I hadn't either until I read about it in a library book.

2. The geep is an animal that's half goat and half sheep.

3. It's not one that occurs naturally.

4. But a number of geep were produced in the early 1980s.

5. Scientists created this strange beast by combining a goat's cells with a sheep's cells at their earliest stages of development.

6. What many people couldn't believe was that the resulting geep's cells still kept either their goat or sheep qualities intact.

7. Therefore, the geep had long straight goat hair on parts of its body and fluffy sheep's wool on other parts.

8. Theres a picture of a geep in the book that I read.

9. Its so weird to look at a goat's head surrounded by curled sheep horns.

10. Lets hope that scientists dont try to make a "cog" or a "dat" in the same way.

Source: Mysteries of Planet Earth (Carlton Books, 1999)

Exercise 2

1. Diane Von Furstenberg is a fashion designer whos famous for inventing the wrap dress.

2. Its a simple, elegant design that helped make her a celebrated businessperson.

3. However, the wrap dress's success isnt her most-cherished memory.

4. Thats another story.

5. Von Furstenberg was on an airplane on the day that shed been featured on the front page of *The Wall Street Journal*.

6. Shed been reading the story and had the newspaper on her lap.

7. A man sitting next to her looked over and said, "Whats a pretty girl like you doing with *The Wall Street Journal*?"

8. She knew that he obviously hadnt seen her picture in the newspaper yet.

9. By pointing out the front-page article, she couldve made him feel terrible.

10. But she didnt do it, and she considers her restraint at that moment one of her highest achievements.

Source: CBS News Sunday Morning, July 20, 2003

Exercise 3

1. Theres an old tongue twister thats getting a new twist these days.

2. "Fuzzy Wuzzy was a bear. Fuzzy Wuzzy had no hair. Fuzzy Wuzzy wasnt fuzzy, was he?"

3. Some black bears in Florida dont have any hair, and its not funny.

4. The bears' fur has been falling out, and it isnt growing back.

5. The hairless animals dont even look like bears anymore.

6. Without their hair, the bears arent as prepared for cold temperatures.

7. Theyre also prone to scratches on their skin, which is usually protected by fur.

8. Bear experts havent been able to find a cure for the bears' balding.

9. Theyve identified the problem as mange, a condition common to dogs.

10. But theyre not sure why some bears have it while others dont.

Source: National Geographic News, January 14, 2003

Exercise 4

1. As I was driving home the other day, I saw a fully equipped camper shell for sale on someone's front lawn, and I shouldve stopped to look at it.

2. At first, I didnt think I wanted a camper for my pickup truck, but now I wish Id gone back for it.

3. I remember that it didnt look brand new: it had a door in the back and windows with curtains that I couldve replaced if I didnt like them.

4. And there wasnt any price posted, so I dont know how much it cost.

5. Its just that, for some reason, I feel as though Ive missed an opportunity.

6. Whenever Im driving on a long trip and pass a truck with a camper on it, I always think of how much fun itd be to park on a beach and spend the night.

7. To get all of the comforts of home, I wouldnt have to stop at a hotel; theyd be right in the back of the truck.

8. A friend of mine whos got a motor home said that it was the best purchase hed ever made because it always gives him a reason to take a trip.

9. A camper shell mightve been just what I needed to bring some adventure into my life.

10. Of course, theres nothing stopping me from buying a new one.

Exercise 5

1. This week, Im helping my sister with her research paper, and shes chosen chocolate as her topic.

2. Weve been surprised by some of the things weve discovered.

3. First, the cocoa beans arent very appetizing in their natural form.

4. They grow inside an odd-shaped, alien-looking pod, and theyre surrounded by white mushy pulp.

5. Once cocoa beans have been removed from the pods, theyre dried, blended almost like coffee beans, and processed into the many types of chocolate foods available.

6. In fact, the Aztecs enjoyed chocolate as a heavily spiced hot drink that was more like coffee than the sweet, creamy chocolate thats popular today.

7. Weve also learned that white chocolate cant be called chocolate at all since it doesnt contain any cocoa solids, only cocoa butter.

8. With an interest in organic foods, wed assumed that organic chocolate would be better than conventional chocolate.

9. But thats not true either because its got to be grown on pesticide-free trees, and theyre the strongest but not the tastiest sources of chocolate.

10. Unfortunately, the best cocoa trees are also the most vulnerable to disease, so they cant be grown organically.

Source: The Chocolate Companion (Simon & Schuster, 1995)

PROOFREADING EXERCISE

Add apostrophes to the ten contractions used in the following paragraph.

If you've ever driven through Lancaster County, Pennsylvania, you might've encountered one of the horse-drawn buggies that the Amish use as their main method of transportation. In the daytime, the black buggies stand out against the vivid landscape. But it isn't as easy to see them when its dark. You wouldn't expect to see an Amish buggy driving down the road with its headlights on. In fact, when it comes to headlights and taillights on Amish buggies, they're usually not there. As a result, the buggies aren't as safe as they could be. Due to their beliefs, the Amish don't use electricity. However, a new kind of LED headlight technology doesn't rely on electricity. It works with solar energy, a form of power accepted by some members of the Amish community. These new headlights and taillights haven't been universally embraced, partly because of their cost.

Source: Mennonite Weekly Review, July 29, 2003

SENTENCE WRITING

Doing exercises will help you learn a rule, but even more helpful is using the rule in writing. Write ten sentences using contractions. You might write about your reaction to this week's big news story, or you can choose your own subject.

Possessives

Words that clarify ownership are called *possessives*. The trick in writing possessives is to ask the question "Who (or what) does the item belong to?" Modern usage has made *who* acceptable when it begins a question. More correctly, of course, the phrasing should be "*Whom* does the item belong to?" or even "*To whom* does the item belong?"

In any case, if the answer to this question does not end in *s* (e.g., *girl, person, people, children, month*), simply add an apostrophe and *s* to show the possessive. Look at the first five examples in the following chart.

However, if the answer to the question already ends in *s* (e.g., *girls, Brahms*), add only an apostrophe after the *s* to show the possessive. See the next two examples in the chart and say them aloud to hear that their sound does not change.

Finally, some *s*-ending words need another sound to make the possessive clear. If you need another *s* sound when you *say* the possessive (e.g., *boss* made possessive is *boss's*), add the apostrophe and another *s* to show the added sound.

a girl (uniform)	Whom does the uniform belong to?	a girl	Add *'s*	a girl's uniform
a person (clothes)	Whom do the clothes belong to?	a person	Add *'s*	a person's clothes
people (clothes)	Whom do the clothes belong to?	people	Add *'s*	people's clothes
children (games)	Whom do the games belong to?	children	Add *'s*	children's games
a month (pay)	What does the pay belong to?	a month	Add *'s*	a month's pay
girls (uniforms)	Whom do the uniforms belong to?	girls	Add *'*	girls' uniforms
Brahms (Lullaby)	Whom does the Lullaby belong to?	Brahms	Add *'*	Brahms' Lullaby
my boss (office)	Whom does the office belong to?	my boss	Add *'s*	my boss's office

The trick of asking "Whom does the item belong to?" will always work, but you must ask the question every time. Remember that the key word is *belong*. If you ask the question another way, you may get an answer that won't help you. Also, notice that the trick does not depend on whether the answer is *singular* or *plural*, but on whether it ends in *s* or not.

To Make a Possessive

1. Ask "Whom (or what) does the item belong to?"

2. If the answer doesn't end in *s*, add an apostrophe and *s*.

3. If the answer already ends in *s*, add just an apostrophe *or* an apostrophe and *s* if you need an extra sound to show the possessive (as in *boss's office*).

E X E R C I S E S

Follow the directions carefully for each of the following exercises. Because possessives can be tricky, we include explanations in some exercises to help you understand them better.

Exercise 1

Cover the right column and see if you can write the following possessives correctly. Ask the question "Whom (or what) does the item belong to?" each time. Don't look at the answer before you try!

1. people (opinions)	*people's op*	people's opinions
2. a jury (verdict)	*jury's*	a jury's verdict
3. Chris (GPA)	*Chris's*	Chris' or Chris's GPA
4. Tiffany (scholarship)	*Tiffany's*	Tiffany's scholarship
5. the Jacksons (new roof)	*Jacksons'*	the Jacksons' new roof
6. Dr. Moss (advice)	*Moss's*	Dr. Moss's advice
7. patients (rights)	*patients'*	patients' rights
8. a fish (gills)	*fish's*	a fish's gills
9. a car (windshield)	*car's*	a car's windshield
10. many cars (windshields)	*cars'*	many cars' windshields

(Sometimes you may see a couple of choices when the word ends in *s*. *Chris' GPA* may be written *Chris's GPA*. That is also correct, depending on how you want your reader to say it. Be consistent when given such choices.)

> **CAUTION** - Don't assume that every word that ends in *s* is a possessive. The *s* may indicate more than one of something, a plural noun. Make sure the word actually possesses something before you add an apostrophe.

A few commonly used words have their own possessive forms and don't need apostrophes added to them. Memorize this list:

our, ours	its
your, yours	their, theirs
his, her, hers	whose

Note particularly *its, their, whose,* and *your.* They are already possessive and don't take an apostrophe. (These words sound just like *it's, they're, who's,* and *you're,* which are *contractions* that use an apostrophe in place of their missing letters.)

Exercise 2

Cover the right column and see if you can write the required form. The answer might be a *contraction* or a *possessive.* If you miss any, go back and review the explanations.

1. Yes, (that) the one I ordered. — *that's*
2. (He) saving his money for summer. — He's
3. Does (you) dog bark at night? — your
4. I don't know (who) backpack that is. — whose
5. (You) been summoned for jury duty? — You've
6. My cat is so old that (it) going bald. — it's
7. (They) taking classes together this spring. — They're
8. My car's paint is losing (it) shine. — its
9. We welcomed (they) suggestions. — their
10. (Who) visiting us this weekend? — Who's

Exercise 3

Here's another chance to check your progress with possessives. Cover the right column again as you did in Exercises 1 and 2, and add apostrophes correctly to any possessives. Each answer is followed by an explanation.

1. My twin brothers are members of our school's orchestra.

    school's (handwritten)

    school's (You didn't add an apostrophe to *brothers* or *members,* did you? The brothers and members don't possess anything.)

2. The cashier asked to see my friends identification, too.

    friend's (if it is one friend) friends' (two or more friends)

3. Both men's and women's tennis are exciting to watch.

    men's, women's (Did you use the "Whom does it belong to" test?)

4. I bought a bad textbook; half of it's pages were printed upside down.

    No apostrophe. *Its* needs no apostrophe unless it means "it is" or "it has."

5. Julia's grades were higher than yours.

    none (handwritten)

    Julia's (*Yours* is already possessive and doesn't take an apostrophe.)

6. I decided to quit my job and gave my boss two weeks notice.

    note (handwritten)

    weeks' (The notice belongs to *two weeks,* and since *weeks* ends in *s,* the apostrophe goes after the *s.*)

7. The Taylors porch light burned out while they were still on vacation.

    Taylors' (The light belongs to the Taylors.)

8. It is every citizens duty to vote in national elections.

    citizen's (The duty belongs to *every citizen,* and since *citizen* doesn't end in *s,* we add an apostrophe and *s.*)

9. The chemistry students evaluated each others results as they cleaned up after the experiment.

    each other's (*Students* is plural, not possessive.)

10. During a long trip, flight attendants attitudes can greatly affect an airline passengers experience.

    attendants', passenger's (Did you use the "Whom do they belong to" test?)

Exercises 4 and 5

Now you're ready to add apostrophes to the possessives that follow. But be careful. *First,* make sure the word really possesses something; not every word ending in *s* is a possessive. *Second,* remember that certain words already have possessive forms and don't use apostrophes. *Third,* even though a word ends in *s,* you can't tell where the apostrophe goes until you ask the question "Whom (or what) does the item belong to?" The apostrophe or apostrophe and *s* should follow the answer to that question. Check your answers at the back of the book after the first set.

Exercise 4

1. The vampire bats habit of sucking an animals blood is aided by a substance that stops the blood from clotting.
2. This same substance might come to a stroke patients aid very soon.
3. Sometimes a persons brain function becomes blocked by a blood clot.
4. This conditions medical label is "ischemic stroke."
5. Obviously, the vampire bats ability to unclot its victims blood would come in handy.
6. Luckily for stroke patients, the substance would be removed from the bat first.
7. Doctors believe that if stroke patients families could get them to the hospital fast enough, the bats enzyme could reduce the clot to avoid brain damage.
8. The enzymes technical name is DSPA.
9. Researchers have tested DSPAs abilities on mice with great success.
10. Perhaps the vampire bats bad reputation will change with the discovery of its healing powers.

Source: The American Heart Association's "Stroke Journal Report," January 9, 2003

Exercise 5

1. Beethovens Ninth Symphony is one of the most famous pieces of music in the world.

2. An original version of the symphonys score fetched a price of three-and-a-half million dollars at auction recently.

3. The score had been transcribed from Beethovens manuscript in order to be sent to the printer.

4. The famous composers handwriting was hard to read.

5. Previously, Beethoven had been satisfied with only one copyists work, and that copyist had died.

6. So the Ninth Symphonys score had to be copied by new copyists who were not as familiar with Beethovens marks.

7. The score that was recently auctioned included scrawled insults that Beethoven wrote in the margins as he was proofreading the new copyists work.

8. Those pencil markings in the masters own handwriting added greatly to the manuscripts value.

9. It also may have been the score used to conduct the symphonys world-premiere performance.

10. Beethoven himself attended the Ninths first performance in 1824.

Source: BBC News, May 22, 2003

PROOFREADING EXERCISE

Find and correct the five errors in the following student paragraph. All of the errors involve possessives.

I've been surprised by peoples' reactions to my recent haircut. My hair's new length is very short, and it's style is kind of a controlled mess. When I first got the haircut, I thought that everyone would hate it, but I was wrong. My previous hair-styles' problem was that it was boring—too long and too straight. Now that it's got some spikiness to it, my hair can reveal my personality's natural quirks'.

SENTENCE WRITING

Write ten sentences using the possessive forms of the names of your family members or the names of your friends. You could write about a recent event that brought your family or friends together. Just tell the story of what happened that day.

REVIEW OF CONTRACTIONS AND POSSESSIVES

Here are two review exercises. First, add the necessary apostrophes to the following sentences. Try not to make the mistake of placing an apostrophe where it isn't needed. Don't excuse an error by saying, "Oh, that was just a careless mistake." A mistake is a mistake. Be tough on yourself.

1. Peoples moods are affected by money.

2. However, moneys power is limited.

3. Ive recently decided to start a savings account.

4. I'd feel great if I had an extra month's pay in the bank.

5. I don't mean that money can buy happiness.

6. Everyone knows that it can't.

7. However, it doesn't hurt to have money.

8. I want my bank statement's "bottom line" to show some good news for a change.

9. That way, I wouldn't feel as if I were working just for the company's benefit.

10. After all, a person's self-worth is the most valuable possession of all.

Second, add the necessary apostrophes to the following short student essay.

A Journal of My Own

I've been keeping a journal ever since I was in high school. I don't write it for my teacher's sake. I wouldn't turn it in even if they asked me to. It's mine, and it helps me remember all of the changes I've gone through so far in my life. The way I see it, a diary's purpose isn't just to record the facts; it's to capture my true feelings.

When I record the day's events in my journal, they aren't written in minute-by-minute details. Instead, if I've been staying at a friend's house for the weekend, I'll write something like this: "Sharon's the only friend I have who listens to my whole sentence before starting hers. She's never in a hurry to end a good conversation. Today we talked for an hour or so about the pets we'd had when we were kids. We agreed that we're both 'dog people.' We can't imagine our lives without dogs. Her favorites are Pomeranians, and mine are golden retrievers." That's the kind of an entry I'd make in my journal. It doesn't mean much to anyone but me, and that's the way it should be.

I know that another person's diary would be different from mine and that most people don't even keep one. I'm glad that writing comes easily to me. I don't think Ill ever stop writing in my journal because it helps me believe in myself and value others beliefs as well.

Words That Can Be Broken into Parts

Breaking words into their parts will often help you spell them correctly. Each of the following words is made up of two shorter words. Note that the word then contains all the letters of the two shorter words.

chalk board	. . .	chalkboard	room mate	. . .	roommate
over due	. . .	overdue	home work	. . .	homework
super market	. . .	supermarket	under line	. . .	underline

Becoming aware of prefixes such as *dis, inter, mis,* and *un* is also helpful. When you add a prefix to a word, note that no letters are dropped, either from the prefix or from the word.

dis appear	disappear	mis represent	misrepresent
dis appoint	disappoint	mis spell	misspell
dis approve	disapprove	mis understood	misunderstood
dis satisfy	dissatisfy	un aware	unaware
inter act	interact	un involved	uninvolved
inter active	interactive	un necessary	unnecessary
inter related	interrelated	un sure	unsure

Have someone dictate the preceding list for you to write and then mark any words you miss. Memorize the correct spellings by noting how each word is made up of a prefix and a word.

Rule for Doubling a Final Letter

Most spelling rules have so many exceptions that they aren't much help. But here's one worth learning because it has very few exceptions (see boxes on page 45).

Double a final letter (consonants only) when adding an ending that begins with a vowel (such as *ing, ed, er*) if all three of the following are true:

1. The word ends in a single consonant,

2. which is preceded by a single vowel (the vowels are *a, e, i, o, u*),

3. and the accent is on the last syllable (or the word has only one syllable).

We'll try the rule on a few words to which we'll add *ing, ed,* or *er.*

begin
1. It ends in a single consonant—*n,*
2. preceded by a single vowel—*i,*
3. and the accent is on the last syllable—be *gin'.*
    Therefore, we double the final consonant and write *beginning, beginner.*

stop
1. It ends in a single consonant—*p,*
2. preceded by a single vowel—*o,*
3. and the accent is on the last syllable (only one).
    Therefore, we double the final consonant and write *stopping, stopped, stopper.*

filter
1. It ends in a single consonant—*r,*
2. preceded by a single vowel—*e,*
3. but the accent isn't on the last syllable. It's on the first—*fil'*ter.
    Therefore, we don't double the final consonant. We write *filtering, filtered.*

keep
1. It ends in a single consonant—*p,*
2. but it isn't preceded by a single vowel. There are two *e*'s.
    Therefore, we don't double the final consonant. We write *keeping, keeper.*

NOTE 1 - Be aware that *qu* is treated as a consonant because *q* is almost never written without *u*. Think of it as *kw*. In words like *equip* and *quit*, the *qu* acts as a consonant. Therefore, *equip* and *quit* both end in a single consonant preceded by a single vowel, and the final consonant is doubled in *equipped* and *quitting.*

NOTE 2 - The final consonants *w, x,* and *y* do not follow this rule and are not doubled when adding *ing, ed,* or *er* to a word (as in *bowing, fixing,* and *enjoying*).

E X E R C I S E S

Add *ing* to these words. Correct each group of ten before continuing so you'll catch any errors early.

Exercise 1

1. bet
2. milk
3. wait
4. park
5. skim

6. admit
7. slap
8. think
9. tap
10. hit

Exercise 2

1. wrap
2. rip
3. peel
4. refer
5. invest

6. order
7. profit
8. scream
9. slip
10. predict

Exercise 3

1. box
2. munch
3. roll
4. mop
5. flavor

6. cash
7. beep
8. talk
9. travel
10. play

Exercise 4

1. painting
2. rowing
3. shivering
4. defending
5. trimming

6. pressing
7. dealing
8. ~~kniting~~ knitting
9. blundering
10. ~~chuging~~ chugging

Exercise 5

1. shout
2. deploy
3. refer
4. equal
5. dig

6. mix
7. drip
8. send
9. hem
10. tax

PROGRESS TEST

This test covers everything you've studied so far. One sentence in each pair is correct. The other is incorrect. Read both sentences carefully before you decide. Then write the letter of the incorrect sentence in the blank. Try to isolate and correct the error if you can.

1. _B_ A. The tutor ~~complemented~~ *Complimented* me on my well-organized essay.

   B. She said that my examples complemented my ideas perfectly.

2. _A_ A. I took two coffee breaks at work today.

   B. Do you know ~~wear~~ *where* I put my keys?

3. _B_ A. Students could ~~of~~ *have* registered two days earlier if there hadn't been an error in the computer program.

   B. That would have made the first day of classes much easier.

4. _A_ A. Pat and Jill have travelled to England many times.

   B. Their trips have never been canceled.

5. _B_ A. When people lie, they are usually bothered by their ~~conscious~~.

   B. We could tell that the first pianist at the recital was feeling self-conscious.

6. _____ A. The childrens' bicycles were lined up in front of the adults' bikes.

   B. One of a child's first major accomplishments is learning to ride a bicycle.

7. _____ A. We've always taken her advice about movies.

   B. We have all ready seen that movie.

8. _____ A. My mother is trying to quit smoking, and it's affecting the whole family.

   B. The harmful affects of smoking are well-known.

9. _____ A. Many people still believe in the principal "Money can't buy everything."

   B. We shouldn't invite Jenny and Joe; they're always late.

10. _____ A. Your the happiest person I know.

   B. When I see your face, it's always got a smile on it.

Using a Dictionary

Some dictionaries are more helpful than others. A tiny pocket-sized dictionary or one that fits on a single sheet in your notebook might help you find the spelling of very common words, but for all other uses, you will need a complete, recently published dictionary. Spend some time at a bookstore looking through the dictionaries to find one that you feel comfortable reading. Look up a word that you have had trouble with in the past, and see if you understand the definition. Try looking up the same word in another dictionary and compare. If all else fails, stick with the big names, and you probably can't go wrong.

Complete the following exercises using a good dictionary. Then you will understand what a valuable resource it is.

1. Pronunciation

Look up the word *punctuate* and copy the pronunciation here.

_____

_____

For help with pronunciation of the syllables, you'll probably find key words at the bottom of one of the two dictionary pages open before you. Note especially that the upside-down *e* (ə) always has the sound of *uh* like the *a* in *ago* or *about*. Remember that sound because it's found in many words.

Slowly pronounce *punctuate,* giving each syllable the same sound as its key word.

Note which syllable has the heavy accent mark. (In most dictionaries the accent mark points to the stressed syllable, but in others it is in front of the stressed syllable.) The stressed syllable in *punctuate* is *punc.* Now say the word, letting the full force of your voice fall on that syllable.

When more than one pronunciation is given, the first is preferred. If the complete pronunciation of a word isn't given, look at the word above it to find the pronunciation.

Find the pronunciation of these words, using the key words at the bottom of the dictionary page to help you pronounce each syllable. Then note which syllable has the heavy accent mark, and say the word aloud.

mortgage   suspense   bologna   facsimile

2. Definitions

The dictionary may give more than one meaning for a word. Read all the meanings for each italicized word, and then write a definition appropriate to the sentence.

1. Our neighbors taught their dog to *heel.* _____

_____

2. He made himself a cup of *instant* coffee. _____

_____

3. When we *land,* I will call my parents. _____

_____

4. The battery was leaking at one of its *poles.* _____

_____

3. Spelling

By making yourself look up each word you aren't sure how to spell, you'll soon become a better speller. When two spellings are given in the dictionary, the first one (or the one with the definition) is preferred.

Use a dictionary to find the preferred spelling for each of these words.

moustache, mustache _____   wagon, waggon   _____

judgement, judgment _____   cancelled, canceled _____

4. Parts of Speech

English has eight parts of speech: noun, pronoun, verb, adjective, adverb, preposition, conjunction, and interjection. At the beginning of each definition for a word, you'll find an abbreviation for the part of speech that the word is performing when so defined (n, pron, v, adj, adv, prep, conj, interj). For more discussion of parts of speech, see page 24.

Identify the parts of speech listed in all the definitions for each of the following words.

coach _____   low _____

every _____   rice _____

5. Compound Words

If you want to find out whether two words are written separately, written with a hyphen between them, or written as one word, consult your dictionary. Look at these examples:

half sister	written as two words
father-in-law	hyphenated
stepson	written as one word

Write each of the following as listed in the dictionary (as two words, as a hyphenated word, or as one word):

bull's eye _____   draw bridge _____

play off _____   in house   _____

6. Capitalization

If a word is capitalized in the dictionary, that means it should always be capitalized. If it is not capitalized in the dictionary, then it may or may not be capitalized, depending on how it is used (see p. 203). For example, *American* is always capitalized, but *college* is capitalized or not, according to how it is used.

Last year, she graduated from college.

Last year, she graduated from Monterey Peninsula College.

Write the following words as they're given in the dictionary (with or without a capital) to show whether they must always be capitalized or not. Take a guess before looking them up.

europe _____   pacific _____

mars _____   scotch _____

7. Usage

Just because a word is in the dictionary doesn't mean that it's in standard use. The following labels indicate whether a word is used today and, if so, where and by whom.

obsolete	no longer used
archaic	not currently used in ordinary language but still found in some biblical, literary, and legal expressions

colloquial, informal	used in informal conversation but not in formal writing
dialectal, regional	used in some localities but not everywhere
slang	popular but nonstandard expression
nonstandard, substandard	not used in Standard Written English

Look up each italicized word and write the label indicating its usage. Dictionaries differ. One may list a word as slang, whereas another will call it colloquial. Still another may give no designation, thus indicating that that particular dictionary considers the word in standard use.

1. Please *gimme* some of that popcorn._____

2. His *deadpan* delivery of the joke is what made it so funny. _____

3. What are the *specs* on that computer?_____

4. Our teacher *freaked out* when we said that we needed more time._____

5. *Alas,* the deadline has been postponed._____

8. Derivations

The derivations or stories behind words will often help you remember the current meanings. For example, if you read that someone is *narcissistic* and you consult your dictionary, you'll find that *narcissism* is a condition named after Narcissus, who was a handsome young man in Greek mythology. One day Narcissus fell in love with his own reflection in a pool, but when he tried to get closer to it, he fell in the water and drowned. A flower that grew nearby is now named for Narcissus. And *narcissistic* has come to mean "in love with oneself."

Look up the derivation of each of these words. You'll find it in square brackets either just before or just after the definition.

Murphy bed _____

Chihuahua_____

goody two-shoes _____

silhouette _____

9. Synonyms

At the end of a definition, a group of synonyms is sometimes given. For example, at the end of the definition of *injure,* you'll find several synonyms, such as *damage* or *harm.* And if you look up *damage* or *harm,* you'll be referred to the same synonyms listed under *injure.*

List the synonyms given for the following words.

profess _____

weep _____

dodge _____

10. Abbreviations

Find the meaning of the following abbreviations.

DVD _____   HMO _____

SAM _____   CDC _____

11. Names of People

The names of famous people will be found either in the main part of your dictionary or in a separate biographical names section at the back.

Identify the following famous people.

Anna Ivanovna _____

Gabriel García Marquez _____

Grace Hopper _____

Frederick Douglass _____

12. Names of Places

The names of places will be found either in the main part of your dictionary or in a separate geographical names section at the back.

Identify the following places.

Killiecrankie _____

Chernobyl _____

Biolystok _____

Zanzibar _____

13. Foreign Words and Phrases

Find the language and the meaning of the italicized expressions.

1. The *hors d'oeuvres* at the party were delicious. _____

   _____

2. I hope to graduate *magna cum laude*. _____

   _____

3. My new sheet music said that it should be played *all' otava*. _____

   _____

4. Beverly's projects were always considered the *crème de la crème*. _____

   _____

14. Miscellaneous Information

Find these miscellaneous bits of information in a good dictionary.

1. What duty is a *devil's advocate* supposed to perform? _____

   _____

2. In what country would you measure liquid by *mutchkin*? _____

   _____

3. Under what circumstances should someone be given *ipecac*? _____

   _____

4. Is a *macaroon* something to eat or something to wear? _____

   _____

5. What part of speech is the expression *yoo-hoo*? _____

   _____

PART 2

Sentence Structure

Sentence structure refers to the way sentences are built using words, phrases, and clauses. Words are single units, and words link up in sentences to form clauses and phrases. Clauses are word groups *with* subjects and verbs, and phrases are word groups *without* subjects and verbs. Clauses are the most important because they make statements—they tell who did what (or what something is) in a sentence. Look at the following sentence for example:

We bought oranges at the farmer's market on Main Street.

It contains ten words, each playing its own part in the meaning of the sentence. But which of the words together tell who did what? *We bought oranges* is correct. That word group is a clause. Notice that *at the farmer's market* and *on Main Street* also link up as word groups but don't have somebody (subject) doing something (verb). Instead, they are phrases to clarify *where* we bought the oranges.

Importantly, you could leave out one or both of the phrases and still have a sentence—*We bought oranges.* However, you cannot leave the clause out. Then you would just have *At the farmer's market on Main Street.* Remember, every sentence needs at least one clause that can stand by itself.

Learning about the structure of sentences helps you control your own. Once you know more about sentence structure, you can understand writing errors and learn how to correct them.

Among the most common errors in writing are fragments, run-ons, and awkward phrasing.

Here are some fragments:

Wandering around the mall all afternoon.

Because I tried to do too many things at once.

By interviewing the applicants in groups.

They don't make complete statements—not one has a clause that can stand by itself. Who was *wandering*? What happened *because you tried to do too many things at once*? What was the result of *interviewing the applicants in groups*? These incomplete sentence structures fail to communicate a complete thought.

In contrast, here are some run-ons:

Computer prices are dropping they're still beyond my budget.

The forecast calls for rain I'll wait to wash my car.

A truck parked in front of my driveway I couldn't get to school.

Unlike fragments, run-ons make complete statements, but the trouble is they make *two* complete statements; the first *runs on* to the second without correct punctuation. The reader has to go back to see where there should have been a break.

So fragments don't include enough information, and run-ons include too much. Another problem occurs when the information in a sentence just doesn't make sense.

Here are a few sentences with awkward phrasing:

The problem from my grades started to end.

It was a time at the picnic.

She won me at chess.

Try to find the word groups that show who did what, that is, the clauses. Once you find them, try to put the clauses and phrases together to form a precise meaning. It's difficult, isn't it? You'll see that many of the words themselves are misused or unclear, such as *from, it,* and *won.* These sentences don't communicate clearly because the clauses, phrases, and even words don't work together. They suffer from awkward phrasing.

Fragments, run-ons, awkward phrasing, and other sentence structure errors confuse the reader. Not until you get rid of them will your writing be clearer and easier to read. Unfortunately, there is no quick, effortless way to learn to avoid errors in sentence structure. First, you need to understand how clear sentences are built. Then you will be able to avoid common errors in your own writing.

This section will describe areas of sentence structure one at a time and then explain how to correct errors associated with the different areas. For instance, we start by helping you find subjects and verbs and understand dependent clauses; then we show you how to avoid fragments. You can go through the whole section yourself to learn all of the concepts and structures. Or your teacher may assign only parts based on errors the class is making.

Finding Subjects and Verbs

The most important words in sentences are those that make up its independent clause—the subject and the verb. When you write a sentence, you write about *something* or *someone.* That's the *subject.* Then you write what the subject *does* or *is.* That's the *verb.*

Lightning strikes.

The word *Lightning* is the thing you are writing about. It's the subject, and we'll underline all subjects once. *Strikes* tells what the subject does. It shows the action in the sentence. It's the verb, and we'll underline all of them twice. Most sentences do not include only two words (the subject and the verb). However, these two words still make up the core of the sentence even if other words and phrases are included with them.

Lightning strikes back and forth from the clouds to the ground very quickly.

Often lightning strikes people on golf courses or in boats.

When many words appear in sentences, the subject and verb can be harder to find. Because the verb often shows action, it's easier to spot than the subject. Therefore, always look for it first. For example, take this sentence:

The neighborhood cat folded its paws under its chest.

Which word shows the action? The action word is folded. It's the verb, so we'll underline it twice. Now ask yourself, who or what folded? The answer is cat. That's the subject, so we'll underline it once.

Study the following sentences until you understand how to pick out subjects and verbs.

Tomorrow our school celebrates its fiftieth anniversary. (Which word shows the action? The action word is celebrates. It's the verb, so we'll underline it twice. Who or what celebrates? The school does. It's the subject. We'll underline it once.)

The team members ate several boxes of chocolates. (Which word shows the action? Ate shows the action. Who or what ate? Members ate.)

Internet users crowd the popular services. (Which word shows the action? The verb is crowd. Who or what crowd? Users crowd.)

Often the verb doesn't show action but merely tells what the subject *is* or *was.* Learn to spot such verbs—*is, am, are, was, were, seems, feels, appears, becomes, looks. . . .* (For more information on these special verbs, see the discussion of sentence patterns on p. 136.)

Marshall is a neon artist. (First spot the verb is. Then ask who or what is? Marshall is.)

The bread appears moldy. (First spot the verb appears. Then ask who or what appears? Bread appears.)

Sometimes the subject comes after the verb, especially when a word like *there* or *here* begins the sentence without being a real subject. It's best not to start sentences with "There is . . ." or "There are . . ." for this reason.

> In the audience were two reviewers from the *Times*. (Who or what were in the audience? Two reviewers from the *Times* were in the audience.)
>
> There was a fortune-teller at the carnival. (Who or what was there? A fortune-teller was there at the carnival.)
>
> There were name tags for all the participants. (Who or what were there? Name tags were there for all the participants.)
>
> Here are the contracts. (Who or what are here? The contracts are here.)

> **Note** - Remember that *there* and *here* (as used in the last three sentences) are not subjects. They simply point to something.

In commands, often the subject is not expressed. An unwritten *you* is understood by the reader.

> Sit down. (You sit down.)
>
> Place flap A into slot B. (You place flap A into slot B.)
>
> Meet me at 7:00. (You meet me at 7:00.)

Commonly, a sentence may have more than one subject.

> Toys and memorabilia from the 1950s are high-priced collectibles.
>
> Celebrity dolls, board games, and even cereal boxes from that decade line the shelves of antique stores.

A sentence may also have more than one verb.

> Water boils at a consistent temperature and freezes at another.
>
> The ice tray fell out of my hand, skidded across the floor, and landed under the table.

E X E R C I S E S

Underline the subjects once and the verbs twice in the following sentences. When you've finished the first set, compare your answers carefully with those at the back of the book.

Exercise 1

1. The summer heat causes many problems for people.
2. Food spoils more quickly in the summer.
3. Insects and other pests seek shelter inside.
4. There are power outages due to excessive use of air conditioners and fans.
5. In some areas, smog levels increase dramatically in the summer.
6. Schoolchildren suffer in overheated classrooms.
7. On the worst days, everyone searches for a swimming pool or drives to the beach.
8. Sleeping comfortably becomes impossible.
9. No activity seems worth the effort.
10. But the heat of summer fades in our minds at the first real break in the weather.

Exercise 2

1. In 1992, Jacquelyn Barrett became the sheriff of Fulton County, Georgia.
2. She was the first African-American woman sheriff in U.S. history.
3. As sheriff of Fulton County, Barrett managed the biggest system of jails in the state of Georgia.
4. Her department had a yearly budget of sixty-five million dollars.
5. Over a thousand people worked for the Fulton County Sheriff's office.
6. Barrett definitely broke the stereotype of southern sheriffs in TV and movies.

7. By 1999, there were over eleven hundred sheriffs in the South.

8. African-American men and women represented just five percent of the total.

9. Only one percent of them were women.

10. However, of the twenty-four female sheriffs in the country, nine were from the South.

Sources: USA Today, December 16, 1999, and *Essence,* July 2000

Exercise 3

1. Katharine M. Rogers recently published her biography of L. Frank Baum.

2. Most people know Baum's work but not his name.

3. L. Frank Baum wrote *The Wonderful Wizard of Oz* and many other children's books and stories.

4. Of course, filmmakers used Baum's tale of the Wizard of Oz in the classic movie of the same name.

5. Baum's memorable character of the Scarecrow has an interesting story behind him.

6. During Baum's childhood, his father bought some farmland.

7. Baum saw scarecrows in the fields and found them fascinating.

8. Unfortunately, his keen imagination led to bad dreams about a scarecrow.

9. The scarecrow in his dreams ran after him but fell into a heap of straw just in time.

10. As a writer, Baum brought the Scarecrow to life in his Oz stories and made him less of a nightmare and more of a friend.

Source: L. Frank Baum: Creator of Oz (St. Martin's Press, 2002)

Exercise 4

1. In 2000, the American Film Institute made a list of "America's Funniest Movies."
2. AFI called the list "100 Years . . . 100 Laughs."
3. Many of the movies had their stars or their directors in common.
4. For instance, Katherine Hepburn and Cary Grant were leading actors in both *Bringing Up Baby* and *The Philadelphia Story.*
5. The films of director Woody Allen appeared five times on the list.
6. Some decades produced more of the best comedies than others.
7. Filmmakers in the 1980s, for example, created twenty-two of the funniest.
8. But there were only two films from the 1990s.
9. Perhaps millennium mania resulted in an increase in scary movies instead of comedies.
10. AFI's list of great comedies offered a resource for people in search of a good movie.

Source: www.afi.com/tv/laughs.asp

Exercise 5

1. There was another cloning breakthrough in the news in 2003.
2. Scientists in Italy cloned a horse.
3. The foal's name was Prometea.
4. Unusually, her mother was also her twin.
5. Prometea's DNA came from a mare.
6. Then that mare carried the cloned filly to term.
7. Upon Prometea's arrival, the two horses were unique in the world.

8. Prometea was the first cloned horse.

9. And her mother was first to carry her own clone to term.

10. Not surprisingly, the success of Prometea's cloning interested horseracing fans.

Source: Science News, August 9, 2003

PARAGRAPH EXERCISE

Underline the subjects once and the verbs twice in the following student paragraph.

I was on the volleyball team in high school, so my high school gym was a special place for me. It was an ordinary gym with bleachers on both sides. There were basketball court lines on the floors and the school's mascot in the center. We stretched a net across the middle for our volleyball games. The pale wooden floors sparkled, sometimes with sweat and sometimes with tears. The gym had a distinct stuffy smell of grimy socks, stale potato chips, and sticky sodas. I liked the smell and remember it fondly. Songs from dances and screams and cheers from games echoed throughout the big old building. In the gym during those high school years, I felt a sense of privacy and community.

SENTENCE WRITING

Write ten sentences about any subject—your favorite snack food, for instance. Keeping your subject matter simple in these sentence-writing exercises will make it easier to find your sentence structures later. After you have written your sentences, go back and underline your subjects once and your verbs twice.

Locating Prepositional Phrases

Prepositional phrases are among the easiest structures in English to learn. Remember that a phrase is just a group of related words (at least two) without a subject and a verb. And don't let a term like *prepositional* scare you. If you look in the middle of that long word, you'll find a familiar one—*position.* In English, we tell the *positions* of people and things in sentences using prepositional phrases.

Look at the following sentence with its prepositional phrases in parentheses:

Our field trip (to the desert) begins (at 6:00) (in the morning) (on Friday).

One phrase tells where the field trip is going (*to the desert*), and three phrases tell when the trip begins (*at 6:00, in the morning,* and *on Friday*). As you can see, prepositional phrases show the position of someone or something in space or in time.

Here is a list of some prepositions that can show positions in space:

under	across	with	against
around	by	inside	at
through	beyond	over	beneath
above	among	on	in
below	near	behind	past
between	without	from	to

Here are some prepositions that can show positions in time:

before	throughout	past	within
after	by	until	in
since	at	during	for

These lists include only individual words, *not phrases.* Remember, a preposition must be followed by an object—someone or something—to create a prepositional phrase. Notice that in the added prepositional phrases that follow, the position of the balloon in relation to the object, *the clouds,* changes completely.

The hot-air balloon floated *above the clouds.*
below the clouds.
within the clouds.
between the clouds.

> *past the clouds.*
>
> *around the clouds.*

Now notice the different positions in time:

> The balloon landed *at 3:30.*
>
> *by 3:30.*
>
> *past 3:30.*
>
> *before the thunderstorm.*
>
> *during the thunderstorm.*
>
> *after the thunderstorm.*

Note - A few words—such as *of, as,* and *like*—are prepositions that do not fit neatly into either the space or time category, yet they are very common prepositions (box *of candy,* note *of apology,* type *of bicycle*—act *as a substitute,* use *as an example,* testified *as an expert*—vitamins *like A, C, and E,* acts *like a child,* moves *like a snake*).

By locating prepositional phrases, you will be able to find subjects and verbs more easily. For example, you might have difficulty finding the subject and verb in a long sentence like this:

> After the rainy season, one of the windows in the attic leaked at the corners of its molding.

But if you put parentheses around all the prepositional phrases like this

> (After the rainy season), <u>one</u> (of the windows) (in the attic) <u>leaked</u> (at the
>
> corners) (of its molding).

then you have only two words left—the subject and the verb. Even in short sentences like the following, you might pick the wrong word as the subject if you don't put parentheses around the prepositional phrases first.

> <u>Two</u> (of the characters) <u>lied</u> (to each other) (throughout the play).
>
> The <u>waves</u> (around the ship) <u>looked</u> real.

> **Note** - Don't mistake *to* plus a verb for a prepositional phrase. Special forms of verbals always start with *to*, but they are not prepositional phrases (see p. 125). For example, in the sentence "I like to run to the beach," *to run* is a verbal, not a prepositional phrase. However, *to the beach* is a prepositional phrase because it begins with a preposition (to), ends with a noun (beach), and shows position in space.

EXERCISES

Put parentheses around the prepositional phrases in the following sentences. Be sure to start with the preposition itself (*in, on, to, at, of . . .*) and include the word or words that go with it (*in the morning, on our sidewalk, to Hawaii . . .*). Then underline the sentences' subjects once and verbs twice. Remember that subjects and verbs are not found inside prepositional phrases, so if you locate the prepositional phrases *first*, the subjects and verbs will be much easier to find. Review the answers given at the back for each set of ten sentences before continuing.

Exercise 1

1. (For nearly thirty years), a phone booth stood (in the middle of the Mojave Desert) (with absolutely nothing) (around it.)
2. It was far (from any sign) (of civilization) but originally served miners in camps far away.
3. The number (for this pay phone) became well-known (over time:) 760-733-9969.
4. People called it (from around the world) and traveled (to it) (for fun and adventure.)
5. Sites (on the Internet) posted the isolated phone's number and offered maps (to its remote location) (near Baker, California.)
6. Individuals camped (outside the booth) and waited (for random calls) (from strangers)
7. Callers never expected an answer (from a phone) (in the middle) (of nowhere.)

8. On many occasions, callers panicked and said nothing for a minute or two.

9. In addition, some of its visitors vandalized the booth and the phone itself.

10. So phone-company workers removed the infamous Mojave phone booth in May 2000.

Source: Washington Post, May 25, 2000

Exercise 2

1. At some point at a restaurant, most people ask for a box or a bag for leftovers.

2. At home, such containers go into the refrigerator and sit for a few days.

3. Sometimes they sit for too many days.

4. Unaware of the age of those leftovers, a person eats them and gets sick.

5. A chain of restaurants in Chicago now labels "doggie bags" with freshness information.

6. Like the dates and warnings on products at supermarkets, these labels for leftovers inform people about food-safety issues.

7. Leftovers need almost immediate refrigeration for safety's sake.

8. Such food stays fresh in the fridge for only a few days.

9. Leftover food also needs special reheating to a specific temperature.

10. With this information, food-safety associations hope to save many people from unnecessary illness.

Source: Newsweek, August 25, 2003

Exercise 3

1. Twiggy the Squirrel is a star in the world of trained animals.

2. Twiggy performs on a pair of tiny water skis and delights crowds at boat shows and other events.

3. Like many other famous animal entertainers, the current Twiggy is not the original.

4. The Twiggy of today is fifth in the line of Twiggys.

5. Lou Ann Best is Twiggy's trainer and continues the work begun by her husband Chuck during the 1970s.

6. In his time, Chuck Best convinced many types of animals to ride on water skis.

7. He had success with everything from a dog to a frog.

8. But Twiggy the Squirrel was a hit with crowds from the beginning.

9. All of the Twiggys seemed happy with their show-biz lifestyles.

10. In fact, the Bests received four of the Twiggys from the Humane Society.

Source: Current Science, May 2, 2003

Exercise 4

1. At 2 A.M. on the first Sunday in April, something happens to nearly everyone in America: Daylight Saving Time.

2. But few people are awake at two in the morning.

3. So we set the hands or digits of our clocks ahead one hour on Saturday night in preparation for it.

4. And before bed on the last Saturday in October, we turn them back again.

5. For days after both events, I have trouble with my sleep patterns and my mood.

6. In spring, the feeling is one of loss.

7. That Saturday-night sleep into Sunday is one hour shorter than usual.

8. But in fall, I gain a false sense of security about time.

9. That endless Sunday morning quickly melts into the start of a hectic week like the other fifty-one in the year.

10. All of this upheaval is due to the Uniform Time Act of 1966.

Exercise 5

1. I saw a news story about an art exhibit with a unique focus and message.

2. All of the pieces in the art show started with the same basic materials.

3. The materials were all of the parts of a huge English oak tree.

4. Most of a tree usually becomes waste except the large trunk section.

5. But in the case of this tree, artists took every last bit and made "art" with it as a tribute to the tree.

6. One artist even made clothes from some of the smallest pieces—tiny branches, sawdust, and leaves.

7. Another artist used thousands of bits of the tree in a kind of mosaic painting.

8. Still another turned one hunk of the tree's timber into a pig sculpture.

9. Other chunks, branches, and even the roots became abstract pieces of art.

10. The tree lives on as art and as a new tree with the sprouting of an acorn in its old location.

PARAGRAPH EXERCISE

Put parentheses around the prepositional phrases in this paragraph from *A Golden Guide: Weather,* by Paul E. Lehr, R. William Burnett, and Herbert S. Zim.

Water Storage

Lakes and ponds obviously store a great deal of water. Not so obvious is the immense reservoir of water stored in the polar ice caps, in glaciers, and in snow on mountains and on the cold northern plains during winter. Winter snows in the mountains determine the water supply for irrigation and for power use. This snow melts with the spring thaw and fills the rivers.

SENTENCE WRITING

Write ten sentences describing your favorite place to relax—or choose any topic you like. When you go back over your sentences, put parentheses around your prepositional phrases and underline your subjects once and your verbs twice.

Understanding Dependent Clauses

All clauses contain a subject and a verb, yet there are two kinds of clauses: *independent* and *dependent.* Independent clauses have a subject and a verb and make complete statements by themselves. Dependent clauses have a subject and a verb but don't make complete statements because of the words they begin with. Here are some of the words (conjunctions) that begin dependent clauses:

after	since	where
although	so that	whereas
as	than	wherever
as if	that	whether
because	though	which
before	unless	whichever
even if	until	while
even though	what	who
ever since	whatever	whom
how	when	whose
if	whenever	why

When a clause starts with one of these dependent words, it is usually a dependent clause. To show you the difference between an independent and a dependent clause, look at this example of an independent clause:

We ate dinner together.

It has a subject (We) and a verb (ate), and it makes a complete statement. But as soon as we put one of the dependent words in front of it, the clause becomes dependent because it no longer makes a complete statement:

After we ate dinner together . . .

Although we ate dinner together . . .

As we ate dinner together . . .

Before we ate dinner together . . .

Since we ate dinner together . . .

That we ate dinner together . . .

When we ate dinner together . . .

While we ate dinner together . . .

Each of these dependent clauses leaves the reader expecting something more. Each would depend on another clause—an independent clause—to make a sentence. For the rest of this discussion, we'll place a broken line beneath dependent clauses.

After we ate dinner together, we went to the evening seminar.

We went to the evening seminar *after* we ate dinner together.

The speaker didn't know *that* we ate dinner together.

While we ate dinner together, the restaurant became crowded.

As you can see in these examples, *when a dependent clause comes before an independent clause, it is followed by a comma.* Often the comma prevents misreading, as in the following sentence:

When he returned, the DVD was on the floor.

Without a comma after *returned,* the reader would read *When he returned the DVD* before realizing that this was not what the author meant. The comma prevents misreading. Sometimes, if the dependent clause is short and there is no danger of misreading, the comma can be left out, but it's safer simply to follow the rule that a dependent clause coming before an independent clause is followed by a comma. You'll learn more about the punctuation of dependent clauses on page 181, but right now just remember the previous rule.

Note that a few of the dependent words (*that, who, which, what*) can do "double duty" as both the dependent word and the subject of the dependent clause:

Thelma wrote a book *that* sold a thousand copies.

The manager saw *what* happened.

Sometimes the dependent clause is in the middle of the independent clause:

The book *that* sold a thousand copies was Thelma's.

The events *that* followed the parade delighted everyone.

The dependent clause can even be the subject of the entire sentence:

What you do also affects me.

How your project looks counts for ten percent of the grade.

Also note that sometimes the *that* of a dependent clause is omitted:

I know *that* you feel strongly about this issue.

I know you feel strongly about this issue.

Everyone received the classes *that* they wanted.

Everyone received the classes they wanted.

Of course, the word *that* doesn't always introduce a dependent clause. It may be a pronoun and serve as the subject or object of the sentence:

That was a long movie.

We knew *that* already.

That can also be an adjective, a descriptive word telling *which one:*

That movie always upsets me.

We took them to *that* park last week.

E X E R C I S E S

Draw a broken line beneath any dependent clauses in the following sentences. Some sentences have no dependent clauses, and others have more than one. The best way to begin is to look for the dependent words (*when, since, that, because, after . . .*) and be sure they are followed by subjects and verbs. Finally, underline the subjects once and the verbs twice in both the independent and dependent clauses. Compare your underlines with those at the back of the book carefully after each set.

Exercise 1

1. When I was on vacation in New York City I loved the look of the Empire State Building at night.

2. I thought that the colored lights at the top of this landmark were just decorative.

3. I did not know that their patterns also have meaning.

4. While I waited at the airport, I read a pamphlet that explained what the patterns mean.

5. Some of the light combinations reveal connections that are obvious.

6. For instance, if the occasion is St. Patrick's Day, the top of the building glows with green lights.

7. Whenever the holiday involves a celebration of America, the three levels of lights shine red, white, and blue.

8. There are other combinations that are less well-known.

9. Red-black-green is a pattern that signals Martin Luther King Jr. Day.

10. Whenever I visit the city again and see pink and white lights at the top of that famous building, I'll know that they are there for breast-cancer awareness.

Exercise 2

1. When Barbara Mitchell ate lunch at a California restaurant in late 1997, she thought that the service was terrible.

2. The lunch that Mitchell ordered consisted of salad, soup, pasta, and iced tea.

3. She received the bill, which came to twenty-four dollars, and charged it to her credit card.

4. Because the service was so bad, Mitchell wrote in a one-cent tip.

5. But when Mitchell saw her credit-card statement, she nearly fainted.

6. The tip that was a penny turned into a charge of ten thousand dollars, in addition to the twenty-four dollars for her food.

7. The waiter told authorities that he entered the huge tip amount by mistake.

8. When the restaurant's manager learned of the error, she suspended the waiter for seven days.

9. Mitchell received a full refund, an apology, and a gift certificate from the restaurant.

10. Mitchell wishes that she paid the bill with cash.

Source: Daily News (Los Angeles), January 8, 1998

Exercise 3

1. In June of 2000, there was another incident of mistaken tipping at a bar in Chicago.
2. This time, a male customer left a real ten-thousand-dollar tip for a waitress who was especially nice to him.
3. At least everyone thought that he gave her that amount until the man later denied his generosity.
4. The customer, who was a London resident on a trip to the United States, did everything to convince the people in the bar that he was serious.
5. Melanie Uczen was the waitress who served the man his drinks, which added up to nine dollars.
6. He told her that he was a doctor and wanted to help with her college plans.
7. When the bar's owner questioned the tip, the customer allowed the owner to make a copy of his passport.
8. He even signed a note that verified the tip's amount.
9. Back in London, the man said that he was not a doctor and claimed that he was drunk when he signed the note.
10. Because the big tip brought the bar so much publicity, the owners paid Melanie Uczen the ten thousand dollars themselves.

Source: Washington Post, June 11, 2000

Exercise 4

1. The happiest ending to a big-tipper story came in July of 2000.

2. It began when Karen Steinmetz, who dispatches cars for Continental Limo company, received a call for a driver and limo at 2:30 in the morning.

3. The most unusual part of the customer's request was that he wanted the driver to take him over nine hundred miles, from southern California to Oregon.

4. When Steinmetz contacted the first driver to see if he wanted the job, he told her that he wanted only sleep at that hour.

5. So Steinmetz called Major Cephas, another driver who worked for Continental.

6. Cephas took the job and picked the customer up in the city of Garden Grove.

7. The two men drove through the night but stopped in Sacramento and other spots along the way for exercise and refreshments.

8. Overall, the trip took nearly eighteen hours, which resulted in a twenty-two-hundred-dollar fare.

9. The passenger paid the fare and gave Cephas a twenty-thousand-dollar tip because Cephas was so patient with him.

10. This time, the tip was as real as the disappointment of the first driver who turned down the job.

Source: Los Angeles Times, July 12, 2000

Exercise 5

1. My coworker told me about a news story that he saw on television.

2. It involved those baby turtles that hatch in the sand at night.

3. Normally, once they hatch, they run as fast as they can toward the comforting waves.

4. As soon as they reach the water, they begin their lives as sea turtles.

5. The story that my friend saw told of a potential danger to these motivated little animals.

6. It seems that the turtles instinctively know which direction leads to the sea.

7. The bright white foam of the waves is the trigger that lures them across the sand to their proper destination.

8. Unfortunately, on some beaches where this phenomenon occurs, the tourist business causes a big problem for the turtles.

9. Tourists who want to see the turtles gather at shoreline restaurants and dance pavilions whose lights are so bright that they prompt the turtles to run in the wrong direction—up the beach away from the water.

10. Stories like these remind us of how delicate the balance of nature is.

PARAGRAPH EXERCISE

Underline the subjects once, the verbs twice, and put a broken line under the dependent clauses in this brief excerpt from *The Handy History Answer Book*.

Today experts disagree over the impact of television on our lives. Some argue that increased crime is a direct outcome of television since programs show crime as an everyday event and since advertisements make people aware of what they don't have. Critics also maintain that television stimulates aggressive behavior, reinforces ethnic stereotyping, and leads to a decrease in activity and creativity. Proponents of television counter [when they cite] increased awareness in world events, improved verbal abilities, and greater curiosity as benefits of television viewing.

SENTENCE WRITING

Write ten sentences about your own relationship with television—the patterns or routines that have developed from your choice of watching or not watching TV. Try to write sentences that have both independent and dependent clauses. Then underline your subjects once, your verbs twice, and put a broken line under your dependent clauses.

Correcting Fragments

Sometimes a group of words looks like a sentence—with a capital letter at the beginning and a period at the end—but it may be missing a subject, a verb, or both. Such incomplete sentence structures are called *fragments.* Here are a few examples:

Just ran around with his arms in the air. (*Who* did? There is no subject.)

Paul and his sister with the twins. (*Did* what? There is no verb.)

Nothing to do at night. (This fragment is missing a subject and a real verb. *To do* is a verbal, see p. 125.)

To change these fragments into sentences, we must make sure each has a subject and a real verb:

The lottery winner just ran around with his arms in the air. (We added a subject.)

Paul and his sister with the twins arrived. (We added a verb.)

The jurors had nothing to do at night. (We added a subject and a real verb.)

Sometimes we can simply attach such a fragment to the previous sentence.

I want a fulfilling job. A teaching position, for example.

I want a fulfilling job—a teaching position, for example.

Or we can add a subject or a verb to the fragment and make it a complete sentence.

I want a fulfilling job. A teaching position is one example.

Phrases

By definition, phrases are word groups without subjects and verbs, so whenever a phrase is punctuated as a sentence, it is a fragment. Look at this example of a sentence followed by a phrase fragment beginning with *hoping* (see p. 125 for more about verbal phrases):

Actors waited outside the director's office. Hoping for a chance at an audition.

We can correct this fragment by attaching it to the previous sentence.

Actors waited outside the director's office, hoping for a chance at an audition.

Or we can change it to include a subject and a real verb.

Actors waited outside the director's office. They hoped for a chance at an audition.

Here's another example of a sentence followed by a phrase fragment:

Philosophy classes are difficult. When taught by great thinkers.

Here the two have been combined into one complete sentence:

Philosophy classes taught by great thinkers are difficult.

Or a better revision might be

Philosophy classes are difficult when taught by great thinkers.

Sometimes, prepositional phrases are also incorrectly punctuated as sentences. Here a prepositional phrase follows a sentence, but the word group is a fragment—it has no subject and verb of its own. Therefore, it needs to be corrected.

I live a simple life. With my family on our farm in central California.

Here is one possible correction:

I live a simple life with my family on our farm in central California.

Or it could be corrected this way:

My <u>family</u> and <u>I</u> <u>live</u> a simple life on our farm in central California.

Dependent Clauses

Dependent clauses punctuated as sentences are still another kind of fragment. A sentence needs a subject, a verb, *and* a complete thought. As discussed in the previous section, a dependent clause has a subject and a verb, but it begins with a word that makes its meaning incomplete, such as *after, while, because, since, although, when, if, where, who, which,* and *that.* (See p. 70 for a longer list of these conjunctions.) To correct such fragments, we need to eliminate the word that makes the clause dependent *or* add an independent clause.

Fragment

While <u>some</u> of us <u>wrote</u> in our journals.

Corrected

<u>Some</u> of us <u>wrote</u> in our journals.

or

While <u>some</u> of us <u>wrote</u> in our journals, the fire <u>alarm</u> <u>rang</u>.

Fragment

Which <u>kept</u> me from finishing my journal entry.

Corrected

The fire <u>alarm</u> <u>kept</u> me from finishing my journal entry.

or

<u>We</u> <u>responded</u> to the fire alarm, *which* <u>kept</u> me from finishing my journal entry.

Are fragments ever permissible? Professional writers sometimes use fragments in advertising and other kinds of writing. But professional writers use these fragments intentionally, not in error. Until you're an experienced writer, it's best to write in complete sentences. Especially in college writing, you should avoid using fragments.

E X E R C I S E S

Some—but not all—of the following word groups are sentences. The sentences include subjects and verbs and make complete statements. Write the word "sentence" next to each of the sentences. Any word groups that do *not* include subjects and verbs and make complete statements are fragments. Write the word "fragment" next to each of these incomplete sentence structures. Then change the fragments into sentences by ensuring that each has a subject and a real verb and makes a complete statement.

Exercise 1

1. I read an article about bananas for my health class in high school.
2. That bananas are in danger of extinction in the near future.
3. Due to a crop disease that infects the banana plants' leaves.
4. The disease makes the bananas get ripe too fast.
5. All of the kinds of bananas that people eat are at risk.
6. Some banana experts warning about no more bananas to eat.
7. No banana cream pies, banana splits, banana muffins, or banana bread.
8. Such an idea is new to a lot of us.
9. Most people never think about plant extinction.
10. Chocolate and coffee similar scares in the past.

Exercise 2

1. In my psychology class, we talk about gender a lot.
2. Especially ways of raising children without gender bias.
3. Meaning different expectations about boys' abilities and girls' abilities.
4. Experts have several suggestions for parents and teachers.
5. Ask girls to work in the yard and boys to do dishes sometimes.
6. Not making a big deal out of it.
7. Give both girls and boys affection as well as helpful criticism.
8. Encouraging physically challenging activities for both genders.

9. Give girls access to tools, and praise boys for kindness.

10. Most of all, value their different approaches to math and computers.

Exercise 3

Correct each phrase fragment by changing or adding words or by attaching the phrase to the complete sentence nearby.

1. The oceanliner *Titanic* sank in April of 1912. ~~Affecting~~ *It affected* thousands of families and inspiring books and movies around the world.

2. With three close relatives on the *Titanic* that April night., The Belman family remembers details of the disaster.

3. Two of the Belmans were lost after the sinking, One ~~surviving~~ *however survived* by swimming along next to a lifeboat and eventually climbing aboard.

4. The survivor, Grandfather Belman, returned to his family in Lebanon, And told them about the terrifying events of that night.

5. He recalled the efforts of the crew and the courage of the passengers. The icy cold water and the reassuring sight of the *Carpathia*.

6. Anthony Belman is Grandfather Belman's descendent. Now living in the United States and working as a bartender.

7. Inspired by the stories of his grandfather's survival and the loss of his other two relatives. Belman has created a cocktail in honor of all those touched by the *Titanic* disaster.

8. It's called the Titanic Iceberg. Made with rum, crème de menthe, and blue Curaçao.

9. After blending the mixture with ice and transferring it to a margarita glass. Belman adds two wedges of vanilla ice cream to the sea-blue drink for icebergs.

10. And as a final touch to remind everyone of the human toll of the disaster. The cocktail calls for two white Lifesaver candies floating on top of the icy blue slush.

Source: Washington Post, March 18, 1998

Exercise 4

Correct each dependent clause fragment by eliminating its dependent word or by attaching the dependent clause to the independent clause before or after it.

1. ~~When~~ Nathan King turned twelve. ~~He~~ *gone* had a heart-stopping experience.

2. Nathan was tossing a football against his bedroom wall, ~~Which~~ made the ball ricochet and land on his bed.

3. In a diving motion, Nathan fell on his bed to catch the ball, ~~As~~ it landed.

4. After he caught the ball. Nathan felt a strange sensation in his chest.

5. To his surprise, he looked down and saw the eraser end of a no. 2 pencil, ~~That~~ had pierced his chest and entered his heart.

6. Nathan immediately shouted for his mother. Who luckily was in the house at the time.

7. Because Nathan's mom is a nurse. She knew not to remove the pencil.

8. If she had pulled the pencil out of her son's chest. He would have died.

9. After Nathan was taken to a hospital equipped for open-heart surgery. He had the pencil carefully removed.

10. Fate may be partly responsible for Nathan's happy birthday story. Since it turned out to be his heart surgeon's birthday too.

Source: Time, March 20, 2000

Exercise 5

All of the following word groups contain subjects and verbs and are therefore clauses. If the *clause does not* begin with a dependent word (a conjunction such as *when, while, after, because, since, as, where, if, who, which,* or *that*), put a period after it. If the *clause does* begin with a dependent word (making it a dependent clause fragment), add an independent clause or revise the dependent clause to make it a sentence. These ten clauses are not about the same topic.

1. One of the people sitting next to me on the train sneezed four times in a row

2. Before intermission, the movie seemed endless

3. Before the paint was dry in the classrooms

4. The judge's question rattled the nerves of the contestants

5. Because there were fewer students in the program this year

6. Since his speech lasted for over an hour

7. Whenever the teacher reminds us about the midterm exam

8. Then we moved to Kentucky and stayed for two years

9. As soon as the order form reaches the warehouse

10. Buildings with odd shapes always interest me

PROOFREADING EXERCISE

Correct the five fragments in the following paragraph.

I love fireworks shows, Backyard displays or huge Fourth of July events. When the whole sky lights up with color and booms with noise. In fact, I have a dream to become a fireworks expert. If I could take a class in pyrotechnics right now, I would. Instead, I have to take general education classes. Like English, math, and psychology. Maybe an appointment with a career counselor would be a good idea. To help me find the right school. With a training program in fireworks preparation.

SENTENCE WRITING

Write ten fragments and then revise them so that they are complete sentences. Or exchange papers with another student and turn your classmate's ten fragments into sentences.

Correcting Run-on Sentences

Any word group having a subject and a verb is a clause. As we have seen, the clause may be independent (making a complete statement and able to stand alone as a sentence), or it may be dependent (beginning with a dependent word and unable to stand alone as a sentence). When two *independent* clauses are written together without proper punctuation between them, the result is called a *run-on sentence.* Here are some examples.

> Classical music is soothing I listen to it in the evenings.
>
> I love the sound of piano therefore, Chopin is one of my favorites.

Run-on sentences can be corrected in one of four ways:

1. **Make the two independent clauses into two sentences.**

> Classical music is soothing. I listen to it in the evenings.
>
> I love the sound of piano. Therefore, Chopin is one of my favorites.

2. **Connect the two independent clauses with a semicolon.**

> Classical music is soothing; I listen to it in the evenings.
>
> I love the sound of piano; therefore, Chopin is one of my favorites.

When a connecting word (transition) such as

also	however	otherwise
consequently	likewise	then
finally	moreover	therefore
furthermore	nevertheless	thus

is used to join two independent clauses, the semicolon comes before the connecting word, and a comma usually comes after it.

> Mobile phones are convenient; however, they are very expensive.
>
> Earthquakes scare me; therefore, I don't live in Los Angeles.
>
> Yasmin traveled to London; then she took the "Chunnel" to Paris.
>
> The college recently built a large new library; thus we have more quiet study areas.

Note - The use of the comma after the connecting word depends on how long the connecting word is. If it is only a short word, like *then* or *thus,* the comma is not necessary.

3. **Connect the two independent clauses with a comma and one of the following seven words (the first letters of which create the word *fanboys*): *for, and, nor, but, or, yet, so.***

> Classical music is soothing, *so* I listen to it in the evenings.
>
> Chopin is one of my favorites, *for* I love the sound of piano.

Each of the *fanboys* has its own meaning (for example, *so* means "as a result," and *for* means "because").

> Swans are beautiful birds, *and* they mate for life.
>
> Students may register for classes by phone, *or* they may do so in person.
>
> I applied for financial aid, *but* I was still working at the time.
>
> Brian doesn't know how to use a computer, *nor* does he plan to learn.

Before you put a comma before a *fanboys,* be sure there are two independent clauses. Note that the first sentence that follows has two independent clauses. However, the second sentence contains one independent clause with two verbs and therefore needs no comma.

> The snow began falling at dusk, and it continued to fall through the night.
>
> The snow began falling at dusk and continued to fall through the night.

4. **Make one of the clauses dependent by adding a dependent word (such as *since, when, as, after, while,* or *because*—see p. 70 for a longer list of these conjunctions).**

> *Since* classical music is soothing, I listen to it in the evenings.
>
> Chopin is one of my favorites *because* I love the sound of piano.

Ways to Correct Run-on Sentences

They were learning a new song. They needed to practice. (two sentences)

They were learning a new song; they needed to practice. (semicolon)

They were learning a new song; therefore, they needed to practice. (semicolon + transition)

They were learning a new song, so they needed to practice. (comma + *fanboys*)

Because they were learning a new song, they needed to practice. (dependent clause first)

They needed to practice because they were learning a new song. (dependent clause last)

Learn these ways to join two clauses, and you'll avoid run-on sentences.

EXERCISES

Exercises 1 and 2

CORRECTING RUN-ONS WITH PUNCTUATION

Most—but not all—of the following sentences are run-ons. If the sentence has two independent clauses, separate them with correct punctuation. For the first two exercises, *don't create any dependent clauses;* use only a period, a semicolon, or a comma to separate the two independent clauses. Remember to insert a comma only when the words *for, and, nor, but, or, yet,* or *so* are used to join two independent clauses.

Exercise 1

1. I just read an article about prehistoric rodents, and I was surprised by their size.

2. Scientists recently discovered the remains of a rat-like creature called *Phoberomys*; it was as big as a buffalo.

3. *Phoberomys* sat back on its large rear feet, and fed itself with its smaller front feet in just the way rats and mice do now.

4. This supersized rodent lived in South America, but luckily that was nearly ten million years ago.

5. At that time, South America was a separate continent. It had no cows or horses to graze on its open land.

6. South America and North America were separated by the sea, so there were also no large cats around to hunt and kill other large animals.

7. Scientists believe that *Phoberomys* thrived and grew large because of the lack of predators and competitors for food.

8. The *Phoberomys'* carefree lifestyle eventually disappeared for the watery separation between North and South America slowly became a land route.

9. The big carnivores of North America could travel down the new land route and the big rodents were defenseless against them.

10. The rodents who survived were the smaller ones who could escape underground and that is the reason we have no buffalo-sized rats today.

Source: Science News, September 20, 2003

Exercise 2

1. One day is hard for me every year. that day is my birthday.

2. I don't mind getting older, I just never enjoy the day of my birth.

3. For one thing, I was born in August, but summer is my least favorite season.

4. I hate the heat and the sun, so even traditional warm-weather activities get me down.

5. Sunblock spoils swimming, smog spoils biking, and crowds spoil the national parks.

6. To most people, the beach is a summer haven, to me, the beach in the summer is bright, busy, and boring.

7. I love to walk on the beach on the cold, misty days of winter or early spring I wear a big sweater and have the whole place to myself.

8. August also brings fire season to most parts of the country therefore, even television is depressing.

9. There are no holidays to brighten up August in fact, it's like a black hole in the yearly holiday calendar—after the Fourth of July but before Halloween and the other holidays.

10. I have considered moving my birthday to February even being close to Groundhog Day would cheer me up.

Exercises 3 and 4

CORRECTING RUN-ONS WITH DEPENDENT CLAUSES

Most—but not all—of the following sentences are run-ons. Correct any run-on sentences by making one or more of the clauses *dependent*. You may rephrase the clauses, but be sure to use dependent words (such as *since, when, as, after, while, because* or the other conjunctions listed on p. 70) to begin dependent clauses. In some sentences, you will want to put the dependent clauses first; in others, you may want to put them last (or in the middle of the sentence). Since various words can be used to start dependent clauses, your answers may differ from those suggested at the back of the book.

Exercise 3

1. You may have seen one of the funniest *Simpsons* episodes in that show dolphins rise from the sea and take over Springfield.

2. The Simpsons and the other residents of Springfield are defenseless against the dolphins the dolphins are smarter than the humans.

3. Of course, dolphins do have amazing abilities these abilities allow them to perform mental and physical feats beyond those of other animals.

4. For this reason, the U.S. government has trained dolphins for certain tasks these tasks cannot be performed as well by machines or humans.

5. In the mid-1960s, Tuffy the dolphin was taught to deliver and retrieve information and supplies hundreds of feet below the ocean's surface to the inhabitants of Sealab II.

6. Since then, dolphins have been put on patrol around ships and piers in many locations throughout the world the ships and piers were in danger of attack.

7. During the Iraq war, the U.S. forces took advantage of dolphins' sonar powers to locate underwater explosives near Iraqi ports.

8. Dolphins have special sonar skills with these skills the dolphins can tell the difference between natural objects and manmade objects as small as pearls.

9. Finding these underwater mines is not dangerous for the dolphins the dolphins can use their sonar skills from far away and alert divers the divers then disarm the explosives.

10. The *Simpsons* episode is funny for a reason dolphins do seem to be better equipped in many ways than we are.

Source: Smithsonian, September 2003

Exercise 4

1. Our town has recently installed a new rapid transit system ~~it~~ *that* uses trains instead of only buses.

2. Freight trains used to run on tracks laid behind the buildings in town the new metro train tracks follow the same old route.

3. I might try this new transportation method the parking on campus has been getting worse every semester.

4. I would have to walk only a few blocks each day the stations are near my house and school.

5. Some students don't live near the train stations they have to take a bus to the train.

6. The old buses are bulky and ugly the new trains are sleek and attractive.

7. The new trains seem to be inspiring many people to be more conscious of their driving habits some people will never change.

8. I would gladly give up my car the convenience just has to match the benefits.

9. The city has plans for additional routes these routes will bring more commuters in from out of town.

10. My town is making real progress I am glad.

Exercise 5

Correct the following run-on sentences using any of the methods studied in this section: adding a period, a semicolon, or a semicolon plus a transition word, a comma before a *fanboys,* or using dependent words to create dependent clauses.

1. It's summer time there will be bugs.
2. People at picnics and backyard barbecues see bees and wasps as pests but they're just being themselves.
3. These creatures build their nests earlier in the year late summer is their vacation time too.
4. They leave their homes and look for sweets they are easy to find at picnics and barbecues.
5. The smell of a soda, for instance, attracts these insects so such drinks should be covered.
6. Also, people wear perfume these people are more likely to attract insects.
7. Even hair spray, body lotion, and soap scents interest bees, wasps, and flies.
8. The picnic location may be near a hive the hive might not be obvious.
9. It is so dangerous to upset or threaten any hive of insects people must be aware of their surroundings.
10. Insects can pose a threat to the peace and safety of summer activities therefore, the best defense is understanding.

Source: Better Homes and Gardens, September 2000

REVIEW OF FRAGMENTS AND RUN-ON SENTENCES

If you remember that all clauses include a subject and a verb, but only independent clauses can be punctuated as sentences (since only they can stand alone), then you will avoid fragments in your writing. And if you memorize these six rules for the punctuation of clauses, you will be able to avoid most punctuation errors.

Punctuating Clauses

I am a student. I am still learning.	(two sentences)
I am a student; I am still learning.	(two independent clauses)
I am a student; therefore, I am still learning.	(two independent clauses connected by a word such as *also, consequently, finally, furthermore, however, likewise, moreover, nevertheless, otherwise, then, therefore, thus*)
I am a student, so I am still learning.	(two independent clauses connected by *for, and, nor, but, or, yet, so*)
Because I am a student, I am still learning.	(dependent clause at beginning of sentence)
I am still learning because I am a student.	(dependent clause at end of sentence) The dependent words are *after, although, as, as if, because, before, even if, even though, ever since, how, if, in order that, since, so that, than, that though, unless, until, what, whatever, when, whenever, where, whereas, wherever, whether, which, whichever, while, who, whom, whose, why.*

It is essential that you learn the italicized words in the previous table—which ones come between independent clauses and which ones introduce dependent clauses.

PROOFREADING EXERCISE

Rewrite the following paragraph, making the necessary changes so there will be no fragments or run-on sentences.

People and animals require different amounts of sleep. People have to balance on two legs all day therefore, we need to get off our feet and sleep for about eight hours each night. Horses, however, are able to rest better standing up. Because their four legs support their bodies without a strain on any one area. When horses lie down, their large bodies press uncomfortably against the earth. Making their hearts and lungs work harder than they do in standing position.

Generally speaking, horses lie on the ground for about two hours a day and they spend only a little of the remaining time drowsy or lightly sleeping while still on their feet.

Source: *Illustrated Horsewatching* (Knickerbocker Press, 1999)

SENTENCE WRITING

Write a sample sentence of your own to demonstrate each of the six ways a writer can use to punctuate two clauses. You may model your sentences on the examples used in the preceding review chart.

Identifying Verb Phrases

Sometimes a verb is one word, but often the whole verb includes more than one word. These are called verb phrases. Look at several of the many forms of the verb *speak*, for example. Most of them are verb phrases, made up of the main verb *(speak)* and one or more helping verbs.

speak	is speaking	had been speaking
speaks	am speaking	will have been speaking
spoke	are speaking	is spoken
will speak	was speaking	was spoken
has spoken	were speaking	will be spoken
have spoken	will be speaking	can speak
had spoken	has been speaking	must speak
will have spoken	have been speaking	should have spoken

Note that words like the following are never verbs even though they may be near a verb or in the middle of a verb phrase:

already	finally	now	probably
also	just	often	really
always	never	only	sometimes
ever	not	possibly	usually

<u>Jason</u> <u>has</u> *never* <u>spoken</u> to his instructor before. <u>She</u> *always* <u>talks</u> with other students.

Two verb forms—*speaking* and *to speak*—look like verbs, but neither can ever be the verb of a sentence. No *ing* word by itself can ever be the verb of a sentence; it must be helped by another verb in a verb phrase. (See the discussion of verbal phrases on p. 125.)

Jeanine speaking French. (not a sentence because there is no complete verb phrase)

<u>Jeanine</u> <u>is speaking</u> French. (a sentence with a verb phrase)

And no verb with *to* in front of it can ever be the verb of a sentence.

Ted to speak in front of groups. (not a sentence because there is no real verb)

<u>Ted</u> <u>hates</u> to speak in front of groups. (a sentence with *hates* as the verb)

These two forms, *speaking* and *to speak,* may be used as subjects, or they may have other uses in the sentence.

adj

<u>Speaking</u> on stage <u>is</u> scary. <u>To speak</u> on stage <u>is</u> scary. <u>Ted</u> <u>had</u> a *speaking* part in that play.

E X E R C I S E S

Underline the subjects once and the verbs or verb phrases twice in the following sentences. It's a good idea to put parentheses around prepositional phrases first. (See p. 63 if you need help in locating prepositional phrases.) The sentences may contain independent *and* dependent clauses, so there could be several verbs and verb phrases. (Remember that *ing* verbs alone and the *to* _____ forms of verbs are never real verbs in sentences. We will learn more about them on p. 125.)

Exercise 1

1. Have you ever felt a craving (for art?)
2. Have you said to yourself, "I need a new painting, or I am going to go crazy"?
3. If you ever find yourself in this situation, you can get instant satisfaction.
4. I am referring to Art-o-Mat machines, of course.
5. These vending machines dispense small pieces of modern art.
6. You insert five dollars, pull a knob on a refurbished cigarette dispenser, and out comes an original art piece.
7. The artists themselves get fifty percent of the selling price.
8. Art-o-Mat machines can be found at locations across the country.
9. Art-o-Mats are currently dispensing tiny paintings, photographs, and sculptures in twelve states.
10. The machines have sold the works of hundreds of contemporary artists.

Source: www.artomat.org

Exercise 2

1. My daughter and I had been seeing commercials for the latest Cirque du Soleil tour on television.
2. The name of the show was *Varekai*, and the commercials promised creative costumes, evocative music, and breathtaking feats of physical skill.
3. We bought our tickets over the Internet and could not wait for the date of our show to arrive.
4. As we were approaching the arena, we caught a glimpse of the company's trademark blue and yellow circus tent in the parking lot.
5. The audience was arriving outside while the performers were warming up inside.
6. From outside the tent, we could hear music and the commotion of pre-show preparations.

7. Once the doors—or should I say flaps—of the tent were opened, the audience members were ushered to their seats.

8. We could not believe how incredible the *Varekai* show was.

9. The acrobats, contortionists, and flying acts dazzled and amazed the whole crowd.

10. The appreciative audience brought the performers out for three standing-ovation curtain calls, and they waved and blew kisses out to everyone.

Exercise 3

1. The largest meteorite that has ever been found on earth was recently at the center of a custody battle.

2. The American Museum of Natural History in New York has owned the Willamette meteorite since the early 1900s, and it was displayed at the Hayden Planetarium.

3. Scientists believe that the car-sized meteor landed between eight thousand and ten thousand years ago in what is now called Oregon.

4. The Wilamette meteorite may actually be the central part of an exploded planet.

5. But to one group of Native Americans, the huge meteor has always been known as "Tomanowos," or "Sky Person."

6. In a lawsuit against the museum, Grand Ronde tribe members claimed that their ancestors had worshiped Tomanowos for thousands of years before it was sold to the museum.

7. They could support their claims with tribal songs and dances that revealed a close relationship between the Grand Ronde people and the meteorite.

8. The museum and the Grand Ronde tribes did settle the dispute in August of 2000.

9. The two sides agreed that the Willamette meteorite would remain on display at the Hayden Planetarium but would be accompanied by a plaque that described the Grand Ronde tribes' connection to the meteor.

10. The museum also agreed to give the Grand Ronde people special access to the Willamette meteorite so that they may continue their relationship with Tomanowos.

Sources: Washington Post, June 23, 2000, and *New York Times Upfront,* March 27, 2000

Exercise 4

1. Bill and Melinda Gates have been two of the wealthiest people in the world for a while now.

2. In 2003, the Gateses donated fifty million dollars to the New York City public school system.

3. The couple is hoping that the gift will be used for the creation of hundreds of smaller schools within the system.

4. The curricula at the downsized schools would focus on single themes, such as law or medicine.

5. Teachers and administrators can cope better with fewer students and can have a greater impact on their pupils.

6. The people of New York City are not complaining about the Gates donation, but some do worry about the results.

7. Changing large academic institutions can be difficult.

8. Some educators question the concept of throwing money at the problem.

9. Others see such donations as good investments in the future.

10. If the Gates gamble pays off, students in New York City will be the winners.

Source: Newsweek, Sepetember 29, 2003

Exercise 5

1. Prehistoric musical instruments have been found before.

2. But the ancient flutes that were discovered in China's Henan Province included the oldest playable instrument on record.

3. The nine-thousand-year-old flute was made from the wing bone of a bird.

4. The bone was hollowed out and pierced with seven holes that produce the notes of an ancient Chinese musical scale.

5. Because one of the holes' pitches missed the mark, an additional tiny hole was added by the flute's maker.

6. The flute is played in the vertical position.

7. People who have studied ancient instruments are hoping to learn more about the culture that produced this ancient flute.

8. Other bone flutes were found at the same time and in the same location, but they were not intact or strong enough for playing. .

9. Visitors to the Brookhaven National Laboratory's Web site can listen to music from the world's oldest working flute.

10. Listeners will be taken back to 7,000 years B.C.

Source: www.bnl.gov

REVIEW EXERCISE

To practice finding all of the sentence structures we have studied so far, mark the following paragraphs from a student essay. First, put parentheses around prepositional phrases, then underline subjects once and verbs or verb phrases twice. Finally, put a broken line beneath dependent clauses. Begin by marking the first paragraph, then check your answers at the back of the book before going on to the next paragraph. (Remember that *ing* verbs alone and the *to* _____ forms of verbs are never real verbs in sentences. We will learn more about them on p. 125.)

My brain feels like a computer's central processing unit. Information is continually pumping into its circuits. I organize the data, format it to my individual preferences, and lay it out in my own style. As I endlessly sculpt existing formulas, they become something of my own. When I need a solution to a problem, I access the data that I have gathered from my whole existence, even my preprogrammed DNA.

Since I am a student, teachers require that I supply them with specific information in various formats. When they assign an essay, I produce several paragraphs. If they need a summary, I scan the text, find its main ideas, and put them briefly into my own words. I know that I can accomplish whatever the teachers ask so that I can obtain a bachelor's degree and continue processing ideas to make a living.

I compare my brain to a processor because right now I feel that I must work like one. As I go further into my education, my processor will be continually updated—just like a Pentium! And with any luck, I will end up with real, not artificial, intelligence.

Using Standard English Verbs

The next two discussions are for those who need to practice using Standard English verbs. Many of us grew up doing more speaking than writing. But in college and in the business and professional world, the use of Standard Written English is essential.

The following charts show the forms of four verbs as they are used in Standard Written English. These forms might differ from the way you use these verbs when you speak. Memorize the Standard English forms of these important verbs. The first verb (*talk*) is one of the regular verbs (verbs that all end the same way according to a pattern); most verbs in English are regular. The other three verbs charted here (*have, be,* and *do*) are irregular and are important because they are used not only as main verbs but also as helping verbs in verb phrases.

Don't go on to the exercises until you have memorized the forms of these Standard English verbs.

Regular Verb: Talk

	Present Time		Past Time
I you we they	talk	I you we they	talked
he, she, it	talks	he, she, it	

Irregular Verb: Have

	Present Time		Past Time
I you we they	have	I you we they	had
he, she, it	has	he, she, it	

Irregular Verb: Be

	Present Time		Past Time
I	am	I	was
you we they	are	you we they	were
he, she, it	is	he, she, it	was

Irregular Verb: Do

Present Time		Past Time	
I you we they	} do	I you we they	} did
he, she, it	does	he, she, it	

Sometimes you may have difficulty with the correct endings of verbs because you don't hear the words correctly. Note carefully the *s* sound and the *ed* sound at the end of words. Occasionally, the *ed* is not clearly pronounced, as in *They tried to help,* but most of the time you can hear it if you listen.

Read the following sentences aloud, making sure that you say every sound.

1. He seems satisfied with his new job.

2. She likes saving money for the future.

3. It takes strength of character to control spending.

4. Todd makes salad for every potluck he attends.

5. I used to know all their names.

6. They supposed that they were right.

7. He recognized the suspect and excused himself from the jury.

8. Shao Ming sponsored Dorothy in the school's charity event.

Now read some other sentences aloud from this text, making sure that you say all of the *s*'s and *ed*'s. Reading aloud and listening to others will help you use the correct verb endings automatically.

E X E R C I S E S

In these pairs of sentences, use the *present* form of the verb in the first sentence and the *past* form in the second. All the verbs follow the pattern of the regular verb *talk* except the irregular verbs *have, be,* and *do.* Keep referring to the tables if you're not sure which form to use. Check your answers in the back of the book after each set.

Exercise 1

1. (have) My brother _has_ a bad cold right now. He _had_ the flu last month.

2. (do) Jennifer _does_ the crossword puzzles in the newspaper. She _did_ them in the *TV Guide* until we canceled our subscription.

3. (be) I _am_ now the president of the chess club on campus. I _was_ just a member of the club last semester.

4. (vote) Pat _votes_ in every election. Pat _voted_ with an absentee ballot in 2003.

5. (have) The twins _have_ similar ideas about the environment. Last year, they _had_ a fund-raiser for their local wildlife preserve.

6. (shop) He _shops_ for almost everything online. He _shopped_ for groceries online last week.

7. (be) They _are_ finally satisfied with their living room. They _were_ embarrassed by it before the remodeling.

8. (pick) I _pick_ out the plants whenever we go to the nursery. Yesterday, I also _picked_ out the paint colors at the home improvement store.

9. (do) We _do_ what we can for the birds in winter. A few years ago, we _did_ our best to save a nearly frozen sparrow.

10. (end) That new movie _ends_ with a big surprise. It _ended_ before I had finished my popcorn.

Exercise 2

1. (be) They _____ rich and famous now. They _____ unknown a year ago.

2. (do) He _____ his best work in class. He _____ not do well on the take-home test.

3. (have) She _____ a new goal. She _____ an unrealistic goal before.

4. (tag) He _____ only the expensive items at his garage sales. In the past, he _____ all of the items.

5. (have) I always _____ a good time with my friends. At Disneyland, I _____ the best time of all.

6. (stuff) She _____ envelopes part time. Yesterday she _____ envelopes for five hours straight.

7. (be) Many of us _____ allergic to milk, so we _____ unable to eat the pizza at the postgame party.

8. (do) They _____ their best to help their parents. They _____ the grocery shopping and the dishes this week.

9. (dance) You _____ very well now. You _____ a little awkwardly in high school.

10. (be) At the moment, they _____ the fastest delivery people in the business. They _____ the second-fastest delivery people just six months ago.

Exercise 3

Underline the Standard English verb forms. All the verbs follow the pattern of the regular verb *talk* except the three irregular verbs *have, be,* and *do.* Keep referring to the tables if you are not sure which form to use.

1. I recently (change, changed) my career plans; now I (want, wants) to be a teacher.

2. Last year, I (have, had) my mind set on becoming a nurse.

3. I (enroll, enrolled) in nursing classes, but they (was, were) different from what I (expect, expected).

4. The classes (was, were) often too stressful, and the teachers (was, were) very demanding.

5. We (does, did) spend part of the semester working in a clinic where we (was, were) able to observe just what a nurse (do, does).

6. The nurse that I (observe, observed) (have, had) several patients to look after.

7. I (watch, watched) him as he (cares, cared) for them and (follow, followed) the doctors' orders.

8. He (have, had) his patients, their families, and the clinic's doctors and staff to worry about all the time.

9. I never (imagine, imagined) that a nurse (have, had) so many responsibilities.

10. A teacher (need, needs) to worry about the students and the school, and those (is, are) responsibilities that I (is, am) ready to take.

Exercise 4

1. My cousin Armina and I (has, have) a lot in common.

2. We both (play, plays) several musical instruments.

3. She (play, plays) the piano, the guitar, and the harp.

4. I (play, plays) the piano, the trumpet, and the clarinet.

5. However, Armina (practice, practices) more often than I (does, do).

6. The result (is, are) better performances.

7. I (is, am) as skilled as she (is, am), but I (is, am) also a little bit lazy.

8. Our parents (remind, reminds) us about practicing all the time.

9. Only Armina really (follow, follows) their advice.

10. We both (has, have) talent, but I (is, am) not as disciplined as she (is, am).

Exercise 5

Correct any of the following sentences that do not use Standard English verb forms.

1. Last semester my drawing teacher hand us an assignment.

2. It was half of a photograph pasted onto a whole piece of paper.

3. We has to draw in the other half of the picture.

4. My picture show a woman sitting against the bottom of a tree trunk.

5. Her shoulders, hat, and umbrella was only partly there.

6. I tried to imagine what the missing parts look like.

7. The tree was easy to fill in because its shape was clear in the photo.

8. Therefore, I starts with the tree, the sky, and the ground.

9. Then I used my imagination to fill in the woman's shoulders, hat, and umbrella.

10. I receives an "A" grade for my drawing.

PROOFREADING EXERCISE

Correct any sentences in the following paragraph that do not use Standard English verb forms.

I like family parties, especially when we invites all of our favorite relatives and friends. My dad usually do all of the shopping for food and supplies. If the party is a potluck, the meat dishes is the most popular. We has sliced beef, baked ham, and roast turkey. I looks forward to trying new salads. I remember that I love the ones that has the glazed walnuts in them. All I have to do is think about the food at our parties, and I starts to get hungry.

SENTENCE WRITING

Write ten sentences about the last party you had or attended. Check your sentences to be sure that they use Standard English verb forms. Try exchanging papers with another student if possible.

Using Regular and Irregular Verbs

All regular verbs end the same way in the past form and when used with helping verbs. Here is a table showing all the forms of some *regular* verbs and the various helping verbs with which they are used.

Regular Verbs				
Base Form	**Present**	**Past**	**Past Participle**	***ing* Form**
(Use after can, may, shall, will, could, might, should, would, must, do, does, did.)			*(Use after have, has, had. Some can be used after forms of be.)*	*(Use after forms of be.)*
ask	ask *(s)*	asked	asked	asking
bake	bake *(s)*	baked	baked	baking
count	count *(s)*	counted	counted	counting
dance	dance *(s)*	danced	danced	dancing
decide	decide *(s)*	decided	decided	deciding
enjoy	enjoy *(s)*	enjoyed	enjoyed	enjoying
finish	finish *(es)*	finished	finished	finishing
happen	happen *(s)*	happened	happened	happening
learn	learn *(s)*	learned	learned	learning
like	like *(s)*	liked	liked	liking
look	look *(s)*	looked	looked	looking
mend	mend *(s)*	mended	mended	mending
need	need *(s)*	needed	needed	needing
open	open *(s)*	opened	opened	opening
start	start *(s)*	started	started	starting
suppose	suppose *(s)*	supposed	supposed	supposing
tap	tap *(s)*	tapped	tapped	tapping
walk	walk *(s)*	walked	walked	walking
want	want *(s)*	wanted	wanted	wanting

Note - When there are several helping verbs, the last one determines which form of the main verb should be used: they *should* finish soon; they should *have* finished an hour ago.

When do you write *ask, finish, suppose, use*? And when do you write *asked, finished, supposed, used*? Here are some rules that will help you decide.

Write *ask, finish, suppose, use* (or their *s* forms) when writing about the present time, repeated actions, or facts:

He *asks* questions whenever he is confused.

They always *finish* their projects on time.

I *suppose* you want me to help you move.

Birds *use* leaves, twigs, and feathers to build their nests.

Write *asked, finished, supposed, used*

1. **When writing about the past:**

   He *asked* the teacher for another explanation.

   She *finished* her internship last year.

   They *supposed* that there were others bidding on that house.

   I *used* to study piano.

2. **When some form of *be* (other than the word *be* itself) comes before the word:**

   He was *asked* the most difficult questions.

   She is *finished* with her training now.

   They were *supposed* to sign at the bottom of the form.

   My essay was *used* as a sample of clear narration.

3. **When some form of *have* comes before the word:**

   The teacher has *asked* us that question before.

   She will have *finished* all of her exams by the end of May.

   I had *supposed* too much without any proof.

   We have *used* many models in my drawing class this semester.

All the verbs in the chart on page 105 are *regular*. That is, they're all formed in the same way—with an *ed* ending on the past form and on the past participle. But many verbs are irregular. Their past and past participle forms change spelling instead of just adding an *ed*. Here's a chart of some *irregular* verbs. Notice that the base, present, and *ing* forms end the same as regular verbs. Refer to this list when you aren't sure which verb form to use. Memorize all the forms you don't know.

Irregular Verbs

Base Form	Present	Past	Past Participle	*ing* Form
(Use after can, may, shall, will, could, might, should, would, must, do, does, did.)			*(Use after have, has, had. Some can be used after forms of be.)*	*(Use after forms of be.)*
be	is, am, are	was, were	been	being
become	become *(s)*	became	become	becoming
begin	begin *(s)*	began	begun	beginning
break	break *(s)*	broke	broken	breaking
bring	bring *(s)*	brought	brought	bringing
buy	buy *(s)*	bought	bought	buying
build	build *(s)*	built	built	building
catch	catch *(es)*	caught	caught	catching
choose	choose *(s)*	chose	chosen	choosing
come	come *(s)*	came	come	coming
do	do *(es)*	did	done	doing
draw	draw *(s)*	drew	drawn	drawing
drink	drink *(s)*	drank	drunk	drinking
drive	drive *(s)*	drove	driven	driving
eat	eat *(s)*	ate	eaten	eating
fall	fall *(s)*	fell	fallen	falling
feel	feel *(s)*	felt	felt	feeling
fight	fight *(s)*	fought	fought	fighting
find	find *(s)*	found	found	finding
forget	forget *(s)*	forgot	forgotten	forgetting
forgive	forgive *(s)*	forgave	forgiven	forgiving
freeze	freeze *(s)*	froze	frozen	freezing
get	get *(s)*	got	got *or* gotten	getting
give	give *(s)*	gave	given	giving
go	go *(es)*	went	gone	going
grow	grow *(s)*	grew	grown	growing
have	have *or* has	had	had	having
hear	hear *(s)*	heard	heard	hearing
hold	hold *(s)*	held	held	holding
keep	keep *(s)*	kept	kept	keeping
know	know *(s)*	knew	known	knowing
lay (to put)	lay *(s)*	laid	laid	laying
lead (like "bead")	lead *(s)*	led	led	leading

Base Form	Present	Past	Past Participle	*ing* Form
leave	leave *(s)*	left	left	leaving
lie (to rest)	lie *(s)*	lay	lain	lying
lose	lose *(s)*	lost	lost	losing
make	make *(s)*	made	made	making
meet	meet *(s)*	met	met	meeting
pay	pay *(s)*	paid	paid	paying
read	read *(s)*	read	read	reading
(pron. "reed")	(pron. "reeds")	(pron. "red")	(pron. "red")	
ride	ride *(s)*	rode	ridden	riding
ring	ring *(s)*	rang	rung	ringing
rise	rise *(s)*	rose	risen	rising
run	run *(s)*	ran	run	running
say	say *(s)*	said	said	saying
see	see *(s)*	saw	seen	seeing
sell	sell *(s)*	sold	sold	selling
shake	shake *(s)*	shook	shaken	shaking
shine (give light)	shine *(s)*	shone	shone	shining
shine (polish)	shine *(s)*	shined	shined	shining
sing	sing *(s)*	sang	sung	singing
sleep	sleep *(s)*	slept	slept	sleeping
speak	speak *(s)*	spoke	spoken	speaking
spend	spend *(s)*	spent	spent	spending
stand	stand *(s)*	stood	stood	standing
steal	steal *(s)*	stole	stolen	stealing
strike	strike *(s)*	struck	struck	striking
swim	swim *(s)*	swam	swum	swimming
swing	swing *(s)*	swung	swung	swinging
take	take *(s)*	took	taken	taking
teach	teach *(es)*	taught	taught	teaching
tear	tear *(s)*	tore	torn	tearing
tell	tell *(s)*	told	told	telling
think	think *(s)*	thought	thought	thinking
throw	throw *(s)*	threw	thrown	throwing
wear	wear *(s)*	wore	worn	wearing
win	win *(s)*	won	won	winning
write	write *(s)*	wrote	written	writing

Sometimes verbs from the past participle column are used after some form of the verb *be* (or verbs that take the place of *be*, such as *appear, seem, look, feel, get, act, become*) to describe the subject or to say something in a passive, rather than an active, way.

> She is contented.
>
> You appear pleased. (You *are* pleased.)
>
> He seems delighted. (He *is* delighted.)
>
> She looked surprised. (She *was* surprised.)
>
> I feel shaken. (I *am* shaken.)
>
> They get bored easily. (They *are* bored easily.)
>
> You acted concerned. (You *were* concerned.)
>
> They were thrown out of the game. (Active: *The referee threw them out of the game.*)
>
> We were disappointed by the news. (Active: *The news disappointed us.*)

Often these verb forms become words that describe the subject; at other times they still act as part of the verb in the sentence. What you call them doesn't matter. The only important thing is to be sure you use the correct form from the past participle column.

EXERCISES

Write the correct form of the verbs in the blanks. Refer to the tables and explanations on the preceding pages if you aren't sure which form to use after a certain helping verb. Check your answers after each exercise.

Exercise 1

1. (live)   I currently __live__ with my parents.
2. (live)   I have __lived__ with them all of my life.
3. (live)   Someday I will __live__ in my own apartment.
4. (live)   Once I am __living__ on my own, things will change for me.
5. (live)   My brother has __lived__ in a dorm ever since he moved to Berkeley.

6. (live)   In his e-mails, he describes the roommates that he _lived_ [lives] with.

7. (live)   I am glad that I can still _live_ at home while I am in college.

8. (live)   My parents seem pleased that I have been _living_ with them for so long.

9. (live)   We know each other's habits, and we _live_ with each other's quirks.

10. (live)   We are all a bit sad that I will soon be _living_ away from home.

Exercise 2

1. (get)   A few months ago, I _got_ a kitten named Samantha. She has silvery gray fur and long white whiskers. Samantha always _gets_ so excited when I sprinkle catnip on the rug.

2. (give)   When my friend Will _gave_ Samantha to me, she was the sleekest, most graceful of his cat's kittens. Since then, I have _given_ her almost all of my attention.

3. (be)   Now I _am_ a certified cat lover, and Sam _is_ a great cat.

4. (think)   Before I had Samantha, my parents _thought_ that I was too irresponsible to own a cat, but I didn't _think_ so, or I wouldn't have taken her in the first place.

5. (grow)   Samantha has _grown_ into a plump, handsome cat. And I _grew_ catnip plants in the backyard.

6. (leave)   Before I _leave_ for school each day, I make sure that Sam is inside the house. Once, I _left_ the kitchen window open, and I found her sitting near the street when I came home.

7. (wave) Sam loves to play with a toy that I made for her. I _____ the bunch of feathers on a string in front of her, and she _____ her paws at them and tries to eat them.

8. (know) Samantha _____ her name and will come when she hears me call. I didn't _____ that cats could do that.

9. (do) Sam _____ many cute things, and I _____ my best to keep her healthy and make her happy.

10. (be) I _____ a little nervous when I first brought Sam home, but I could not _____ happier with a pet than I _____ now.

Exercise 3

1. (take, suppose) My brother Jeff _____ me to the movies last Tuesday afternoon even though I was _____ to be in school.

2. (be, go) It _____ the only time that Jeff could _____ to the movies with me.

3. (call, leave, feel) So I _____ my teacher and _____ a message that I didn't _____ well enough to go to class.

4. (imagine, be) I never _____ that I would get caught, but I _____ wrong.

5. (buy, drive, see) Just as Jeff and I were _____ our tickets, my teacher _____ by and _____ us.

6. (feel, know, be) I _____ such panic because I _____ that my teacher would _____ disappointed in me.

7. (try, go) I _____ to explain myself when I _____ back to school the next day.

8. (be, undo) The damage had _____ done, however, and nothing could _____ it.

9. (wish, take)   Now I _____ that I could _____ back that day.

10. (do, be)   I _____ not have much fun with Jeff, and the movie _____ not even good.

Exercise 4

1. (use, have)   Many people _____ cell phones that _____ voice-recognition capabilities.

2. (do, speak, dial)   With such a system, callers _____ not have to dial phone numbers by hand. Instead, they just _____ into the phone, and the phone _____ the number.

3. (be, be)   When driving a car, callers _____ then free to watch the road and steer the car without distraction. These phones _____ much safer.

4. (be, like, start)   Voice dialing _____ almost always optional, but so many people _____ the system that most people have _____ to use it.

5. (do, want)   My mom _____ not trust such systems; she _____ to have complete control over her own dialing.

6. (trust, be)   She barely even _____ cell phones, so she _____ definitely suspicious of voice dialing.

7. (imagine, dial)   I can _____ her as a teenager in the sixties. In my mind, she is _____ one of those rotary-operated princess phones.

8. (ask, tell, be)   I was _____ my mom about phones the other day, and I _____ her how old-fashioned she _____.

9. (look, smile)   She just _____ at me and _____.

10. (have)   My mom _____ a way of saying a lot with just a smile.

Exercise 5

1. (sit, see)   I was _____ in the lobby of the haircutting place near my house when I _____ one of my old high school teachers, Mr. Blair.

2. (be, appear)   He _____ obviously waiting for a haircut too and _____ to be nervous about it.

3. (flip, turn, look)   As he _____ through a magazine, he _____ his face toward the big front window and _____ longingly in the direction of his car.

4. (be, wear,

think, be)   During my high school years, Mr. Blair _____ well-liked because he _____ his hair in a pony tail, so everyone _____ that he _____ cool.

5. (pass, seem)   As the minutes _____ in the hair salon, Mr. Blair _____ to calm down.

6. (wait, cut)   I was _____ to see whether Mr. Blair would really _____ his pony tail off after all these years.

7. (call, watch,

recognize)   When my name was _____ I _____ Mr. Blair's face to see whether he would _____ me.

8. (look, figure, be)   He didn't _____ up, so I _____ that he _____ too busy worrying about his own hair to notice me.

9. (get, chat, be)   I _____ my usual simple cut, and as I _____ with my haircutter, I _____ surprised to see Mr. Blair's haircutter finish his cut within just a few minutes.

10. (come, leave)   Mr. Blair had apparently just _____ in for a trim, and he _____ the lobby with the water from his long wet hair soaking into the top of his shirt.

PROGRESS TEST

This test covers everything you've learned in the Sentence Structure section so far. One sentence in each pair is correct. The other is incorrect. Read both sentences carefully before you decide. Then write the letter of the incorrect sentence in the blank. Try to name the error and correct it if you can.

1. _B_   **A.** My roommates had already put up all of the balloons by the time I arrived.

  B. I was looking forward to a night of decorating so I was disappointed.

2. _B_   **A.** Summer school goes by very quickly.

  B. Leaving us only a little time to do our assignments. frag.

3. _B_   **A.** Chris works at a home improvement center.

  B. He use to work at a pet store.

4. _A_   **A.** We looked everywhere for the theater tickets before I found them.

  B. They were laying on the floor beside the couch.

5. _A_   **A.** After eating a snack in the afternoon.

  B. I was able to work for several hours before dinner.

6. _A_   **A.** We have took taken many classes together.

  B. Last semester, we enrolled in three of the same classes.

7. _B_   **A.** Laverne likes every kind of restaurant.

  (f **B.** Whenever we go out to dinner.

8. _B_   **A.** Their field trip took them far into the desert.

  B. Their teacher was driving, he knew the road well.

9. _B_   **A.** We are learning about dependent clauses in my English class.

  (**B.**) Especially how they can be fragments if they are used alone.

10. _B_   **A.** I was suppose to pick up my sister after school.

  B. But she forgot and started walking home.

Maintaining Subject/Verb Agreement

As we have seen, the subject and verb in a sentence work together, so they must always agree. Different subjects need different forms of verbs. When the correct verb follows a subject, we call it subject/verb agreement.

The following sentences illustrate the rule that *s* verbs follow most singular subjects but not plural subjects.

One turtle walks.	Three turtles walk.
The baby cries.	The babies cry.
A democracy listens to the people.	Democracies listen to the people.
One child plays.	Many children play.

The following sentences show how forms of the verb *be* (*is, am, are, was, were*) and helping verbs (*be, have,* and *do*) are made to agree with their subjects.

This puzzle is difficult.	These puzzles are difficult.
I am amazed.	You are amazed.
He was sleeping.	They were sleeping.
That class has been canceled.	Those classes have been canceled.
She does not want to participate.	They do not want to participate.

The following words are always singular and take an *s* verb or the irregular equivalent (*is, was, has, does*):

one	anybody	each
anyone	everybody	
everyone	nobody	
no one	somebody	
someone		

Someone feeds my dog in the morning.

Everybody <u>was</u> at the party.

Each <u>does</u> her own homework.

Remember that prepositional phrases often come between subjects and verbs. You should ignore these interrupting phrases, or you may mistake the wrong word for the subject and use a verb form that doesn't agree.

<u>Someone</u> from the apartments <u>feeds</u> my dog in the morning. (*Someone* is the subject, not *apartments*.)

<u>Everybody</u> on the list of celebrities <u>was</u> at the party. (*Everybody* is the subject, not *celebrities*.)

<u>Each</u> of the twins <u>does</u> her own homework. (*Each* is the subject, not *twins*.)

However, the words *some, any, all, none,* and *most* are exceptions to this rule of ignoring prepositional phrases. These words can be singular or plural, depending on the words that follow them in prepositional phrases.

<u>Some</u> of the *pie* <u>is</u> gone.

<u>Some</u> of the *cookies* <u>are</u> gone.

<u>Is</u> <u>any</u> of the *paper* still in the supply cabinet?

<u>Are</u> <u>any</u> of the *pencils* still in the supply cabinet?

<u>All</u> of her *work* <u>has</u> been published.

<u>All</u> of her *poems* <u>have</u> been published.

<u>None</u> of the *jewelry* <u>is</u> missing.

<u>None</u> of the *clothes* <u>are</u> missing.

On July 4th, <u>most</u> of the *country* <u>celebrates</u>.

On July 4th, <u>most</u> of the *citizens* <u>celebrate</u>.

When a sentence has more than one subject joined by *and,* the subject is plural:

The <u>teacher</u> *and* the <u>tutors</u> <u>eat</u> lunch at noon.

A glazed <u>donut</u> *and* an onion <u>bagel</u> <u>were</u> sitting on the plate.

However, when two subjects are joined by *or*, then the subject *closest* to the verb determines the verb form:

Either the <u>teacher</u> *or* the <u>tutors</u> <u>eat</u> lunch at noon.

Either the <u>tutors</u> *or* the <u>teacher</u> <u>eats</u> lunch at noon.

A glazed <u>donut</u> *or* an onion <u>bagel</u> <u>was</u> sitting on the plate.

In most sentences, the subject comes before the verb. However, in some cases, the subject follows the verb, and subject/verb agreement needs special attention. Study the following examples:

Over the building <u>flies</u> a solitary <u>flag</u>. (flag flies)

Over the building <u>fly</u> several <u>flags</u>. (flags fly)

There <u>is</u> a good <u>reason</u> for my actions. (reason is)

There <u>are</u> good <u>reasons</u> for my actions. (reasons are)

E X E R C I S E S

Underline the correct verbs in parentheses to maintain subject/verb agreement in the following sentences. Remember to ignore prepositional phrases, unless the subjects are *some, any, all, none,* or *most.* Check your answers ten at a time.

Exercise 1

1. Bulletproof windows (has, have) been used for protection for a long time.

2. Of course, they (was, were) only helpful from one direction.

3. There (was, were) no way to shoot back from inside the bulletproof glass.

4. Now there (is, are) a new kind of bulletproof window.

5. The new window (allow, allows) someone to shoot through it from inside and still be protected from bullets fired at it from outside.

6. A bullet (travel, travels) out through the new multilayered substance.

7. As the bullet (break, breaks) through on its way out, it (melt, melts) the substance and (seal, seals) it again.

8. Police departments (is, are) very interested in this new technology.

9. They (realize, realizes) how useful such a substance could be for their officers.

10. The cost of the new windows (is, are) high, but the benefits (is, are) worth it.

Source: Discover, November 2003

Exercise 2

1. There (is, are) a Web site that (rate, rates) movies based on how accurately they (portray, portrays) the laws of physics.

2. The site (is, are) called Intuitor.com.

3. Examples of bad physics in movies (include, includes) bullets that (spark, sparks) on contact, cars that (explode, explodes) in crashes, and laser beams that (is, are) visible to the naked eye.

4. The reviewers at Intuitor.com (give, gives) movies one of the following ratings: GP, PGP, PGP-13, RP, XP, and NR.

5. These labels (rank, ranks) the physics in a particular movie from good [GP] to pretty good [PGP] to totally unbelievable [XP].

6. Those movies that (get, gets) the RP rating are the ones that (is, are) so flawed in portraying the laws of physics that they (make, makes) the Intuitor reviewers "retch."

7. The NR label (is, are) reserved for the movies that (is, are) not rated because of their obvious focus on imaginative, not scientific, possibilities.

8. The recent classic films *Titanic, Speed,* and *The Terminator* (was, were) rated GP or PGP.

9. The worst rating of RP (was, were) handed out to both *A.I. Artificial Intelligence* and *Independence Day* and to all of *The Matrix* movies.

10. Both *Spider-Man* and *The Hulk* (was, were) creative films that (was, were) given the NR label.

Exercise 3

1. In his book *Catwatching,* Desmond Morris (explain, explains) why cats (seem, seems) to be able to feel earthquakes before they (happen, happens).
2. First of all, the cat (feel, feels) sensations that we humans (doesn't, don't).
3. Earthquakes (begin, begins) with movements far under ground, and cats often (react, reacts).
4. Some of these reactions (is, are) among the reasons why cats (has, have) been thought to have magical powers.
5. Another explanation for cats' predictions (is, are) that they (sense, senses) changes in static electricity or in the earth's magnetic fields.
6. Most of us (doesn't, don't) notice such changes, but some people (get, gets) headaches before earthquakes, headaches that may be caused by the change.
7. A human being just (isn't, aren't) able to tell the difference between a pre-earthquake headache and a regular stress-related one.
8. Cats (does, do) seem to have such abilities.
9. Many people (has, have) witnessed what cats (does, do) when an earthquake (is, are) approaching.
10. Cats suddenly (look, looks) scared and (run, runs) back and forth or in and out of a house or building; research (have, has) shown that we humans should pay close attention when they (does, do).

Source: Catwatching (Three Rivers Press, 1986)

Exercise 4

1. Some of our ancestors' customs (sound, sounds) strange to us today.

2. One of those customs (was, were) button collecting, (explain, explains) Catherine Roberts in a book about buttons.

3. The first organized button collectors in America (was, were) young unmarried women living in the middle to late 1800s.

4. Their aim in collecting buttons (was, were) to make what (was, were) called Charm Strings.

5. All of the girls had the same goal, which (was, were) to gather exactly 999 buttons on a string.

6. The rules of the game (was, were) strict and known by all, and breaking the rules (was, were) severely frowned upon.

7. A girl and her friends (was, were) supposed to get each button from a different person as a gift; some button trading (was, were) allowed, but not the use of duplicates.

8. Each of the girls (was, were) expected to remember when each of her buttons (was, were) given to her and by whom.

9. During the process of acquiring their buttons, the young women (was, were) eager to hear each other tell the stories of their Charm Strings.

10. In a final note that (show, shows) how far we (has, have) come in the last century, the Victorians believed that any girl who accidentally collected a thousandth button (was, were) destined to become an "old maid."

Source: Who's Got the Button? (David McCay Co., 1962)

Exercise 5

1. An old rhyme about sneezing (give, gives) a sneeze on each day of the week special meaning.

2. The poem (sound, sounds) a lot like the one that (begin, begins) "Monday's child (is, are) full of woe."

3. This poem about sneezing also (connect, connects) Monday with a negative outcome.

4. It (say, says) that a sneeze on Monday (mean, means) "danger."

5. A Tuesday sneeze (forecast, forecasts) a meeting with a "stranger."

6. Wednesday and Thursday (is, are) days when sneezes (mean, means) we will receive a "letter" or "something better," respectively.

7. There (is, are) no TGIF celebrations for sneezes on Friday, for they (foretell, foretells) "sorrow."

8. But a sneeze on Saturday (mean, means) the visit of a loved one "tomorrow."

9. Sunday sneezes (is, are) left out of the poem altogether.

10. Such day-of-the-week rhymes from the past (seem, seems) to reveal a lot about us.

Source: Schott's Original Miscellany (Bloomsbury, 2003)

PROOFREADING EXERCISE

Find and correct the ten subject/verb agreement errors in the following paragraph.

With today's high food prices, you should choose your produce wisely. However, buying ripe fruits and vegetables are a tricky process. How can you tell if an apple or a bunch of bananas are ready to buy or eat? A good rule of thumb for apples, oranges, and lemons is to judge the weight of the fruit. If the fruit are heavy, then it will probably be juicy and tasty. Lightweight fruits tends to lack juice and be tasteless. A melon, on the other hand, are almost always heavy, but a good one sloshes when you shakes it. And the stem end of a ripe cantaloupe will give slightly when you presses on it. Vegetables needs to be chosen carefully, too. If there is sprouted eyes on a potato, you should pass that one by. The sprouted eyes shows a change in the chemical structure of the potato, and it is not a good idea to eat them. When in doubt, you can ask the produce clerk, who should know a lot about the merchandise.

SENTENCE WRITING

Write ten sentences in which you describe the classes you are taking right now. Use verbs in the present time. Then go back over your sentences—underline your subjects once, underline your verbs twice, and be sure they agree.

Avoiding Shifts in Time

People often worry about using different time frames in writing. Let common sense guide you. If you begin writing a paper in past time, don't shift back and forth to the present unnecessarily; and if you begin in the present, don't shift to the past without good reason. In the following paragraph, the writer starts in the present and then shifts to the past, then shifts again to the present:

In the novel *To Kill a Mockingbird*, Jean Louise Finch is a little girl who lives in the South with her father, Atticus, and her brother, Jem. Everybody in town calls Jean Louise "Scout" as a nickname. When Atticus, a lawyer, chose to defend a black man against the charges of a white woman, some of their neighbors turned against him. Scout protected her father by appealing to the humanity of one member of the angry mob. In this chapter, five-year-old Scout turns out to be stronger than a group of adult men.

All the verbs should be in the present:

> In the novel *To Kill a Mockingbird,* Jean Louise Finch is a little girl who lives in the South with her father, Atticus, and her brother, Jem. Everybody in town calls Jean Louise "Scout" as a nickname. When Atticus, a lawyer, chooses to defend a black man against the charges of a white woman, some of their neighbors turn against him. Scout protects her father by appealing to the humanity of one member of the angry mob. In this chapter, five-year-old Scout turns out to be stronger than a group of adult men.

This sample paragraph discusses only the events that happen within the novel's plot, so it needs to maintain one time frame—the present, which we use to write about literature and repeated actions.

However, sometimes you will write about the present, the past, and even the future together. Then it may be necessary to use these different time frames within the same paragraph, each for its own reason. For example, if you were to give biographical information about Harper Lee, author of *To Kill a Mockingbird,* within a discussion of the novel and its influence, you might need to use all three time frames:

> Harper Lee grew up in Alabama, and she based elements in the book on experiences from her childhood. Like the character Atticus, Lee's father was a lawyer. She wrote the novel in his law offices. *To Kill a Mockingbird* is Harper Lee's most famous work, and it received the Pulitzer Prize for fiction in 1960. Lee's book turned forty years old in the year 2000. It will always remain one of the most moving and compassionate novels in American literature.

This paragraph uses past (*grew, based, was, wrote, received, turned*), present (*is*), and future (*will remain*) in the same paragraph without committing the error of shifting. Shifting occurs when the writer changes time frames *inconsistently* or *for no reason,* confusing the reader (as in the first example given).

PROOFREADING EXERCISES

Which of the following student paragraphs shift *unnecessarily* back and forth between time frames? In those that do, change the verbs to maintain one time frame, thus making the entire paragraph read smoothly. (First, read the paragraphs to determine whether unnecessary shifting takes place. One of the paragraphs is correct.)

1. The last time I took my car in for a scheduled service, I noticed a few problems when I pick it up. I check the oil dipstick, and it has really dark oil still on it. Also, there was a screwdriver balancing on my air-filter cover. I can't believe it when I see it, but as soon as I showed the tool to the service manager, he calls the mechanic over to take my car back to the service area. After another hour, my car is ready, the dipstick has clean oil on it, and the service manager cleared the bill so that I didn't have to pay anything.

2. Back in the early 1900s, Sears Roebuck sold houses through the mail. The houses are listed along with the rest of the products in Sears' famous catalog. The house kits arrived in thousands of pieces, and people will put them together themselves. Or they get a builder to help them. In 1919, one company, Standard Oil, places an order for an entire town's worth of houses as shelter for its employees. The house kits even included the paint that the homeowners use to paint the houses when they will be finished. The ability to order a whole house from the Sears catalog ended in 1940, but thousands of them are still being lived in by people across America.

Source: CBS News Sunday Morning, May 18, 2003

3. Richard Barton invented the Lapotron, which is a device used by swimmers. In 1998, Barton was a member of Quince Orchard High School's swim team. While practicing, he had trouble concentrating while keeping track of his laps. So he decided to put his knowledge of machines to work. He combined a counter, a touch sensor, a timer, and a display into one device that is positioned at the end of the swim lane. He entered the invention in several competitions and won thousands of dollars in bonds and scholarships. As a result of his Lapotron, Barton is one of the most recent inductees into the National Gallery of America's Young Inventors wing of the Inventors Hall of Fame.

Source: Washington Post, February 17, 2000

Recognizing Verbal Phrases

We know (from the discussion on p. 92) that a verb phrase is made up of a main verb and at least one helping verb. But sometimes certain forms of verbs are used not as real verbs but as some other part of a sentence. Verbs put to other uses are called *verbals.*

A verbal can be a subject:

> *Skiing* is my favorite Olympic sport. (*Skiing* is the subject, not the verb. The verb is *is.*)

A verbal can be a descriptive word:

> His *bruised* ankle healed very quickly. (*Bruised* describes the subject, *ankle. Healed* is the verb.)

A verbal can be an object:

> I like *to read* during the summer. (*To read* is the object. *Like* is the verb.)

Verbals link up with other words to form *verbal phrases.* To see the difference between a real verb phrase and a verbal phrase, look at these two sentences:

> I was bowling with my best friends. (*Bowling* is the main verb in a verb phrase. Along with the helping verb *was,* it shows the action of the sentence.)

> I enjoyed *bowling* with my best friends. (Here, the real verb is *enjoyed. Bowling* is not the verb; it is part of a verbal phrase—*bowling with my best friends*—which is what I enjoyed.)

Three Kinds of Verbals

1. *ing* verbs used without helping verbs (*running, thinking, baking . . .*)
2. verb forms that often end in *ed, en,* or *t* (*tossed, spoken, burnt . . .*)
3. verbs that follow *to* (*to walk, to eat, to cause . . .*)

Look at the following sentences using the previous chart's examples in verbal phrases:

> *Running two miles a day* is great exercise. (real verb = is)
>
> She spent two hours *thinking of a title for her essay*. (real verb = spent)
>
> We had such fun *baking those cherry vanilla cupcakes*. (real verb = had)
>
> *Tossed in a salad*, artichoke hearts add zesty flavor. (real verb = add)
>
> *Spoken in Spanish*, the dialogue sounds even more beautiful. (real verb = sounds)
>
> The gourmet pizza, *burnt by a careless chef*, shrunk to half its normal size. (real verb = shrunk)
>
> I like *to walk around the zoo by myself*. (real verb = like)
>
> *To eat exotic foods* takes courage. (real verb = takes)
>
> They actually wanted *to cause an argument*. (real verb = wanted)

EXERCISES

Each of the following sentences contains at least one verbal or verbal phrase. Double underline the real verbs or verb phrases and put brackets around the verbals and verbal phrases. Remember to locate the verbals first (*running, wounded, to sleep* . . .) and include any word(s) that go with them (*running a race, wounded in the fight, to sleep all night*). Real verbs will never be inside verbal phrases. Check your answers after the first set before going on to the next.

Exercise 1

1. I love to drive my new car on the freeway and on winding country roads.

2. Its convertible roof folds back into the trunk to allow for a feeling of complete freedom.

3. At high speeds, I hear the rush of wind and feel it whipping my hair around.

4. Wind-blown hair is the only drawback to owning a convertible.

5. Sometimes I wear a hat or a bandana to keep my hair from looking too crazy when I get home.

6. One time, after taking a long drive around the lake, I couldn't even comb my hair out without using a detangling shampoo.

7. In fact, humid weather combined with wind seems to make matters worse.

8. I am still happy to have my new car.

9. I will accept a little inconvenience in exchange for owning such a great automobile.

10. And now I know all of the best places to buy hats and bandanas.

Exercise 2

1. To paraphrase Mark Twain, golfing is just a way to ruin a good walk.

2. In fact, becoming a golfer can be dangerous.

3. Golf professionals commonly suffer a couple of injuries per year resulting from long hours of practicing their swings.

4. Amateur golfers tend to injure themselves much more often.

5. Most injuries come from the twisting, squatting, and bending involved in golfing.

6. And moving the heavy bags of clubs from cars to carts can wrench the backs of potential golfers before they even begin to play.

7. Of course, there are the unfortunate incidents of people on golf courses being struck by lightning.

8. But some of the sources of golfers' ailments may be surprising.

9. Cleaning the dirt and debris off the golf balls by licking them, for instance, may have serious repercussions.

10. After swallowing the chemicals sprayed on the turf of the golf course, players can develop liver problems.

Source: I'm Afraid, You're Afraid: 448 Things to Fear and Why (Hyperion, 2000)

Exercise 3

1. Do you remember receiving your first greeting card that played a song when you opened it?
2. You have probably also seen characters in recent movies looking through the pages of enchanted books.
3. The magical books contain moving pictures, similar to video.
4. Thinking logically, you might have said to yourself, "Books don't have pictures that move, but I wish that they did."
5. Actually, the technology necessary to include bits of video in magazines, newspapers, and books may not be too far away.
6. In simple terms, the e-ink will display moving images after being jolted with electricity.
7. Such technology is already used to change black letters on a white background.
8. It may be hard to imagine this, but the video-on-paper will appear in full color.
9. Many companies are competing to perfect the video e-paper process.
10. Someday soon you will be able to watch clips from sports or world events in your newspaper—as if by magic.

Source: Science News, September 27, 2003

Exercise 4

1. Why do plumbing emergencies always happen on the weekends?
2. Toilets, sinks, and tubs seem to know when plumbers' rates go up.
3. Some emergencies—a slow-draining sink, for instance—can be tolerated for a couple of days.
4. And a dripping shower faucet may cause annoyance, but not panic.

5. However, a backed-up sewer pipe definitely can't wait until Monday.

6. No one wants to see that water rising and overflowing the rim of the bowl.

7. At that point, the only question is which "rooter" service to call.

8. Finding the main drainage line often takes more time than clearing it.

9. Once the plumber has finished fixing the problem, he or she usually eyes future potential disasters and offers to prevent them with even more work.

10. After getting the final bill, I hope that my children will grow up to be not doctors but plumbers.

Exercise 5

1. In the past, the library was the perfect place to study or to do research or homework.

2. But lately is has become a place to meet friends.

3. Things changed when students began to access the Internet.

4. Now two or three students gather near each terminal and show each other the best sites to visit on the Web.

5. Library officials have designated certain rooms as "talking areas."

6. However, such territories are hard to enforce.

7. The old image of the librarian telling everyone to be quiet is just that— an old image.

8. So people talk to each other and giggle right there in the reading room.

9. One of the librarians told me about a plan to take the Internet-access computers out of the main study room and to put them into the "talking areas."

10. I hate to read in a noisy room, so I hope that he was right.

PARAGRAPH EXERCISE

Double underline the real verbs or verb phrases and put brackets around the verbals and verbal phrases in the following paragraphs from the Time-Life book called *Odd and Eccentric People.*

The Wright brothers would have applauded truckdriver Larry Walters's inventiveness. From readily available and inexpensive materials, he built an aircraft, of sorts, flew it to an altitude of 16,000 feet near Long Beach, California, then landed safely. The ninety-minute maiden voyage took place on the sunny morning of July 2, 1982, fulfilling Walters's twenty-year dream of a free-floating airborne adventure.

The amateur's flying machine could scarcely have been simpler. It consisted of an aluminum lawn chair buoyed by forty-odd helium weather balloons arranged in four tiers. When Walters took off from his girlfriend's backyard in San Pedro, his equipment included a portable CB radio and a BB pistol, with which he planned to pop balloons for his descent. Sensibly cautious, Walters wore a parachute and, of course, buckled his seat belt before the chair's tether cables were finally cast off.

Although Walters had no experience flying any kind of aircraft, he felt reasonably confident that the wind would waft him to the Mojave Desert, located some fifty miles northeast of San Pedro. He was mistaken. His chair zipped upward at a startling rate and headed southeast toward Long Beach.

It was chilly up there and dangerous besides, for Walters soon found himself bobbing amid commercial jets approaching the Long Beach airport. He radioed air-traffic controllers, shot ten weather balloons with his BB pistol, and began his descent, praying earnestly. Floating low over a Long Beach neighborhood, Walters ran into a power line, but the police had seen him coming and had shut off the electricity. He disembarked unscathed fifteen miles from his liftoff point.

SENTENCE WRITING

Write ten sentences that contain verbal phrases. Use the ten verbals listed here to begin your verbal phrases: *thinking, folding, skiing, marking, to take, to get, to paste, to exercise, planned, given.* The last two may seem particularly difficult to use as verbals. There are sample sentences listed in the Answers section at the back of the book. But first, try to write your own so that you can compare the two.

Correcting Misplaced or Dangling Modifiers

When we modify something, we change whatever it is by adding something to it. We might modify a car, for example, by adding special tires. In English, we call words, phrases, and clauses *modifiers* when they add information to part of a sentence. To do its job properly, a modifier should be in the right spot—as close to the word it describes as possible. If we put new tires on the roof of the car instead of where they belong, they would be misplaced. In the following sentence, the modifier is too far away from the word it modifies to make sense. It is a misplaced modifier:

Swinging from tree to tree, we watched the monkeys at the zoo.

Was it *we* who were swinging from tree to tree? That's what the sentence says because the modifying phrase *Swinging from tree to tree* is next to *we*. It should be next to *monkeys*.

At the zoo, we watched the monkeys swinging from tree to tree.

The next example has no word at all for the modifier to modify:

At the age of eight, my family finally bought a dog.

Obviously, the family was not eight when it bought a dog. Nor was the dog eight. The modifier *At the age of eight* is dangling there with no word to attach itself to, no word for it to modify. We can get rid of the dangling modifier by turning it into a dependent clause. (See p. 70 for a discussion of dependent clauses.)

When I was eight, my family finally bought a dog.

Here the clause has its own subject and verb—*I was*—and there's no chance of misunderstanding the sentence. Here's another dangling modifier:

After a two-hour nap, the train pulled into the station.

Did the train take a two-hour nap? Who did?

After a two-hour nap, I awoke just as the train pulled into the station.

EXERCISES

Carefully rephrase any of the following sentences that contain misplaced or dangling modifiers. Some sentences are correct.

Exercise 1

1. Even when taken by amateurs, digital cameras produce beautiful pictures.

2. They noticed a wallet walking past a bench in the park.

3. Let's get the roof fixed before the rainy season begins.

4. The teacher read a story about a scary troll character sitting on a little chair in front of the preschoolers.

5. Watching television all weekend, my homework never got done.

6. Carl received a raise with his promotion.

7. After making it to the movie on time, our popcorn was stale.

8. Geology students read about different kinds of rock formations in their textbooks.

9. Loaded with potatoes, two shoppers were almost hurt by falling boxes.

10. Home for the weekend, our parents took us to all of our favorite places again.

Exercise 2

1. Smeared with mustard or ketchup, everyone enjoys eating corndogs.

2. Before asking for an extension, the teacher told us that we had a few extra days to finish our papers.

3. They spotted a hawk and its babies looking through their binoculars.

4. After I finished my audition, the director released everyone else.

5. I called the doctor on the roof.

6. We sat on the lawn and waited for further instructions on how to prune the roses.

7. Screeching to a stop, I got on the bus and took my seat among the rest of the passengers.

8. Without onions, I can't eat a hamburger.

9. Given as a token of friendship, that ring means a lot to me.

10. We had to write a paragraph about the weather in our notebooks.

Exercise 3

1. Baked in an odd-shaped pan, the kids at the party still enjoyed the cake.

2. We sat quietly at our desks as we took the quiz.

3. Loaded with butter and sour cream, I looked at the baked potato and wondered how I would eat it because I am allergic to dairy products.

4. Paul contacted his travel agent through e-mail.

5. Without natural talent, the violin is almost impossible to learn.

6. Riding on a bus into town, the sunshine felt warm on my arm.

7. They were locked out of the building by accident.

8. Telling one bad joke after another, I have given up on that comedian.

9. Blue paint mixed with yellow paint usually produces green paint.

10. I loved the presents I received from my friends tied with pretty bows.

Exercise 4

1. Taking an aspirin before my nap, my headache was gone.

2. I drove my new car home full of gas.

3. After thirteen months of planning, the reunion was a success.

4. She wrapped all the gifts in her pajamas.

5. The students watched the video in a dark room.

6. Before walking out, the bus drivers made their final offer.

7. Gathered in a bunch, the children gave the daisies to their teacher.

8. Skipping across the water, I watched the stone reach the middle of the lake.

9. Trying to look happy, his heart was breaking.

10. All along the sidewalk, we saw weeds.

Exercise 5

1. Feeling the thrill of a day at the amusement park, my blisters didn't bother me.

2. Full of touching scenes, my friends and I saw the new tearjerker.

3. My classmates and I always turned our essays in on time.

4. Practicing for an hour a day, her piano has improved.

5. Gasoline prices fluctuate with politics.

6. Sitting on a bench all day, an idea came to her.

7. On the road to their cousins' house, they discovered a new outlet mall.

8. He felt the pressure of trying to get a good job from his parents.

9. I enjoy talking to new people at parties.

10. Written in chalk, the notes on the board were hard to read.

PROOFREADING EXERCISE

Find and correct any misplaced or dangling modifiers in the following paragraph.

Walking into my neighborhood polling place during the last election, a volunteer greeted me and checked my name and address. Being misspelled slightly on their printout, he couldn't find me at first. I pointed to what I thought was my name. At least upside down, I thought it was mine. But actually, it was another person's name. Once turned toward me, I could see the printout more clearly. My name was there, but it had an extra letter stuck on the end of it. The volunteer handed me a change-of-name form with a polite smile. I filled it out and punched my ballot. Stuck on my wall at home, I have my voting receipt to remind me to check my name carefully when the next election comes around.

SENTENCE WRITING

Write five sentences that contain misplaced or dangling modifiers; then revise those sentences to put the modifiers where they belong. Use the examples in the explanations as models.

Following Sentence Patterns

Sentences are built according to a few basic patterns. For proof, rearrange each of the following sets of words to form a complete statement (not a question):

apples a ate raccoon the   *the raceon ate a apple*

the crashing beach were waves the on

your in am partner I life

been she school has to walking

you wonderful in look green

There are only one or two possible combinations for each due to English sentence patterns. Either *A raccoon ate the apples,* or *The apples ate a raccoon,* and so on. But in each case, the verb or verb phrase makes its way to the middle of the statement.

To understand sentence patterns, you need to know that verbs can do three things.

1. Verbs can show actions:

   The raccoon ate the apples.

   The waves were crashing on the beach.

   She has been walking to school.

2. Verbs can link subjects with descriptive words:

   I am your partner in life.

   You look wonderful in green.

3. Verbs can help other verbs form verb phrases:

   The waves were crashing on the beach.

   She has been walking to school.

Look at these sentences for more examples:

Mel grabbed a slice of pizza. (The verb *grabbed* shows Mel's action.)

His slice was the largest one in the box. (The verb *was* links *slice* with its description as *the largest one.*)

Mel had been craving pizza for a week. (The verbs *had* and *been* help the main verb *craving* in a verb phrase.)

Knowing what a verb does in a clause helps you gain an understanding of the three basic sentence patterns:

Subject + Action Verb + Object Pattern

Some action verbs must be followed by a person or an object that receives the action.

S   AV   Obj
Sylvia completed the difficult math test. (*Sylvia completed* makes no sense

without being followed by the object that she completed—*test*.)

Subject + Action Verb (+ No Object) Pattern

At other times, the action verb itself completes the meaning and needs no object after it.

S   AV
She celebrated at home with her family. (*She celebrated* makes sense alone.

The two prepositional phrases—*at home* and *with her family*—are not needed to understand the meaning of the clause.)

Subject + Linking Verb + Description Pattern

A special kind of verb that does not show an action but links a subject with a description is called a *linking verb*. It acts like an equal sign in a clause. Learn to recognize the most common linking verbs: *is, am, are, was, were, seem, feel, appear, become, look.*

S   LV   Desc
Sylvia is very intelligent. (*Very intelligent* describes *Sylvia*.)

S   LV   Desc
Sylvia has become an excellent student. (*Sylvia* equals *an excellent student*.)

> **Note** - We learned on page 92 that a verb phrase includes a main verb and its helping verbs. Helping verbs can be used in any of the sentence patterns.

S   AV
Sylvia is going to Seattle for a vacation. (Here the verb *is* helps the main verb

going, which is an action verb with no object followed by two prepositional phrases—*to Seattle* and *for a vacation*.)

The following chart outlines the patterns using short sentences that you could memorize:

Three Basic Sentence Patterns

S + AV + Obj

<u>Kids</u> <u><u>trade</u></u> candy.

S + AV

<u>They</u> <u><u>play</u></u> (with their friends) (on the playground).

not objects

S + LV + Desc

<u>They</u> <u><u>are</u></u>   fourth-graders.

<u>They</u> <u><u>look</u></u> happy.

These are the basic patterns for most of the clauses used in English sentences. Knowing them can help you control your sentences and improve your use of words.

E X E R C I S E S

First, put parentheses around any prepositional phrases. Next, underline the subjects once and the verbs or verb phrases twice. Then mark the sentence patterns above the words. Remember that the patterns never mix together. For example, unlike an action verb, a linking verb will almost never be used alone (for example, "He seems."), nor will an action verb be followed by a description of the subject (for example, "She took tall."). And if there are two clauses, each one may have a different pattern. Check your answers after the first set of ten.

Exercise 1

1. Wendy Hasnip lives in England.
2. She does not speak French.
3. At the age of forty-seven, Hasnip had a stroke.
4. For two weeks after the stroke, she could not talk.

5. Eventually, Hasnip regained her speaking ability.

6. But suddenly, she spoke with a distinct French accent.

7. Strangely, this condition is a known—but extremely rare—post-brain-injury symptom.

8. Doctors call it the Foreign Accent Syndrome.

9. One man in Russia recovered from a brain injury.

10. Now he can speak and understand ninety-three languages.

Sources: Moscow Times, December 1999, *Salt Lake Tribune,* June 13, 2000, and *Current Science,* October 6, 2000

Exercise 2

1. Local news programs are all alike.

2. They begin with the top stories of the day.

3. These stories may be local, national, or international.

4. They might include violent crimes, traffic jams, natural disasters, and political upheavals.

5. After the top stories, one of the anchors offers a quick weather update.

6. Then a sportscaster covers the latest scores and team standings.

7. At some point, a "human interest" story lightens the mood of the broadcast.

8. And then we hear the latest entertainment news.

9. Near the end of the half hour, the weatherperson gives the full weather forecast.

10. News programs could use an update of their own.

Exercise 3

1. My friend and I studied in the library yesterday.

2. We stopped at the "New Books" shelf.

3. I found so many books of interest there.

4. One of them traced the history of tools.

5. Another book was a collection of essays about children and sports.

6. Biographies are always interesting to me.

7. I especially love books about art and artists.

8. The pictures and stories take me away from my daily problems.

9. I chose a book about the life of Frida Kahlo.

10. I saw the movie about her and liked it a lot.

Exercise 4

1. Some facts about coins in America might surprise you.

2. An average American handles six hundred dollars in coins every year.

3. Most Americans keep small stashes of pennies, nickels, dimes, quarters, half-dollars, and dollar coins at home.

4. The total of these unused coins may be ten billion dollars at any one time.

5. Researchers have asked people about their coin use.

6. Some people use coins in place of small tools.

7. Others perform magic with them.

8. Younger people are more careless with their coins.

9. They might toss a penny in the trash.

10. Older Americans would save the penny instead.

Source: Discover, October 2003

Exercise 5

1. Charles Osgood is a writer, editor, TV host, and radio personality.

2. He has edited a new book.

3. The book's title is *Funny Letters from Famous People.*

4. In his book, Osgood shares hilarious letters from history.

5. Thomas Jefferson wrote to an acquaintance about rodents eating his wallet.

6. Benjamin Franklin penned the perfect recommendation letter.

7. Franklin did not know the recommended fellow at all.

8. Beethoven cursed his friend bitterly in a letter one day.

9. In a letter the following day, Beethoven praised the same friend excessively and asked him for a visit.

10. Osgood ends the book with a letter by Julia Child and includes her secrets for a long life.

PARAGRAPH EXERCISE

Label the sentence patterns in the following paragraph from the book *Guess Who? A Cavalcade of Famous Americans,* by Veronica Geng. It helps to surround prepositional phrases with parentheses and verbal phrases with brackets first to isolate them from the main words of the sentence patterns. Then label the subjects, the verbs, and any objects after action verbs or descriptions after linking verbs (*is, am, are, was, were, become, appear, seem,* and so on).

Thomas Alva Edison

Slow in school and poor at math, Edison quit school at twelve to work as a newsboy on a train. He used his wages to buy chemicals, for he loved experimenting. He even built a little lab in the baggage car on the train. Later he worked as a telegraph operator and learned about electricity. By 1876, he had his own lab and . . . a staggering series of inventions: a phonograph, a practical light bulb, a strip of motion picture film, and many others. By trial and error, sleepless nights, and tireless work, Edison became the most productive inventor of practical devices that America has ever seen. He was also probably the only inventor who was as well-known to every American as the most famous movie star.

SENTENCE WRITING

Write ten sentences describing the weather today and your feelings about it—make your sentences short and clear. Then go back and label the sentence patterns you have used.

Avoiding Clichés, Awkward Phrasing, and Wordiness

Clichés

A cliché is an expression that has been used so often it has lost its originality and effectiveness. Whoever first said "light as a feather" had thought of an original way to express lightness, but today that expression is worn out. Most of us use an occasional cliché in speaking, but clichés have no place in writing. The good writer thinks up fresh new ways to express ideas.

Here are a few clichés. Add some more to the list.

the bottom line
older but wiser
last but not least
in this day and age
different as night and day
out of this world

white as a ghost
sick as a dog
tried and true
at the top of their lungs
the thrill of victory
one in a million
busy as a bee
easier said than done
better late than never

Clichés lack freshness because the reader always knows what's coming next. Can you complete these expressions?

the agony of . . .
breathe a sigh of . . .
lend a helping . . .
odds and . . .
raining cats and . . .
as American as . . .
been there . . .
worth its weight . . .

Clichés are expressions too many people use. Try to avoid them in your writing.

Awkward Phrasing

Another problem—awkward phrasing—comes from writing sentence structures that *no one* else would use because they break basic sentence patterns, omit necessary words, or use words incorrectly. Like clichés, awkward sentences might *sound* acceptable when spoken, but as polished writing, they are usually unacceptable.

Awkward

There should be great efforts in terms of the communication between teachers and their students.

Corrected

Teachers and their students must communicate.

Awkward

During the experiment, the use of key principles was essential to ensure the success of it.

Corrected

The experiment was a success. *or* We performed the experiment carefully.

Awkward

My favorite was when the guy with the ball ran the wrong way all the way across the field in the movie.

Corrected

In my favorite part of the movie, the receiver ran across the field in the wrong direction.

Wordiness

Good writing is concise writing. Don't use ten words if you can say it better in five. "In today's society" isn't as effective as "today," and it's a cliché. "At this point in time" could be "presently" or "now."

Another kind of wordiness comes from saying something twice. There's no need to write "in the month of August" or "9 A.M. in the morning" or "my personal opinion." August *is* a month, 9 A.M. *is* morning, and anyone's opinion *is* personal. All you need to write is "in August," "9 A.M.," and "my opinion."

Still another kind of wordiness comes from using expressions that add nothing to the meaning of the sentence. "The point is that we can't afford it" says no more than "We can't afford it."

Here is a sample wordy sentence:

The construction company ~~actually~~ worked on that ~~particular~~ building for ~~a period of~~ six months.

And here it is after eliminating wordiness:

The construction company worked on that building for six months.

Wordy Writing	Concise Writing
advance planning	planning
an unexpected surprise	a surprise
ask a question	ask
at a later date	later
basic fundamentals	fundamentals
but nevertheless	but (or nevertheless)

combine together	combine
completely empty	empty
down below	below
each and every	each (or every)
end result	result
fewer in number	fewer
free gift	gift
green in color	green
in order to	to
in spite of the fact that	although
just exactly	exactly
large in size	large
new innovation	innovation
on a regular basis	regularly
past history	history
rectangular in shape	rectangular
refer back	refer
repeat again	repeat
serious crisis	crisis
sufficient enough	sufficient (or enough)
there in person	there
two different kinds	two kinds
very unique	unique

EXERCISES

Exercise 1

Rewrite the following sentences to eliminate *clichés* and *awkward phrasing*. If a whole sentence is a cliché, eliminate it.

1. I believe that, when there's a will, there's a way.

2. And I've got determination a mile long and a yard wide.

3. ~~So when~~ I decided to learn how to juggle, there was no stopping me.

4. It was as easy ~~as pie~~ to ~~get the hang of~~ passing two beanbags from hand to hand.

5. But introducing that third bag into the mix was easier said than done.

6. I would be going along just fine, and then it would all fall apart.

7. A friend of mine who knows the ins and outs of juggling told me I was going about it all wrong.

8. He said that I needed to get the circular movement hardwired into my circuits by practicing without catching the bags before I should attempt the real thing.

9. Well, that advice was just what the doctor ordered, and I was tossing three bags like a pro before long.

10. The bottom line is I learned how to juggle with the help of some good advice.

Exercise 2

Rewrite the following sentences to eliminate *wordiness*. See how few words you can use without changing the meaning of the sentence.

1. I was recently looking through a book the other day, and it was written on the subject of inventions.

2. The inventions that the book was about were inventions of the 1800s.

3. I learned that in order for anyone who has invented something to get credit for the invention, he or she has to apply for a legal document called a patent.

4. Some of the patents described in the book had to do with the invention of useful things that most of us take for granted these days, such as automobiles, can openers, safety pins, and vending machines.

5. However, there were a few other patents for inventions in the book that made me wonder how they ever got patented in the first place because the inventions seemed so strange and so unnecessary for people to use in their everyday lives.

6. One example of just such an invention from 1872 was one that was for a device that was made of leather strips that were supposed to cover a man's moustache while he ate so that the food he was eating didn't get all over his moustache.

7. Still another example of an odd invention was the 1879 patent that described a big, stiff fabric parachute that was supposed to be strapped onto a person's head along with thick spongy pads to be put on the feet to allow the person to float safely down from any tall height in case of emergencies.

8. The inventor had not figured out three obvious facts: that a parachute has to fit around a person's body instead of just the head, that no one would be able to carry around all of the invention's equipment all the time, and that people don't always land on their feet.

9. In the same silly category as the man's moustache cover, there was a patent for the invention of a veil like the others that ladies in the 1890s were wearing, but this veil had some pink shading added to the usual black mesh at the cheek areas so that the woman looked like she had rosy cheeks even from outside her veil.

10. The best part of the book that I read about these old-time inventions was the drawings that were used at the time of the patents to illustrate both the serious and the oddball inventions in the book.

Source: Inventing the 19th Century: 100 Inventions that Shaped the Victorian Age (New York University Press, 2001)

Exercise 3

Revise the sentences in the remaining exercises to eliminate any *clichés*, *awkward phrasing*, and *wordiness*.

1. In today's society, many shoppers at the supermarkets are on the look-out for organic meats and vegetables.

2. In fact, they don't draw the line at fresh foods; these same shoppers' eyes light up whenever they see an organic label on a can or any other package.

3. I know this for a fact since I work as an employee at the supermarket in the middle of the busiest section of town.

4. It's not only people with a lot of money that want the foods grown without pesticides and hormones.

5. It's just about everybody that walks in the door.

6. I guess that what's going on is that people are taking a good long look at their lives and caring about their children's eating habits, too.

7. I do have to admit that the organic eggs I buy taste pretty good when you get right down to it.

8. Knowing that the eggs come from happy, free-ranging chickens makes me feel good about eating them.

9. Of course, the bottom line for some people will always be price.

10. If organic foods cost more than traditionally grown foods, some of the shoppers are going to keep passing them by on the supermarket shelves.

Exercise 4

1. I just saw a story on the news about an animal that didn't look like anything I'd ever seen before.

2. It kind of looks like a teddy bear and a little monkey and a miniature dog all rolled into one.

3. I found out that this little guy has his own Web site and in fact was quite a celebrity in his own right.

4. The name of this odd creature is Mr. Winkle, and on his home page, even they say they don't know what he is.

5. On the Web site, a bunch of questions flash across the screen while it's loading, questions like is it an "alien?" a "stuffed animal?" a "hamster with a permanent?"

6. One thing I can say for sure is that he is pretty cute.

7. I can see why his owner stopped her car one day when she saw the strange-looking beast walking by the side of the road and took him home with her.

8. Since she found him that day, she has taken a whole bunch of pictures of him in quirky little costumes and even one of him running in a hamster wheel.

9. Of course, all of these pictures are available for purchase at the click of the mouse in the form of posters and calendars, and I must say the prices are relatively reasonable.

10. And there's no need to go hunting around for the Web address at which these products and pictures and stories can be found; just head to mrwinkle.com.

Exercise 5

1. As with any widely used goods or services, network television must be somewhat responsive to the demands of the people who watch it.

2. One thing that one must bear in mind when judging something as widespread as television is the kind of people that watch it, namely, just about everyone.

3. To say that TV is not giving the American public the kind of programming it wants is to say that the American public all want the same kind of programming, and of course, that is not the case.

4. First of all, for TV to satisfy everyone, there would have to be a separate channel for each person that showed only those kinds of things that person wanted to see.

5. There are a couple of products that let people customize their viewing opportunities, but they have not caught on yet because there is an extra cost.

6. That brings me to my next point, network TV is free, so what more does everyone want?

7. Sure, we have to sit there and watch while some "typical" person has an experience with paper towels that changes her life.

8. But sometimes I find that the commercials are often more educational or at least more entertaining than the regular programs.

9. And what's more is that people can watch as much TV as they want at a given time.

10. The American people need different things to watch at different times, and that's the only way to make everyone happy.

PROOFREADING EXERCISE

Revise the sentences in the following paragraph to eliminate any *clichés, awkward phrasing,* or *wordiness.*

I have a friend who used to be one of those struggling actors who couldn't find a steady job, but now she has become a professional house sitter, and it has really paid off in more ways than one. First of all, she joined a house sitters' organization that is supposed to find out about all of the house-sitting opportunities that are available at any one time and match house sitters up with each of them. Then she landed her first house-sitting job at a house in Malibu. You're not going to believe this, but she got paid to live in a house on the beach in Malibu and even got her meals and movie rentals for free. All she had to do to do the job she was paid for was to watch out for the house and feed one cat. The cat was even an indoor cat. Now my friend is house-sitting in Sedona, watching a house for friends of the same people who own the Malibu house. Well, I'll tell you, I want a job like that and am thinking seriously about trying it out for myself.

SENTENCE WRITING

Go back to the sentences you wrote for the Sentence Writing exercise on page 23 or page 104 and revise them to eliminate any *clichés, awkward phrasing,* or *wordiness.*

Correcting for Parallel Structure

Your writing will be clearer and more memorable if you use parallel structure. That is, when you write two pieces of information or any kind of list, put the items in similar form. Look at this sentence, for example:

My favorite movies are comic, romantic, or the ones about outer space.

The sentence lacks parallel structure. The third item in the list doesn't match the other two. Now look at this sentence:

My favorite movie categories are comedies, love stories, and sci-fi fantasies.

Here the items are parallel; they are all plural nouns. Or you could write the following:

I like movies that make me laugh, that make me cry, and that make me think.

Again the sentence has parallel structure because all three items in the list are dependent clauses. Here are some more examples. Note how much easier it is to read the sentences with parallel structure.

Without Parallel Structure	With Parallel Structure
I like to hike, to ski, and going sailing.	I like to hike, to ski, and to sail. (all "to" verbs)
The office has run out of pens, paper, ink cartridges, and we need more toner, too.	The office needs more pens, paper, ink cartridges, and toner. (all nouns)
They decided that they needed a change, that they could afford a new house, and wanted to move to Arizona.	They decided that they needed a change, that they could afford a new house, and that they wanted to move to Arizona. (all dependent clauses)

The parts of an outline should always be parallel. Following are two brief outlines about food irradiation. The parts of the outline on the *left* are not parallel. The first subtopic (I.) is a question; the other (II.) is just a noun. And the supporting points (A., B., C.) are written as nouns, verbs, and even clauses. The parts of the outline on the *right* are parallel. Both subtopics (I. and II.) are plural nouns, and all details (A., B., C.) are action verbs followed by objects.

Not Parallel	Parallel
Food Irradiation	Food Irradiation
I. How is it good?	I. Benefits
A. Longer shelf life	A. Extends shelf life
B. Using fewer pesticides	B. Requires fewer pesticides
C. Kills bacteria	C. Kills bacteria
II. Concerns	II. Concerns
A. Nutritional value	A. Lowers nutritional value
B. Consumers are worried	B. Alarms consumers
C. Workers' safety	C. Endangers workers

Using parallel structure will make your writing more effective. Note the parallelism in these well-known quotations:

A place for everything and everything in its place.

Isabella Mary Beeton

Ask not what your country can do for you; ask what you can do for your country.

John F. Kennedy

We hold these truths to be self-evident, that all men are created equal, that they are endowed by their creator with certain unalienable rights, that among these are Life, Liberty, and the pursuit of Happiness.

Thomas Jefferson

E X E R C I S E S

Most—but not all—of the following sentences lack parallel structure. In some, you will be able to cross out the part that is not parallel and write the correction above. Other sentences will need complete rephrasing.

Exercise 1

1. I ~~started preparations~~ for my winter vacation last week, and ~~that's when~~ ~~I~~ realized that my luggage and the coat that I use in cold weather are completely inadequate for a trip to Chicago. *[handwritten: prepared]*

2. My brother lives in "The Windy City," and he says that it gets very cold there.

3. Temperatures in San Francisco hardly ever dip below the forties, or they might get as low as the thirties.

4. The jacket I normally use is lightweight, and it does not have a liner of any kind.

5. I'll need to buy a coat made of down or maybe one of the fleece ones that skiers wear.

6. My suitcases are inadequate as well; they are soft-bodied, and they're duffel-bag style with several outer compartments closed by zippers.

7. I have taken these cases on car trips to Seattle, but it wouldn't be a good idea to travel by plane with them.

8. Anyone can access the zippered compartments while my bags are waiting in a luggage area.

9. I don't want to worry about things being stolen or that a pocket might rip or something.

10. As a result of these deficiencies, I'm currently looking for new luggage, and I need to buy a proper winter coat.

Exercise 2

1. In October of 2003, Matt McNally won the title of U.S. National Monopoly Champion.

2. Along with McNally's title came a prize of over fifteen thousand dollars.

3. Before winning the national title, McNally together with forty-seven fellow contestants traveled on a special train.

4. The chartered train was called the "Reading Railroad," and it ran from Chicago going to Atlantic City.

5. The outside of the train was decorated with images from the Monopoly board: the property cards, the playing pieces, and there were pictures of the "Chance" and "Community Chest" cards as well.

6. Contestants played Monopoly on the train: those who lost the games became spectators; the winning players went on to compete in the championship games in Atlantic City.

7. The prize money included $1,000 for fourth place, $2,500 for the third spot, $5,000 to the runner-up, in addition to the big prize of $15,140, which equals the amount of fake money in a Monopoly game.

8. To participate in the Monopoly Championship, contestants first had to visit the Monopoly site online, then take a quiz, or they were competitors in Monopoly championships in the past.

9. Matt turns out to be a lucky name and a lucky way to spell it for would-be Monopoly champions.

10. At the previous National Monopoly Championship in Las Vegas, Matt Gissel won first prize.

Source: www.hasbro.com/monopoly

Exercise 3

1. Going to the new car wash in my neighborhood is like a trip to paradise.

2. It has a plush lounge that offers free coffee, cookies, and there are even pretzels for those who don't like sweets.

3. The leather furniture comforts weary customers as they wait for their cars to be cleaned.

4. Full plate-glass windows line the front wall of the lounge so that people can see their vehicles being dried, and sometimes they even check out the cars of the people around them.

5. For those who don't like to sit down, a full assortment of greeting cards lines the back wall of the lounge, as well as car accessories too.

6. To keep things interesting, every hour there is a drawing for a free car wash; I haven't ever won one of those though.

7. Whenever I am waiting in the luxurious setting of the car wash, I wonder about two things.

8. Why do people talk on cell phones when they could be resting, and how can you explain that some people stand up when they could be sitting on a nice leather sofa?

9. I will always love going to my neighborhood car wash.

10. It's the modern equivalent of going to the barbershop or to get a new hairdo at the beauty parlor.

Exercise 4

1. On June 26, 2000, scientists and their machines completed the extraordinary task of writing out the code for human life, also known as the human genome.

2. Joining the scientists were car-sized robots, and there were also massive computers that worked continuously to analyze the most basic structures of human tissues.

3. The genome project has already cost nearly four billion dollars, and ten years have gone by since it was started.

4. Now that they have our genetic code on paper, scientists will try to learn how it works.

5. The code is made up of billions of combinations of letters standing for four different chemicals: "A" for adenine, "C" for cystosine, "G" for guanine, and finally there's "T" for thymine.

6. What nobody knew before June 26, 2000, was the ordering of those four chemicals along the human genome or chain of human DNA.

7. Within DNA, genes are the smaller groupings of chemicals that instruct the different cells of the body, but the problem is that the genome includes fifty thousand genes.

8. In simpler terms, the genome is similar to a huge anthology of fifty thousand stories (genes) written so closely together that no one can tell where one ends and another begins.

9. The future of human life, disease, and how long we live may all be affected once the experts begin to identify the individual genes.

10. Some people look forward to that day optimistically, but the fear that it fills others with is just as real.

Source: Current Science, September 8, 2000

Exercise 5

Rephrase the sentences in the following list to incorporate the use of parallel structures.

1. The U.S. Surgeon General makes the following recommendations for living a healthy life and to make it a happy one too.

2. Eating well is one way to enhance your life, especially if your daily intake includes the right amount of fruits, vegetables, and don't forget to eat meat and dairy products (or their vegetarian equivalents).

3. To see a doctor regularly and getting all the usual tests and checkups can lead to a better life as well.

4. Of course, it is also very important to know about any illnesses or conditions that run in your family.

5. Getting enough rest and to sleep for a sufficient time each night obviously helps improve your overall health.

6. Along with relaxation comes communication with your friends and family, and that's another recommendation that the Surgeon General makes.

7. Some steps can be taken to prevent harm that can be avoided, wearing seatbelts, for example, and other safety devices such as helmets.

8. Drug use and alcohol consumption can have mixed results, some beneficial, but most are extremely harmful.

9. Probably the strongest recommendation is not to smoke or breathing in second-hand smoke if you can avoid it.

10. The Surgeon General's recommendations and the warnings that go with them make very good sense.

Source: Biography, August 2003

PROOFREADING EXERCISE

Proofread the following student paragraph, and revise it to correct any errors in parallel structure.

Every year in late spring, a long caravan of vehicles arrives at the park in my neighborhood. The caravan consists of a combination of trucks, campers, and vans, as well as a bunch of trailers full of folded-up kiddy rides. All of the residents and even just the people who drive by the park can tell that the fair has come to town. It isn't a big fair, but one that is small and child-friendly. Most people remember these fairs from when they were growing up. In childhood, the rides seemed huge and scary, but when you're an adult, they look almost silly in their smallness. As the fair is being set up in the park for a few days, the kids in the neighborhood can't wait to get on one of those "wild" rides. What their parents start to look forward to, of course, is the "fair food": the popcorn that comes either sweet or salty, those mouth-watering corndogs and deep-fried candy bars, and everybody loves the juicy snow cones. I can't wait until next year's fair; I'm getting hungry just thinking about it.

SENTENCE WRITING

Write ten sentences that use parallel structure. You may choose your own subject, or you may describe the process of studying for an important test. Be sure to include pairs and lists of objects, actions, locations, or ideas.

Using Pronouns

Nouns name people, places, things, and ideas—such as *students, school, computers,* and *cyberspace.* Pronouns take the place of nouns to avoid repetition and to clarify meaning. Look at the following two sentences:

> Naomi's father worried that the children at the party were too loud, so Naomi's father told the children that the party would have to end if the children didn't calm down.

> Naomi's father worried that the children at the party were too loud, so *he* told *them* that *it* would have to end if *they* didn't calm down.

Nouns are needlessly repeated in the first sentence. The second sentence uses pronouns in their place. *He* replaces *father, they* and *them* replace *children,* and *it* takes the place of *party.*

Of the many kinds of pronouns, the following cause the most difficulty because they include two ways of identifying the same person (or people), but only one form is correct in a given situation:

Subject Group	Object Group
I	me
he	him
she	her
we	us
they	them

Use a pronoun from the Subject Group in two instances:

1. Before a verb as a subject:

   He is my cousin. (*He* is the subject of the verb *is.*)

   He is taller than *I.* (The sentence is not written out in full. It means "*He* is taller than *I* am." *I* is the subject of the verb *am.*)

Whenever you see *than* in a sentence, ask yourself whether a verb has been left off the end of the sentence. Add the verb, and then you'll automatically use the correct pronoun. In both speaking and writing, always add the verb. Instead of saying, "She's smarter than (I, me)," say, "She's smarter than I *am.*" Then you will use the correct pronoun.

2. After a linking verb (*is, am, are, was, were*) as a pronoun that renames the subject:

The ones who should apologize are *they*. (*They* are *the ones who should apologize.*
Therefore, the pronoun from the Subject Group is used.)

The winner of the lottery was *she*. (*She* was *the winner of the lottery.*)

Therefore, the pronoun from the Subject Group is used.)

Modern usage allows some exceptions to this rule, however. For example, *It's me* or *It is her* (instead of the grammatically correct *It is I* and *It is she*) may be common in spoken English.

Use pronouns from the Object Group for all other purposes. In the following sentence, *me* is not the subject, nor does it rename the subject. It follows a preposition; therefore, it comes from the Object Group.

My boss went to lunch with Jenny and *me*.

A good way to tell whether to use a pronoun from the Subject Group or the Object Group is to leave out any extra name (and the word *and*). By leaving out *Jenny and,* you will say, *My boss went to lunch with me.* You would never say, *My boss went to lunch with I.*

My father and *I* play chess on Sundays. (*I* play chess on Sundays.)

She and her friends rented a video. (*She* rented a video.)

We saw Kevin and *them* last night. (We saw *them* last night.)

The teacher gave *us* students certificates. (Teacher gave *us* certificates.)

The coach asked Craig and *me* to wash the benches. (Coach asked *me* to wash the benches.)

Pronoun Agreement

Just as subjects and verbs must agree, pronouns should agree with the nouns they refer to. If the word referred to is singular, the pronoun should be singular. If the word referred to is plural, the pronoun should be plural.

Each classroom has *its* own chalkboard.

The pronoun *its* refers to the singular noun *classroom* and therefore is singular.

Both classrooms have *their* own chalkboards.

The pronoun *their* refers to the plural noun *classrooms* and therefore is plural.

The same rules that we use to maintain the agreement of subjects and verbs also apply to pronoun agreement. For instance, ignore any prepositional phrases that come between the noun and the pronoun that takes its place.

The *box* of chocolates has lost *its* label.

Boxes of chocolates often lose *their* labels.

A *player* with the best concentration usually beats *her or his* opponent.

Players with the best concentration usually beat *their* opponents.

When a pronoun refers to more than one word joined by *and,* the pronoun is plural:

The *teacher* <u>and</u> the *tutors* eat *their* lunches at noon.

The *salt* <u>and</u> *pepper* were in *their* usual spots on the table.

However, when a pronoun refers to more than one word joined by *or,* then the word closest to the pronoun determines its form:

Either the teacher <u>or</u> the *tutors* eat *their* lunches in the classroom.

Either the tutors <u>or</u> the *teacher* eats *her* lunch in the classroom.

Today many people try to avoid gender bias by writing sentences like the following:

If anyone wants help with the assignment, he or she can visit me in my office.

If anybody calls, tell him or her that I'll be back soon.

Somebody has left his or her pager in the classroom.

But those sentences are wordy and awkward. Therefore some people, especially in conversation, turn them into sentences that are *not* grammatically correct.

If anyone wants help with the assignment, they can visit me in my office.

If anybody calls, tell them that I'll be back soon.

Somebody has left their pager in the classroom.

Such ungrammatical sentences, however, are not necessary. It just takes a little thought to revise each sentence so that it avoids gender bias and is also grammatically correct:

Anyone who wants help with the assignment can visit me in my office.

Tell anybody who calls that I'll be back soon.

Somebody has left a pager in the classroom.

Probably the best way to avoid the awkward *he or she* and *him or her* is to make the words plural. Instead of, "Each actor was in his or her proper place on stage," write, "All the actors were in their proper places on stage," thus avoiding gender bias and still writing a grammatically correct sentence.

Pronoun Reference

A pronoun replaces a noun to avoid repetition, but sometimes the pronoun sounds as if it refers to the wrong word in a sentence, causing confusion. Be aware that when you write a sentence, *you* know what it means, but your reader may not. What does this sentence mean?

> The students tried to use the school's computers to access the Internet, but they were too slow, so they decided to go home.

Who or what was too slow, and who or what decided to go home? We don't know whether the two pronouns (both *they*) refer to the students or to the computers. One way to correct such a faulty reference is to use singular and plural nouns:

> The students tried to use a school computer to access the Internet, but it was too slow, so they decided to go home.

Here's another sentence with a faulty reference:

> Calvin told his father that he needed a haircut.

Who needed the haircut—Calvin or his father? One way to correct such a faulty reference is to use a direct quotation:

> Calvin told his father, "You need a haircut."
> Calvin said, "Dad, I need a haircut."

Or you could always rephrase the sentence completely:

> Calvin noticed his father's hair was sticking out in odd places, so he told his father to get a haircut.

Another kind of faulty reference is a *which* clause that appears to refer to a specific word, but it doesn't really.

> I wasn't able to finish all the problems on the exam, which makes me worried.

The word *which* seems to replace *exam*, but it isn't the exam that makes me worried. The sentence should read

I am worried because I wasn't able to finish all the problems on the exam.

The pronoun *it* causes its own reference problems. Look at this sentence, for example:

When replacing the ink cartridge in my printer, it broke, and I had to call the technician to come and fix it.

Did the printer or the cartridge break? Here is one possible correction:

The new ink cartridge broke when I was putting it in my printer, and I had to call the technician for help.

EXERCISES

Exercise 1

Underline the correct pronoun. Remember the trick of leaving out the extra name to help you decide which pronoun to use. Use the correct grammatical form even though an alternate form may be acceptable in conversation.

1. My brother Martin, a few friends, and (I, me) went skiing over the holidays.
2. Martin usually enjoys skiing more than (I, me).
3. This time, however, both (he and I, him and me) challenged ourselves.
4. Since Martin is less safety conscious than (I, me), he usually doesn't want to ski with my group down the gentle slopes.
5. Every time (he and I, him and me) have been skiing before, Martin has just met my buddies and (I, me) back at the cabin at the end of the day.
6. But the one who was the most daring this time was (I, me).
7. Martin may be more of a daredevil than (I, me) most of the time, but he needed coaxing to try the steep slopes that my friends and (I, me) sailed down this time.
8. Just between (you and me, you and I), I think Martin was really scared.
9. Martin was thrilled when a ski instructor came up to (he and I, him and me) and asked, "You've been skiing for a long time, haven't you?"

10. Instead of going off on his own in the future, Martin will stay close to my friends and (I, me).

Exercise 2

Underline the pronoun that agrees with the word the pronoun replaces. If the correct answer is *his or her,* revise the sentence to eliminate the need for this awkward expression. Check your answers as you go through the exercise.

1. A good parent gives (his or her, their) children advice.
2. Most parents don't like to interfere in (his or her, their) children's lives.
3. Giving advice is not the same as interfering, however; (it's, they're) a completely different thing.
4. A child often looks to (his or her, their) parents for guidance in difficult times.
5. For instance, a child might have encountered a bully at (his or her, their) elementary school.
6. The other schoolchildren might tell the child to keep (his or her, their) mouth shut about it.
7. A parent would probably offer (his or her, their) child very different advice—to speak to the principal about the problem right away.
8. A bully can only get away with (his or her, their) activities if everyone else is too scared or too uninformed to stop (him or her, them).
9. Dealing with bullies is just one example of how parents can offer helpful advice to (his or her, their) children.
10. Most kids would rather have parents who are involved in (his or her, their) lives than parents who only think about (himself or herself, themselves).

Exercise 3

Underline the correct pronoun. Again, if the correct answer is *his or her,* revise the sentence to eliminate the need for this awkward expression.

1. When it comes to dog-training strategies, no one knows as much as (he, him).
2. The swimming coach gave the new students and (we, us) a few pointers about breathing.
3. (He and she, Him and her) find many of the same things funny.
4. I recently found out that my algebra tutor is actually younger than (I, me).
5. Each of the ushers wore a badge on (his or her, their) jacket.
6. That carpet store has (its, their) own unique methods of advertising.
7. Every member of the club has (his or her, their) special duty to perform at the fund-raiser.
8. The bat that flies around our backyard every night seems to have lost (its, their) family.
9. The winner of the slogan contest was (she, her).
10. Would you like to come to the movies with (he and I, him and me)?

Exercises 4 and 5

Most—but not all—of the sentences in the next two sets aren't clear because we don't know what word the pronoun refers to. Revise such sentences, making the meaning clear. Since there are more ways than one to rewrite each sentence, yours may be as good as the ones at the back of the book. Just ask yourself whether the meaning is clear.

Exercise 4

1. The school issued new student ID cards and mailed them out yesterday.
2. I finished my painting, put my supplies in my art box, and waited for it to dry.
3. Kelly told her friend that there was a backpack on top of her car.
4. We worked at the car wash this weekend, which made us all sore.
5. Trent's dad let him drive his car to the prom.

6. When I placed my key in the lock, it broke.

7. Janel told my sister that she didn't like her.

8. As we were spreading the blanket on the grass, it ripped.

9. Our teacher writes lots of comments on our essays, which helps us correct our mistakes.

10. Carl asked his new boss why he couldn't work late.

Exercise 5

1. She put ketchup on her hamburger and then handed it to her friend.

2. As he clipped his rabbit's front claws, he felt much better.

3. Whenever my car's transmission shifts into a higher gear, it makes a high-pitched noise.

4. Shawn's dentist told him to floss his teeth more often.

5. The Jenkins family built a new gazebo, but it still isn't as popular as the Hill family.

6. Some people buy hardback novels because they're so attractive.

7. The coaches trained the athletes in their own backyards.

8. She wrote the essay on her computer and then deleted it by mistake.

9. I watched the sun set as it got darker and darker.

10. The student asked the teacher why he was doing so badly.

PROOFREADING EXERCISE

The following paragraph contains errors in the use of pronouns. Find and correct the errors.

Rude drivers have one thing in common: they think that they know how to drive better than anybody else. The other day, as my friends and me were driving to school, we stopped at an intersection. A very old man who used a cane to help him walk started across it in front of my friends and I just before the light was ready to change. So we waited. But while we waited for him, a male driver behind us started to honk his horn since he couldn't see him. I wondered, "Does he want us to hit him, or what?" Finally, it was clear. He pulled his car up beside ours, opened his window, and yelled at us before it sped away. The old man reached the other side safely, but he hardly noticed.

SENTENCE WRITING

Write ten sentences about a conversation between you and someone else. Then check that your pronouns are grammatically correct, that they agree with the words they replace, and that references to specific nouns are clear.

Avoiding Shifts in Person

To understand what "person" means when using pronouns, imagine a conversation between two people about a third person. The first person speaks using "I, me, my. . ."; the second person would be called "you"; and when the two of them talked of a third person, they would say "he, she, they. . . ." You'll never forget the idea of "person" if you remember it as a three-part conversation.

First person—*I, me, my, we, us, our*

Second person—*you, your*

Third person—*he, him, his, she, her, hers, they, them, their, one, anyone*

You may use all three of these groups of pronouns in a paper, but don't shift from one group to another without a good reason.

Wrong: Few people know how to manage *their* time. *One* need not be an efficiency expert to realize that *one* could get a lot more done if *he* budgeted *his* time. Nor do *you* need to work very hard to get more organized.

Better: *Everyone* should know how to manage *his or her* time. *One* need not be an efficiency expert to realize that *a person* could get a lot more done if *one* budgeted *one's* time. Nor does *one* need to work very hard to get more organized. (Too many *one's* in a paragraph make it sound overly formal, and they lead to the necessity of avoiding sexism by using *s/he* or *he or she*, etc. Sentences can be revised to avoid using either *you* or *one*.)

Best: Many of *us* don't know how to manage *our* time. *We* need not be efficiency experts to realize that *we* could get a lot more done if *we* budgeted *our* time. Nor do *we* need to work very hard to get more organized.

Often students write *you* in a paper when they don't really mean *you, the reader.*

You wouldn't believe how many times I saw that movie.

Such sentences are always improved by getting rid of the *you.*

I saw that movie many times.

PROOFREADING EXERCISES

Which of the following student paragraphs shift *unnecessarily* between first-, second-, and third-person pronouns? In those that do, revise the sentences to eliminate such shifting, thus making the entire paragraph read smoothly. (First, read the paragraphs to determine whether unnecessary shifting takes place. One of the paragraphs is correct.)

1. Everyone knows that, to pitch a baseball well, you need a strong arm. But it might surprise most of us to know that it also requires powerful legs. Scientists at Johns Hopkins University in Baltimore have studied pitchers and their movements. They used a specially designed pitching mound, and they wired the pitchers' joints with sensors for the experiment. Their research revealed that the energy

or force of a pitch begins in the leg that the pitcher stands on, flows from there to the leg that the pitcher lands on, then travels up the body and out the end of the arm that the pitcher throws with.

Source: Current Science, September 8, 2000

2. I was reading about superstitions for my psychology class, and I learned that a lot of these beliefs concern brooms and sweeping. One superstition says that, whenever you change your residence, you should get a new broom. People should not take their old brooms with them because the brooms might carry any bad luck that was swept up at the old place and bring it to the new one. Also, if you sweep dirt out an open door, make it the back door so that the bad luck will depart forever. If you sweep dirt out the front way, the same bad luck will come right back in again. Finally, I learned never to walk across a fallen broomstick unless I never want to get married, for that is the fate for anyone who steps over a broomstick. I bet most people would be surprised by how many things can go wrong when you pick up a broom.

3. Most of us in America could use more vacation time. We hear about citizens of other countries getting several weeks—and sometimes even months—off every year to rest their bodies, recharge their energies, and lift their spirits. But in the United States, we have to fight for and often forfeit our one- or two-week vacations. In fact, if we complain too loudly about needing a break, we could be the newest person on the unemployment line. It's time for all of us to stand up for our right to sit down and take a rest.

REVIEW OF SENTENCE STRUCTURE ERRORS

One sentence in each pair contains an error. Read both sentences carefully before you decide. Then write the letter of the *incorrect* sentence in the blank. Try to name the error and correct it if you can. You may find any of these errors:

awk   awkward phrasing

cliché   overused expression

dm   dangling modifier

frag   fragment

mm   misplaced modifier

pro   incorrect pronoun

pro agr   pronoun agreement error

pro ref   pronoun reference error

ro   run-on sentence

shift   shift in time or person

s/v agr   subject/verb agreement error

wordy   wordiness

//   not parallel

1. _____   A. I've been working twenty-four seven on my art project.

         B. The teacher gave special instructions to Cora and me.

2. _____   A. The first student to hear the news was she.

         B. I received a message on my cell phone and quickly erased it.

3. _____   A. The total, including air fare and hotel, over two thousand dollars.

         B. Traveling is much harder and more expensive than it used to be.

4. _____   A. The fog-making device often distracted the ballet dancers.

         B. Sneezing as softly as possible, her tutu barely shook during her swan number.

5. _____   A. Neither she nor I was prepared for the pop quiz.

         B. Neither she nor I were prepared for the pop quiz.

6. _____   **A.** I had an idea for an invention and I created the prototype.

    B. Then I discovered that a device just like my invention had already been patented.

7. _____   **A.** True friends are hard to find and harder to keep.

    B. A true friend is not afraid to tell their other friends the truth.

8. _____   **A.** We walked across the quad, up the stairs, and into the auditorium.

    B. When we got there, we saw so many people that we couldn't even believe that many people could fit into one building.

9. _____   **A.** At the age of two, my parents gave my brother a little piano.

    B. He started banging on that toy piano immediately.

10. _____   **A.** Just between you and I, the band's new song sounds terrible.

    B. I think that they need more practice.

11. _____   **A.** Fires are supposed to be a natural part of the cycle of forest life.

    B. Like starting over from scratch when they're done.

12. _____   **A.** The porter escorted them to their room, and they see a huge basket of goodies waiting for them.

    B. Everyone in the wedding party got the same basket.

13. _____   **A.** Some people like wall calendars others prefer desk calendars.

    B. Many people don't use calendars at all.

14. _____   **A.** Our teachers may have more facts than we.

    B. However, we have more fun than them.

15. _____   **A.** I received a very unique gift as a present from my boss last week.

    B. It was a sterling silver memo pad holder with my name engraved on it.

PROOFREADING EXERCISE

The following is an insightful student essay. Revise it to eliminate wordiness and to correct any errors in sentence structure.

Getting Involved

Getting involved in other people's business can be a right and a wrong thing. It all depends on the relationship you have with that person and what situation that person is going through. For example, a friend of yours is having trouble in a bad relationship and you are concerned about their well-being. Getting involved not only shows that as a friend you love them, but it can help them solve their problems.

On the other hand, some people just like to be nosey. I feel that most people who do get involved in other people's business just for fun have a boring life. They need to know about others so that their lives can be more interesting. I have been in many situations where peers have tried to learn about my life and problems so that they could show and tell. All of the things they said turned into rumors.

Since I have learned from others' mistakes about not minding your own business, I would never get involved in other people's business. If it is not going to benefit them in some way. Therefore, people should better their own lives and not worry about anyone else's. This would make the world a better place.

PART 3

Punctuation and Capital Letters

Period, Question Mark, Exclamation Point, Semicolon, Colon, Dash

Every mark of punctuation should help the reader. Here are the rules for six marks of punctuation. The first three you have known for a long time and probably have no trouble with. The one about semicolons you learned when you studied independent clauses (p. 84). The ones about the colon and the dash may be less familiar.

Put a period (.) at the end of a sentence and after most abbreviations.

> The students elected Ms. Daniels to represent the class.
> Sept.   Mon.   in.   sq.   ft.   lbs.

Put a question mark (?) after a direct question but not after an indirect one.

> Will we be able to use our notes during the test? (direct)
> I wonder if we will be able to use our notes during the test. (indirect)

Put an exclamation point (!) after an expression that shows strong emotion. This mark is used mostly in dialogue or informal correspondence.

> I can't believe I did so well on my first exam!

Put a semicolon (;) between two independent clauses in a sentence unless they are joined by one of the connecting words *for, and, nor, but, or, yet, so.*

> My mother cosigned for a loan; now I have my own car.
>
> Some careers go in and out of fashion; however, people will always need teachers.

To be sure that you are using a semicolon correctly, see if a period and capital letter can be used in its place. If they can, you are putting the semicolon in the right spot.

> My mother cosigned for a loan. Now I have my own car.
>
> Some careers go in and out of fashion. However, people will always need teachers.

Put a colon (:) after a complete statement that introduces one of the following elements: a name, a list, a quotation, or an explanation.

> The company announced its Employee of the Month: Lee Jones. (The sentence before the colon introduces the name that follows it.)
>
> That truck comes in the following colors: red, black, blue, and silver. (The complete statement before the colon introduces the list that follows it.)
>
> That truck comes in red, black, blue, and silver. (Here the list is simply part of the sentence. There is no complete statement used to introduce the list and set it off from the rest of the sentence.)
>
> Thoreau had this to say about time: "Time is but the stream I go a-fishin in." (The writer introduces the quotation with a complete statement. Therefore, a colon comes between them.)
>
> Thoreau said, "Time is but the stream I go a-fishin in." (Here the writer leads directly into the quotation; therefore, no colon—just a comma—comes between them.)

Use dashes (—) to isolate inserted information, to signal an abrupt change of thought, or to emphasize what follows.

> Lee Jones—March's Employee of the Month—received his own special parking space.
>
> I found out today—or was it yesterday?—that I have inherited a fortune.
>
> We have exciting news for you—we're moving!

E X E R C I S E S

Add to these sentences the necessary punctuation (periods, question marks, exclamation points, semicolons, colons, and dashes). The commas used within the sentences are correct and do not need to be changed.

Exercise 1

1. Have you ever had one of those days ?.

2. You wake up feeling great then you notice that your alarm did not go off

3. You take several steps to avoid being late to your first class skip your shower, throw on the first clothes you see, and walk out the door without coffee or breakfast

4. You open your car door, sit in the driver's seat, and turn the key your car battery is dead

5. You go back inside the house and call your friend Tracy she has a reliable car

6. Tracy's roommate the one who doesn't like you answers the phone out of a sound sleep

7. The roommate tells you that Tracy has already gone to school

8. You try Tracy's cell phone number you get her message as usual

9. All of your efforts to save the day have failed there is only one option left

10. You make yourself coffee and a big breakfast you sit in front of the TV and turn it on

Exercise 2

1. What have spiders done for you lately

2. In the near future, a spider may save your life

3. Researchers in New York have discovered the healing power of one species in particular the Chilean Rose tarantula

4. This spider's venom includes a substance that could stop a human's heart attack once it begins

5. The substance has the ability to restore the rhythm of a heart that has stopped beating

6. A scientist in Connecticut is experimenting with the killing power of another arachnid the creature he is studying is the Australian funnel-web spider

7. Currently, pesticides that destroy insects on crops also end up killing animals accidentally

8. The funnel-web spider's venom is lethal to unwanted insects however, it's harmless to animals

9. Scientists would have to reproduce the funnel-web spider's venom artificially in order to have enough to use in fields

10. As a result of these studies into the power of spider venom, you may live longer and enjoy pesticide-free foods

Source: Discover, September 2000

Exercise 3

This exercise also includes two titles of books that have subtitles. Use a colon to separate the main titles from the subtitles.

1. The change from one millennium to another has prompted us to look back over the twentieth century and wonder what its most important elements were

2. Writers of history books whose usual topics are influential people are choosing these days to write about indispensable things

3. The twentieth century saw the rise of two particularly important objects the banana and the pointed screw

4. Virginia Scott Jenkins has written *Bananas An American History*

5. And Witold Rybczynski is the author of *One Good Turn A Natural History of the Screwdriver and the Screw*

6. Jenkins' book includes facts and stories about the banana's rise in popularity during the twentieth century in America

7. Before 1900, the banana was an unfamiliar fruit in the United States now each American consumes about seventy-five bananas per year

8. Rybczynski points out that the basic ideas for the screwdriver and the screw have been around since the ancient Greeks however, screws did not have sharpened points until the twentieth century

9. So for thousands of years, builders had to drill holes first only then could they get the screws' threads to take hold

10. Where would we be without bananas and self-starting screws

Exercise 4

1. Thunderstorms are spectacular demonstrations of nature's power

2. Do you know where the safest places are during a thunderstorm

3. One relatively safe place is inside a building that has plumbing pipes or electrical wires those channels can absorb the electrical energy unleashed by lightning

4. Of course, once inside such a building, people should stay away from the end sources of plumbing and wiring faucets, hoses, phone receivers, and computer terminals

5. Buildings without pipes or wires are not safe shelters during lightning strikes these might include pergolas, dugouts, and tents

6. Outside, lightning can move over the ground therefore, you should be aware of a position that emergency officials call the "lightning squat"

7. This emergency position involves curling up into the smallest ball you can while balancing on the balls of your feet and covering your ears

8. That way, there is less of you in contact with the ground if lightning strikes

9. Lightning is electrical energy consequently, it can travel far from the actual storm clouds

10. In fact, lightning has struck as far as twenty miles away from the storm that caused it

Source: *Current Health I,* October 2003

Exercise 5

1. "Daddy, am I going to get old like Grandpa"

2. This question is typical of the ones children ask their parents about aging luckily, there are books that help parents answer them

3. Lynne S. Dumas wrote the book *Talking with Your Child about a Troubled World* in it, she discusses children's concerns and suggests ways of dealing with them

4. In response to the question about getting old "like Grandpa," Dumas stresses one main point be positive

5. Too often, Dumas says, parents pass their own fears on to children parents who focus on the negative aspects of aging will probably have children who worry about growing old

6. Other subjects homelessness, for instance require special consideration for parents

7. Dumas explains that children carefully observe how parents deal with a person asking for spare change or offering to wash windshields for money

8. The unplanned nature of these encounters often catches parents off guard therefore, they should try to prepare a uniform response to such situations

9. Dumas also suggests that parents take positive action involving children in charitable donations and activities, for example in order to illustrate their compassion for the homeless

10. The most important aspect in communicating with children is honesty the second and third most important are patience and understanding

PROOFREADING EXERCISE

Can you find the punctuation errors in this student paragraph? They all involve periods, question marks, exclamation points, semicolons, colons, and dashes. Any commas used within the sentences are correct and should not be changed.

The ingredients you will need to make delicious beef stew include—beef cubes, potatoes, onions, and carrots; tomatoes are optional. First, at the bottom of a big heavy pot on high heat, you should brown the meat cubes: after dusting them with a little flour, salt, and pepper. Once the meat chunks have been browned on all sides; it's time to add the water and seasonings. You can use beef bouillon; or beef stew seasoning mix. Or you can add any blend of seasonings to fit your own taste. Next, you put in the vegetables they should be no larger than bite-sized pieces! Heat the watery stew mixture on medium heat until it begins to boil Finally, lower the temperature and cook the stew the longer the better until a thick and tasty gravy develops. Add a little flour cooked in butter if you need to thicken the broth? Bon appétit.

SENTENCE WRITING

Write ten sentences of your own that use periods, question marks, exclamation points, semicolons, colons, and dashes correctly. Imitate the examples used in the explanations if necessary. Write about an interesting assignment you have done for a class, or choose your own topic.

Comma Rules 1, 2, and 3

Commas and other pieces of punctuation guide the reader through your sentence structures in the same way that signs guide drivers on the highway. Imagine what effects misplaced or incorrect road signs would have. Yet students often randomly place commas in their sentences. Try not to use a comma unless you know there is a need for it. Memorize this rhyme about comma use: *When in doubt, leave it out.*

Among all of the comma rules, six are most important. Learn these six rules, and your writing will be easier to read. You have already studied the first rule on page 85.

1. **Put a comma before *for, and, nor, but, or, yet, so* (remember these seven words as the *fanboys*) when they connect two independent clauses.**

   The neighbors recently bought a minivan, and now they take short trips every weekend.

   We wrote our paragraphs in class today, but the teacher forgot to collect them.

   Karen was recently promoted, so she has moved to a better office.

If you use a comma alone between two independent clauses, the result is an error called a *comma splice.*

   The cake looked delicious, it tasted good too. (comma splice)

   The cake looked delicious, and it tasted good too. (correct)

Before using a comma, be sure such words do connect two independent clauses. The following sentence is merely one independent clause with one subject and two verbs. Therefore, no comma should be used.

   The cake looked delicious and tasted good too.

2. **Use a comma to separate three or more items in a series.**

> Students in literature classes are reading novels, stories, poems, and plays.
>
> Today I did my laundry, washed my car, and cleaned my room.

Occasionally, writers leave out the comma before the *and* connecting the last two items in a series, but it is more common to use it to separate all of the items equally.

Some words work together and don't need commas between them even though they do make up a kind of series.

> The team members wanted to wear their brand new green uniforms.
>
> The bright white sunlight made the room glow.

To see whether a comma is needed between words in a series, ask yourself whether *and* could be used naturally between them. It would sound all right to say *novels and stories and poems and plays;* therefore, commas are used. But it would not sound right to say *brand and new and green uniforms* or *bright and white sunlight;* therefore, no commas are used.

If an address or date is used in a sentence, put a comma after every item, including the last.

> My father was born on August 19, 1941, in Mesa, Arizona, and grew up there.
>
> Shelby lived in St. Louis, Missouri, for two years.

When only the month and year are used in a date, no commas are needed.

> My aunt graduated from Yale in May 1985.

3. **Put a comma after an introductory expression (a word, a phrase, or a dependent clause) or before a tag comment or question at the end.**

> Finally, he was able to get through to his insurance company.
>
> During her last performance, the actress fell and broke her foot.
>
> Once I have finished my homework, I will call you.
>
> He said he needed to ruminate, whatever that means.
>
> The new chairs aren't very comfortable, are they?

E X E R C I S E S

Add commas to the following sentences according to the first three comma rules. Some sentences may not need any commas, and some may need more than one.

Any other punctuation already in the sentences is correct. Check your answers after the first set.

Exercise 1

1. Chickens are the subject of riddles jokes and sayings.

2. We think of funny ways to respond to the "Why did the chicken cross the road?" question and we endlessly ponder the answer to "Which came first—the chicken or the egg?"

3. A person who runs around in a hurry is often compared to "a chicken with its head cut off."

4. Although we try not to visualize the image of the last comparison most people understand the reference to a fowl's final moments of frantic activity.

5. Anyone who has heard the story of Mike "the headless chicken" will consider the popular saying differently from that moment on for it will come to mean having a strong determination to live in spite of major setbacks.

6. On September 10 1945 a farmer in Fruita Colorado chose one of his chickens to have for dinner that night.

7. But after having his head cut off the rooster didn't die didn't seem to be in pain and continued to act "normally."

8. In fact Mike went on to become a national celebrity and his owner took him around the country so that people could see him for themselves.

9. When both *Time* and *Life* magazines ran feature stories complete with photos of Mike in October 1945 the public became fascinated by the details of Mike's ability to eat drink hear and move without a head.

10. Mike lived for eighteen months after his date with a chopping block and would have lived longer but he died by accidentally choking in 1947.

Source: The Official Mike the Headless Chicken Book (Fruita Times, 2000)

Exercise 2

1. Whenever I need to borrow some blueberries an onion or a teaspoon of ginger I go next door to my neighbor's apartment.

2. My neighbor's name is Albert and he is originally from Belgium.

3. Albert always has the season's best fruits the tastiest vegetables and the freshest spices.

4. Albert feels comfortable borrowing things from me too.

5. He doesn't ask for blueberries onions or ginger but he will ask to borrow a hammer a wrench or a Phillips-head screwdriver.

6. Albert and I have learned to offset each other's household purchases perfectly.

7. If I buy myself a new dustpan I buy an extra one for Albert.

8. When he visits the farmer's market on Thursdays Albert picks up an extra basket of strawberries for me.

9. I could not have planned to have a better next-door neighbor.

10. Whatever one of us doesn't buy the other one will.

Exercise 3

1. As if people didn't have enough to worry about Melinda Muse has written a book called *I'm Afraid, You're Afraid: 448 Things to Fear and Why.*

2. In her book Muse points out the dangers of common places objects foods months days and activities.

3. One place that the author warns about is Las Vegas casinos and the reason is that paramedics can't get to ailing gamblers due to the crowds and huge size of the buildings.

4. Another dangerous spot is the beauty parlor where people suffer strokes caused by leaning their heads back too far into the shampoo sink.

5. New clothes need to be washed before they are worn or they may transfer dangerous chemicals to the wearers' eyes skin and lungs.

6. Grapefruit juice can interfere with certain medications' effectiveness and nutmeg contains hallucinogenic substances so these are among the foods to be avoided.

7. The month of July ranks highest in certain kinds of accidental injuries and poisonings due to Independence Day celebrations and other summer activities.

8. Mondays have two dangerous distinctions for more suicides and heart attacks occur on Mondays than on any other day of the week.

9. Even joining a large choir can permanently damage singers' ears.

10. After reading *I'm Afraid, You're Afraid* it's possible to be afraid of almost everything.

Exercise 4

1. Speaking of worst-case scenarios there is a book about how to survive them and it's called *The Worst-Case Scenario Survival Handbook*.

2. The coauthors of this self-help book are aware that most of us will never have to overpower an alligator or make an emergency landing on an airplane yet they want us to be prepared nonetheless.

3. In the "About the Authors" section of the book readers learn that Joshua Piven is a first-time writer but he has survived encounters with robbers muggers and stalled subway trains.

4. About Piven's coauthor we discover that David Borgenicht has written two other books and has had his share of worst-case scenarios especially while traveling.

5. Although the overall tone of the book is somewhat humorous because it covers such outlandish topics the information it shares is deadly serious and could save a life.

6. There are drawings in each section of the book to help the reader picture the emergency and how to survive it.

7. One of the best examples illustrates a way to avoid being attacked by a mountain lion and that is to try to appear as large as possible so the drawing shows a man holding the sides of his jacket out wide like bat wings to scare the lion away.

8. If readers wonder whether they can trust the advice on escaping from quicksand they can just flip to the list of sources consulted for each section in this case an expert on the physics of natural phenomena at the University of Sydney Australia.

9. Wisely Piven and Borgenicht begin the book by warning readers to seek professional help whenever possible instead of trying the survival techniques themselves.

10. The authors know that if people go looking for trouble they'll probably find it.

Exercise 5

1. Fish may be considered "brain food" but I've never liked it.

2. While everyone is saying how delicious a big salmon steak is or how yummy the shrimp tastes you'll find me grimacing and munching on a piece of bread and butter.

3. Part of the problem with fish is the smell but my friends who love to eat fish also love the smell of fish cooking.

4. I always thought that was strange but it makes sense doesn't it?

5. If someone hates the taste of onions that person probably also hates the smell of onions cooking.

6. Come to think of it my husband hates to eat sweets and doesn't like the smell of them either.

7. When we walk into a bakery together he practically has to hold his nose the way I would in a fish market.

8. To me that's odd but my aversion must be just as odd to someone who loves fish.

9. Our daughter loves the taste of bacon but she hates the smell of bacon frying.

10. So I guess there are exceptions to the agreement of our senses of taste and smell.

PROOFREADING EXERCISE

Apply the first three comma rules to the following paragraph:

During the last thirty years of the twentieth century the number of broken arm injuries rose more than forty percent in Rochester Minnesota. Experts at the Mayo Clinic studied the number of forearm bone fractures during that time and they found that young people are the most susceptible to these injuries. Between the ages of ten and sixteen youngsters break their arms while skating skiing and participating in team sports. Looking for a reason for the startling rise in the number of broken arm bones researchers point to the common practice of drinking sodas instead of milk. Young people are getting less calcium and their bones may be paying the price.

Source: *Journal of the American Medical Association*, September 17, 2003

SENTENCE WRITING

Combine the following sets of sentences in different ways using all of the first three comma rules. You may need to reorder the details and change the phrasing.

The test was long and difficult.
Most students completed it on time.

The gardeners arrive at 7:00 in the morning.

They start up their leaf blowers.

No one in the neighborhood can sleep in anymore.

I was a child in the 1960s.

People rode in cars without seatbelts.

Children did not have protective car seats.

Air bags had not been introduced yet.

Comma Rules 4, 5, and 6

The next three comma rules all involve using pairs of commas to enclose what we like to call "scoopable" elements. Scoopable elements are certain words, phrases, and clauses that can be taken out of the middle of a sentence without affecting its meaning. Notice that the comma (,) is shaped somewhat like the tip of an ice cream scoop? Let this similarity help you remember to use commas to enclose *scoopable* elements. Two commas are used, one before and one after, to show where scoopable elements begin and where they end.

4. Put commas around the name of a person spoken to.

Did you know, Danielle, that you left your backpack at the library?

We regret to inform you, Mr. Davis, that your policy has been canceled.

5. **Put commas around expressions that interrupt the flow of the sentence (such as *however, moreover, therefore, of course, by the way, on the other hand, I believe, I think*).**

> I know, of course, that I have missed the deadline.
>
> They will try, therefore, to use the rest of their time wisely.
>
> Today's exam, I think, was only a practice test.

Read the previous examples *aloud*, and you'll hear how these expressions surrounded by commas interrupt the flow of the sentence. Sometimes such expressions flow smoothly into the sentence and don't need commas around them.

> Of course he checked to see if there were any rooms available.
>
> We therefore decided to stay out of it.
>
> I think you made the right decision.

Remember that when a word like *however* comes between two independent clauses, that word needs a semicolon before it. It may also have a comma after it, especially if there seems to be a pause between the word and the rest of the sentence. (See p. 84.)

> The bus was late; *however,* we still made it to the museum before it closed.
>
> I am improving my study habits; *furthermore,* I am getting better grades.
>
> She was interested in journalism; *therefore,* she took a job at a local newspaper.
>
> I spent hours studying for the test; *finally,* I felt prepared.

Thus, you've seen a word like *however* or *therefore* used in three ways:

1. as a "scoopable" word that interrupts the flow of the sentence (needs commas around it)

2. as a word that flows into the sentence (no commas needed)

3. as a connecting word between two independent clauses (semicolon before and often a comma after)

6. **Put commas around additional information that is not needed in a sentence.**

Certain additional information is "scoopable" and should be surrounded by commas whenever the meaning would be clear without it. Look at the following sentence:

> Maxine Taylor, who organized the fund-raiser, will introduce the candidates.

The clause *who organized the fund-raiser* is not needed in the sentence. Without it, we still know exactly who the sentence is about and what she is going to do: "Maxine Taylor will introduce the candidates." Therefore, the additional information is surrounded by commas to show that it is scoopable. Now read the following sentence:

The woman who organized the fund-raiser will introduce the candidates.

The clause *who organized the fund-raiser* is necessary in this sentence. Without it, the sentence would read as follows: "The woman will introduce the candidates." The reader would have no idea *which woman*. The clause *who organized the fund-raiser* cannot be left out because it identifies which woman. Therefore, the clause is not scoopable, and no commas are used around it. Here is another sample sentence:

Hamlet, Shakespeare's famous play, has been made into a movie many times.

The additional information *Shakespeare's famous play* is scoopable. It could be left out, and we would still understand the meaning of the sentence: "*Hamlet* has been made into a movie many times." Therefore, the commas surround the scoopable information to show that it could be taken out. Here is the same sentence with the information reversed:

Shakespeare's famous play *Hamlet* has been made into a movie many times.

Here, the title of the play is necessary. Without it, the sentence would read as follows: "Shakespeare's famous play has been made into a movie many times." The reader would have no idea which of Shakespeare's famous plays has been made into a movie many times. Therefore, the title is not scoopable, and commas should not be used around it.

The trick in deciding whether additional information is scoopable or not is to remember, "If I can scoop it out and still understand the sentence, I'll put commas around it."

E X E R C I S E S

Surround any "scoopable" elements with commas according to Comma Rules 4, 5, and 6. Any commas already in the sentences follow Comma Rules 1, 2, and 3. Some sentences may be correct. Check your answers after the first set.

Exercise 1

1. This year's office party I believe was worse than last year's.

2. I believe this year's office party was worse than last year's.

3. Lee's lasagna however was better than ever.

4. However Lee's lasagna was better than ever.

5. The clerk who works in the claims division didn't bring a dessert even though he signed up for one.

6. Justin Banks who works in the claims division didn't bring a dessert even though he signed up for one.

7. And Mr. Hopkins who planned the party needed to think of a few more party games.

8. And the person who planned the party needed to think of a few more party games.

9. As usual, no one it seems had time to decorate beyond a few balloons.

10. As usual, it seems that no one had time to decorate beyond a few balloons.

Exercise 2

1. We hope of course that people will honor their summons for jury duty.

2. Of course we hope that people will honor their summons for jury duty.

3. People who serve as jurors every time they're called deserve our appreciation.

4. Thelma and Trevor Martin who serve as jurors every time they're called deserve our appreciation.

5. We should therefore be as understanding as we can be about the slow legal process.

6. Therefore we should be as understanding as we can be about the slow legal process.

7. A legal system that believes people are innocent until proven guilty must offer a trial-by-jury option.

8. The U.S. legal system which believes people are innocent until proven guilty offers a trial-by-jury option.

9. With that option, we hope that no one will receive an unfair trial.

10. With that option, no one we hope will receive an unfair trial.

Exercise 3

1. Bobble-head dolls those figurines with heads that bob up and down have become the souvenir of choice for many modern teams and companies.

2. The history of the bobble-head doll might go back as far as the seventeenth century when figurines with moving heads were popular in China.

3. Others say these types of ceramic nodding figures called "nodder" dolls in Europe originated there in the 1800s.

4. Much more recently in the 1960s to be exact Japan began producing what some call "bobbinheads" as souvenirs to sell at baseball parks in the United States.

5. The first four baseball nodders celebrated the careers of Roberto Clemente, Mickey Mantle, Roger Maris, and Willie Mays.

6. Two of the most famous people of the twentieth century President Kennedy and Elvis Presley were immortalized as bobble-head dolls.

7. In the year 2000, Cal Ripken's nodding doll was issued just prior to his retirement.

8. Now some cereal boxes traditionally the showplaces for athletic triumphs include tiny bobble-heads as prizes inside.

9. Even William Rehnquist Chief Justice of the U.S. Supreme Court has a bobble-head doll in his likeness.

10. The Rehnquist bobble-head a must-have for any nodding-doll collector was commissioned by a law journal to encourage people to read about legal issues.

Source: www.charleston.net, July 13, 2003

Exercise 4

1. The Ironman competition one of the most grueling athletic races in the world takes place in Hawaii every year.

2. The Hawaii Ironman race challenges those who enter it in three areas of physical activity.

3. They must swim over two miles, ride a bike for 112 miles, and finally run a marathon.

4. As if that race weren't enough for some fitness fanatics, it is followed soon after by the XTerra World Championship another attraction for triathletes from around the world.

5. The Xterra an obstacle course through the extreme Hawaiian landscape takes participants over ocean waves, blistering sand, dried lava, fallen tree limbs, exposed roots, and huge chunks of coral.

6. Again, the men and women who enter the race must swim, bike, and run their way to the finish line.

7. Some triathletes participate in both races Ironman and Xterra in what triathletes refer to as The Double.

8. Nobody has ever won both Ironman and Xterra in the same year.

9. Due to the short recovery time, it is possible that no one ever will.

10. However, the male and female athletes with the best times overall in both races are considered winners of The Double; they earn a thousand dollars and an invaluable title World's Toughest Athlete.

Source: Newsweek, October 23, 2000

Exercise 5

1. One of the weirdest competitions on earth the Wife Carrying World Championships takes place in Finland once a year.

2. These load-carrying races which may have begun as training rituals for Finnish soldiers have become popular in the United States and all over the world.

3. Each pair of participants made up of one man and one "wife" has to make it through an obstacle course in the shortest time possible.

4. The "wife" half of the team has to weigh at least 49 kilos 108 pounds.

5. She does not have to be married to the man who carries her; she can indeed be someone else's wife or even unmarried.

6. The wife-carrying course includes two sections a part on land and a part in water.

7. The contest rules are few: make it to the finish line first, have fun, and don't drop the wife along the way.

8. The wife-dropping penalty which is fifteen seconds added to the pair's time is enough to disqualify most couples.

9. Contest officials allow one piece of equipment a belt that the man can wear so that the "wife" has something to hold on to during the race.

10. The winning couple wins a prize, but the coveted title Wife Carrying World Champion is reward enough for most.

Source: www.sonkajarvi.fi and *Sports Illustrated for Kids,* July 2003

PROOFREADING EXERCISE

Insert the necessary commas into this paragraph according to Comma Rules 4, 5, and 6.

There are two types of punctuation internal punctuation and end punctuation. Internal punctuation is used within the sentence, and end punctuation is used at the end of the sentence. There are six main rules for the placement of commas the most important pieces of internal punctuation. Semicolons the next most important have two main functions. Their primary function separating two independent clauses is also the most widely known. A lesser-known need for semicolons to separate items in a list already containing commas occurs rarely in college writing. Colons and dashes have special uses within sentences. And of the three pieces of end punctuation—periods, question marks, and exclamation points—one is obviously the most common. That piece is the period which signals the end of the majority of English sentences.

SENTENCE WRITING

Combine the following sets of sentences in different ways according to Comma Rules 4, 5, and 6. Try to combine each set in a way that needs commas and in a way that doesn't need commas. In other words, try to make an element "scoopable" in one sentence and not "scoopable" in another. You may reorder the details and change the phrasing as you wish. Sample responses are provided in the Answers section.

I think about that restaurant's dress code.
That restaurant's dress code is old-fashioned and may be bad for business.

He bought a pack of gum.
The gum was cinnamon.
Cinnamon was his favorite flavor.

A woman was standing on the corner at the time.
She answered the question correctly and won a thousand dollars in cash.
The woman's name was Molly Price.

Review of the Comma

Six Comma Rules

1. Put a comma before *for, and, nor, but, or, yet, so* when they connect two independent clauses.

2. Put a comma between three or more items in a series.

3. Put a comma after an introductory expression or before a tag comment or question.

4. Put commas around the name of a person spoken to.

5. Put commas around words like *however* or *therefore* when they interrupt a sentence.

6. Put commas around unnecessary additional ("scoopable") information.

COMMA REVIEW EXERCISE

Add the missing commas, and identify which one of the six comma rules applies in the brackets at the end of each sentence. Each of the six sentences illustrates a different rule.

We're writing you this e-mail Lena to give you directions to the reunion this weekend. [   ] We know that you will be driving with a few others but we want to be sure that everyone knows the way. [   ] When we contacted some of our classmates over the Internet several of the messages were returned as "undeliverable." [   ] We hope therefore that this one gets through to you. [   ] We can't wait to see everyone again: Michelle Tom Olivia and Brad. [   ] Dr. Milford our favorite professor will be there to welcome all of the returning students. [   ]

SENTENCE WRITING

Write at least one sentence of your own to demonstrate each of the six comma rules.

Quotation Marks and Underlining/*Italics*

Put quotation marks around a direct quotation (the exact words of a speaker) but not around an indirect quotation.

> The officer said, "Please show me your driver's license." (a direct quotation)
>
> The officer asked to see my driver's license. (an indirect quotation)

If the speaker says more than one sentence, quotation marks are used before and after the entire speech.

> She said, "One of your brake lights is out. You need to take care of the problem right away."

If the quotation begins the sentence, the words telling who is speaking are set off with a comma unless the quotation ends with a question mark or an exclamation point.

> "I didn't even know it was broken," I said.
>
> "Do you have any questions?" she asked.
>
> "You mean I can go!" I shouted.
>
> "Yes, consider this just a warning," she said.

Notice that each of the previous quotations begins with a capital letter. But when a quotation is interrupted by an identifying phrase, the second part doesn't begin with a capital letter unless the second part is a new sentence.

> "If you knew how much time I spent on the essay," the student said, "you would give me an A."

"A chef might work on a meal for days," the teacher replied. "That doesn't mean the results will taste good."

Put quotation marks around the titles of short stories, poems, songs, essays, TV program episodes, or other short works.

I couldn't sleep after I read "The Lottery," a short story by Shirley Jackson.

My favorite Woodie Guthrie song is "This Land Is Your Land."

We had to read George Orwell's essay "A Hanging" for my speech class.

Jerry Seinfeld's troubles in "The Puffy Shirt" episode are some of the funniest moments in TV history.

Underline titles of longer works such as books, newspapers, magazines, plays, record albums or CDs, movies, or the titles of TV or radio series.

<u>The Color Purple</u> is a novel by Alice Walker.

I read about the latest discovery of dinosaur footprints in <u>Newsweek</u>.

<u>Gone with the Wind</u> was re-released in movie theaters in 1998.

My mother listens to <u>The Writer's Almanac</u> on the radio every morning.

You may choose to *italicize* instead of underlining if your word processor gives you the option. Just be consistent throughout any paper in which you use underlining or italics.

The Color Purple is a novel by Alice Walker.

I read about the latest discovery of dinosaur footprints in *Newsweek*.

Gone with the Wind was re-released in movie theaters in 1998.

My mother listens to *The Writer's Almanac* on the radio every morning.

EXERCISES

Correctly punctuate quotations and titles in the following sentences by adding quotation marks or underlining (*italics*). Check your answers often.

Exercise 1

1. I am reading a book called Don't: A Manual of Mistakes & Improprieties More or Less Prevalent in Conduct and Speech.

2. The book's contents are divided into chapters with titles such as At Table, In Public, and In General.

3. In the section about table don'ts, the book offers the following warning: Don't bend over your plate, or drop your head to get each mouthful.

4. The table advice continues by adding, Don't bite your bread. Break it off.

5. This book offers particularly comforting advice about conducting oneself in public.

6. For instance, it states, Don't brush against people, or elbow people, or in any way show disregard for others.

7. When meeting others on the street, the book advises, Don't be in a haste to introduce. Be sure that it is mutually desired before presenting one person to another.

8. In the section titled In General, there are more tips about how to get along in society, such as Don't underrate everything that others do, and overstate your own doings.

9. The Don't book has this to say about books, whether borrowed or owned: Read them, but treat them as friends that must not be abused.

10. And one can never take the following warning too much to heart: Don't make yourself in any particular way a nuisance to your neighbors or your family.

Exercise 2

1. Have you been to the bookstore yet? Monica asked.

2. No, why? I answered.

3. They've rearranged the books, she said, and now I can't find anything.

4. Are all of the books for one subject still together? I wondered.

5. Yes, they are, Monica told me, but there are no markers underneath the books to say which teacher's class they're used in, so it's really confusing.

6. Why don't we just wait until the teachers show us the books and then buy them? I replied.

7. That will be too late! Monica shouted.

8. Calm down, I told her, you are worrying for nothing.

9. I guess so, she said once she took a deep breath.

10. I sure hope I'm not wrong, I thought to myself, or Monica will really be mad at me.

Exercise 3

1. Stopping by Woods on a Snowy Evening is a poem by Robert Frost.

2. Once you finish your responses, the teacher said, bring your test papers up to my desk.

3. I subscribe to several periodicals, including Time and U.S. News & World Report.

4. Our country is the world, William Lloyd Garrison believed, our country-men are all mankind.

5. Do you know, my teacher asked, that there are only three ways to end a sentence?

6. Edward Young warned young people to Be wise with speed. A fool at forty is a fool indeed.

7. In Shakespeare's play Romeo and Juliet, Mercutio accidentally gets stabbed and shouts, A plague on both your houses!

8. There is no such thing as a moral or an immoral book, Oscar Wilde writes in his novel The Picture of Dorian Gray; Books are either well written, or badly written.

9. Molière felt that One should eat to live, and not live to eat.

10. Did you say, I'm sleepy or I'm beeping?

Exercise 4

1. Women's Wit and Wisdom is the title of a book I found in the library.

2. The book includes many great insights that were written or spoken by women throughout history.

3. England's Queen Elizabeth I noted in the sixteenth century that A clear and innocent conscience fears nothing.

4. Nothing is so good as it seems beforehand, observed George Eliot, a female author whose real name was Mary Ann Evans.

5. Some of the women's quotations are funny; Alice Roosevelt Longworth, for instance, said, If you don't have anything good to say about anyone, come and sit by me.

6. If life is a bowl of cherries, asked Erma Bombeck, what am I doing in the pits?

7. Some of the quotations are serious, such as Gloria Steinem's statement, The future depends on what each of us does every day.

8. Maya Lin, the woman who designed Washington D.C.'s Vietnam Veterans Memorial, reminded us that, as she put it, War is not just a victory or a loss. . . . People die.

9. Emily Dickinson had this to say about truth: Truth is such a rare thing, it is delightful to tell it.

10. Finally, columnist Ann Landers advised one of her readers that The naked truth is always better than the best-dressed lie.

Exercise 5

1. In his book Who's Buried in Grant's Tomb? A Tour of Presidential Gravesites, Brian Lamb records the final words of American presidents who have passed away.

2. Some of their goodbyes were directed at their loved ones; for example, President Zachary Taylor told those around him, I regret nothing, but I am sorry that I am about to leave my friends.

3. Other presidents, such as William Henry Harrison, who died after only one month in office, addressed more political concerns; Harrison said, I wish you to understand the true principles of the government. I wish them carried out. I ask for nothing more.

4. John Tyler became president due to Harrison's sudden death; Tyler served his term, lived to be seventy-one, and said, Perhaps it is best when his time came.

5. At the age of eighty-three, Thomas Jefferson fought to live long enough to see the fiftieth anniversary of America's independence; on that day in 1826, Jefferson was one of only three (out of fifty-six) signers of the Declaration of Independence still living, and he asked repeatedly before he died, Is it the fourth?

6. John Adams, one of the other three remaining signers, died later the same day—July 4, 1826—and his last words ironically were Thomas Jefferson still survives.

7. The third president to die on the Fourth of July (1831) was James Monroe; while he was president, people within the government got along so well that his time in office was known as the era of good feelings.

8. Doctors attempted to help James Madison live until the Fourth of July, but he put off their assistance; on June 26, 1836, when a member of his family became alarmed at his condition, Madison comforted her by saying, Nothing more than a change of mind, my dear, and he passed away.

9. Grover Cleveland, who had suffered from many physical problems, was uneasy at his death; before losing consciousness, he said, I have tried so hard to do right.

10. Finally, George Washington, our first president, also suffered greatly but faced death bravely; I die hard, he told the people by his bedside, but I am not afraid to go. 'Tis well.

PARAGRAPH EXERCISE

Correctly punctuate quotations and titles in the following paragraph by adding quotation marks or underlining (*italics*).

We read part of The Autobiography of Benjamin Franklin in class the other day. In the section we read, Franklin spells out the details of his concept of Order: Let all your things have their places; let each part of your business have its time. Then a few pages later, he includes a chart of what he calls the twenty-four hours of a natural day. Along with the notations of Work, Read, and Sleep that Franklin filled in were two questions to consider. At the start of each new day, he would ask himself, What good shall I do this day? And at the end of each day, he would ask, What good have I done to-day? After reading this brief section of Franklin's Autobiography, I am not surprised that he accomplished so much during his lifetime.

SENTENCE WRITING

Write ten sentences that list and discuss your favorite songs, TV shows, characters' expressions, movies, books, and so on. Be sure to punctuate quotations and titles correctly. Refer to the rules at the beginning of this section if necessary.

Capital Letters

1. **Capitalize the first word of every sentence.**

   Peaches taste best when they are cold.

   A piece of fruit is an amazing object.

2. **Capitalize the first word of every direct quotation.**

   She said, "I've never worked so hard before."

   "I have finished most of my homework," she said, "but I still have a lot to do." (The *but* is not capitalized because it does not begin a new sentence.)

   "I love my speech class," she said. "Maybe I'll change my major." (*Maybe* is capitalized because it begins a new sentence.)

3. **Capitalize the first, last, and every important word in a title. Don't capitalize prepositions (such as** *in, of, at, with*)**, short connecting words (such as** *and, but, or*)**, the** *to* **in front of a verb, or** *a, an,* **or** *the.*

   I saw a copy of Darwin's *The Origin of Species* at a yard sale.

   The class enjoyed the essay "How to Write a Rotten Poem with Almost No Effort."

   Shakespeare in Love is a film based on Shakespeare's writing of the play *Romeo and Juliet.*

4. **Capitalize specific names of people, places, languages, races, and nationalities.**

Rev. Jesse Jackson	China	Cesar Chavez
Ireland	Spanish	Japanese
Ryan White	Philadelphia	Colorado Blvd.

5. **Capitalize names of months, days of the week, and special days, but not the seasons.**

March	Fourth of July	spring
Tuesday	Easter	winter
Valentine's Day	Labor Day	fall

6. **Capitalize a title of relationship if it takes the place of the person's name. If** *my* **(or** *your, her, his, our, their***) is in front of the word, a capital is not used.**

I think Mom wrote to him.	*but*	I think my mom wrote to him.
We visited Aunt Sophie.	*but*	We visited our aunt.
They spoke with Grandpa.	*but*	They spoke with their grandpa.

7. **Capitalize names of particular people or things, but not general terms.**

I admire Professor Washborne.	*but*	I admire my professor.
We saw the famous Potomac River.	*but*	We saw the famous river.
Are you from the South?	*but*	Is your house south of the mountains?
I will take Philosophy 4 and English 100.	*but*	I will take philosophy and English.
She graduated from Sutter High School.	*but*	She graduated from high school.
They live at 119 Forest St.	*but*	They live on a beautiful street.
We enjoyed the Monterey Bay Aquarium.	*but*	We enjoyed the aquarium.

E X E R C I S E S

Add all of the necessary capital letters to the sentences that follow. Check your answers after the first set.

Exercise 1

1. i have always wanted to learn another language besides english.

2. right now, i am taking english 410 in addition to my writing class.

3. the course title for english 410 is basic grammar.

4. english 410 is a one-unit, short-term class designed to help students with their verb forms, parts of speech, phrases, and clauses.

5. i hope that learning more about english grammar will help me understand the grammar of another language more easily.

6. now i must decide whether i want to take spanish, french, italian, or chinese.

7. i guess i could even take a class in greek or russian.

8. when i was in high school, i did take french for two years, but my clearest memory is of the teacher, mrs. gautier.

9. she was one of the best teachers that hillside high school ever had.

10. unfortunately, i did not study hard enough and can't remember most of the french that mrs. gautier taught me.

Exercise 2

1. when people think of jazz, they think of *down beat* magazine.

2. *down beat*'s motto may be "jazz, blues & beyond," but some people think that the magazine has gone too far "beyond" by including two guitarists in the *down beat* hall of fame.

3. the two musicians in question are jimi hendrix and frank zappa.

4. jimi hendrix was inducted into the hall of fame in 1970.

5. *down beat* added frank zappa to the list in 1994.

6. since then, readers and editors have been debating whether hendrix and zappa belong in the same group as duke ellington, john coltrane, and miles davis.

7. those who play jazz guitar have some of the strongest opinions on the subject.

8. russell malone, mark elf, and john abercrombie all agree that hendrix and zappa were great guitarists but not jazz guitarists.

9. others like steve tibbetts and bill frisell don't have any problem putting hendrix on the list, but tibbetts isn't so sure about including zappa.

10. it will be interesting to see who *down beat*'s future inductees will be.

Source: Down Beat, July 1999

Exercise 3

1. i grew up watching *it's a wonderful life* once a year on tv in the winter.

2. that was before the colorized version and before every station started showing it fifteen times a week throughout the months of november and december.

3. i especially remember enjoying that holiday classic with my mother and brothers when we lived on seventh avenue.

4. "hurry up!" mom would yell, "you're going to miss the beginning!"

5. my favorite part has always been when jimmy stewart's character, george bailey, uses his own money to help the people of bedford falls and to save his father's building and loan.

6. george's disappointment turns to happiness after he and donna reed's character, mary, move into the abandoned house on their honeymoon.

7. of course, mean old mr. potter takes advantage of uncle billy's carelessness at the bank, and that starts george's breakdown.

8. in his despair, george places the petals of his daughter zuzu's flower in his pocket, leaves his house, and wants to commit suicide.

9. luckily, all of george's good deeds have added up over the years, and he is given a chance to see that thanks to a character named clarence.

10. when george feels zuzu's petals in his pocket, he knows that he's really made it home again, and the people of bedford falls come to help him.

Exercise 4

1. most people don't know the name elzie crisler segar.

2. segar was the creator of the comic character popeye.

3. segar based popeye and many of his fellow characters on residents of the town of chester, illinois, where segar was born.

4. popeye's inspiration was a chester bartender named frank "rocky" fiegel.

5. fiegel was a brawler by nature and might have even been a sailor at some point.

6. segar learned how to draw by taking a correspondence course.

7. one of segar's bosses at a chester movie house, j. william schuchert, was the prototype for wimpy.

8. segar introduced olive oyl's character in his *thimble theater* comic strip.

9. olive was based on a chester store owner, dora paskel.

10. the town of chester celebrates the work of elzie crisler segar with a yearly popeye picnic, the popeye museum, a popeye statue, and segar memorial park.

Source: Biography, November 2003

Exercise 5

1. helen hunt has been acting on tv and in movies since she was nine years old.

2. she portrayed the cyclone-chasing scientist named jo harding in *twister.*

3. she gave an oscar-winning performance alongside jack nicholson in *as good as it gets.*

4. her most recognizable and long-lasting tv character so far has been jamie buckman in *mad about you,* which costarred paul reiser.

5. having wanted to act with kevin spacey since she saw *american beauty,* hunt took the part of haley joel osment's mom in *pay it forward.*

6. she also worked with famous director robert altman and actor richard gere on the film *dr. t and the women.*

7. hunt played tom hanks' love interest in *cast away.*

8. she and mel gibson starred together in the romantic comedy *what women want.*

9. in addition to acting, hunt loves the olympics and even worked event tickets into her contract with nbc while she was making *mad about you.*

10. hunt has collected souvenir pins like any normal fan at the olympic games in atlanta and in sydney, australia.

Source: Los Angeles Times, September 10, 2000

REVIEW OF PUNCTUATION AND CAPITAL LETTERS

Punctuate these sentences. They include all the rules for punctuation and capitalization you have learned. Compare your answers carefully with those at the back of the book. Sentences may require several pieces of punctuation or capital letters.

1. tower bridge is one of the most famous landmarks in london

2. have you ever read eb whites essay goodbye to 48th street

3. constance and jennifer drove up the coast from los angeles to san francisco

4. how many years of spanish have you taken my counselor asked

5. we received your application ms tomkins we would like you to call us to set up an appointment for an interview

6. the person who wins the contest will fly to italy

7. i am majoring in architecture and my best friend is in the nursing program

8. due to the shortage of qualified applicants the financial aid office has extended its deadline

9. the drama club needs new costumes new sets and new scripts

10. neil armstrong said the famous words one small step for man, one giant leap for mankind at the moment when he first set foot on the moon

11. my parents gave me the following advice trust your own instincts whenever you face difficult decisions

12. we need a new car however we cant afford one right now

13. because i could not stop for death is a famous poem by emily dickinson

14. jk rowling is the author of the harry potter books

15. the overlooked bus passenger ran into the street and yelled come back here

COMPREHENSIVE TEST

In these sentences you'll find all the errors that have been discussed in the entire text. Try to name the error in the blank before each sentence, and then correct the error if you can. You may find any of the following errors:

apos	apostrophe
awk	awkward phrasing
c	comma needed
cap	capitalization
cliché	overused expression
cs	comma splice
dm	dangling modifier
frag	fragment
mm	misplaced modifier
p	punctuation
pro	incorrect pronoun
pro agr	pronoun agreement
pro ref	pronoun reference
ro	run-on sentence
shift	shift in time or person
sp	misspelled word
s/v agr	subject/verb agreement
wordy	wordiness
ww	wrong word
//	not parallel

A perfect—or almost perfect—score will mean you've mastered the first part of the text.

1. _____ The scary scenes in the movie really effected me; I couldn't sleep that night.
2. _____ The police asked us what time the theft had occured.
3. _____ There are a few positive steps that can be taken toward a solution to our problems with money.
4. _____ Last semester, I took art history, spanish, and geography.
5. _____ The department store hired my friend and I as gift wrappers for the holidays.
6. _____ In just six weeks, we learned to find main ideas, to remember details, and how we can integrate new words into our vocabulary.
7. _____ The chairs should be straightened and the chalkboard should be erased before the next class.
8. _____ Hopping into the room, the students noticed a tiny frog from the biology lab.
9. _____ He tells the same joke in every speech, and people laughed.
10. _____ I bring pies to potluck parties because they are always appreciated.
11. _____ We don't know if the buses run that late at night?
12. _____ The womens' teams have their own trophy case across the hall.
13. _____ At the age of twenty-one, my mom handed me a beer.
14. _____ Their car wouldn't start the battery was dead.
15. _____ I asked the car salesman to cut to the chase and spill the beans about the price.
16. _____ In my own personal opinion, that restaurant serves terrible food.
17. _____ Everybody in the audience raised their hand.
18. _____ Because the lines were long and we couldn't find our friends.
19. _____ I plan to stay in town for spring break, it's more restful that way.
20. _____ Each of the kittens have white paws.

PART 4

Writing

Aside from the basics of word choice, spelling, sentence structure, and punctuation, what else do you need to understand to write better? Just as sentences are built according to accepted patterns, so are other "structures" of English—paragraphs and essays, for example.

Think of writing as including levels of structures, beginning small with words connecting to form phrases, clauses, and sentences. Then sentences connect to form paragraphs and essays. Each level has its own set of "blueprints." To communicate clearly in writing, you must choose and spell your words correctly. Sentences must have a subject, a verb, and a complete thought. Paragraphs must be indented and should contain a main idea supported with sufficient detail. Each of your essays should explore a valuable topic in several coherent paragraphs, usually including an introduction, a body, and a conclusion.

Not everyone approaches writing as structure, however. You can write better without thinking about structure at all. A good place to start might be to write what you care about and care about what you write. You can make an amazing amount of progress by simply being *genuine*, being who you are naturally. No one has to tell you to be yourself when you speak, but you might need encouragement to be yourself in your writing.

Writing is almost never done without a reason. The reason may come from an experience, such as receiving an unfair parking ticket, or from a requirement in a class. And when you are asked to write, you often receive guidance in the form of an assignment: tell a story to prove a point, paint a picture with your words, summarize an article, compare two subjects, share what you know about something, explain why you agree with or disagree with an idea.

Learning to write well is important, one of the most important things you will do in your education. Confidence is the key. The Writing sections will help you build confidence, whether you are expressing your own ideas or summarizing and responding to the ideas of others. Like the Sentence Structure sections, the Writing sections are best taken in order. However, each one discusses an aspect of writing that you can review on its own at any time.

What Is the Least You Should Know about Writing?

"Unlike medicine or the other sciences," William Zinsser points out, "writing has no new discoveries to spring on us. We're in no danger of reading in our morning newspaper that a breakthrough has been made in how to write [clearly]. . . . We may be given new technologies like the word processor to ease the burdens of composition, but on the whole we know what we need to know."

One thing we know is that we learn to write by *writing*—not by reading long discussions about writing. Therefore the explanations and instructions in this section are as brief as they can be, followed by samples from student and professional writers.

Understanding the basic structures and learning the essential skills covered in this section will help you become a better writer.

Basic Structures	Writing Skills
I. The Paragraph	**III.** Writing in Your Own Voice
II. The Essay	**IV.** Finding a Topic
	V. Organizing Ideas
	VI. Supporting with Details
	VII. Revising Your Papers
	VIII. Presenting Your Work
	IX. Writing about What You Read

Basic Structures

I. The Paragraph

A paragraph is unlike any other structure in English. Visually, it has its own profile: the first line is indented about five spaces, and sentences continue to fill the space between both margins until the paragraph ends (which may be in the middle of the line):

_____
_____ . _
_____
_____
_____
_____ .

As a beginning writer, you might forget to indent your paragraphs, or you may break off in the middle of a line within a paragraph, especially when writing in class. You must remember to indent whenever you begin a new paragraph and fill the space between the margins until it ends. (*Note:* In business writing, paragraphs are not indented but double-spaced in between.)

Defining a Paragraph

A typical paragraph centers on one idea, usually phrased in a topic sentence from which all the other sentences in the paragraph radiate. The topic sentence does not need to begin the paragraph, but it most often does, and the other sentences support it with specific details. (For more on topic sentences and organizing paragraphs, see p. 230.) Paragraphs usually contain several sentences, though no set number is required. A paragraph can stand alone, but more commonly paragraphs are part of a larger composition, an essay. There are different kinds of paragraphs, based on the jobs they are supposed to do.

Types of Paragraphs

Sample Paragraphs in an Essay

Introductory paragraphs begin essays. They provide background information about the essay's topic and usually include the thesis statement or main idea of the essay. (See p. 228 for information on how to write a thesis statement.) Here is the introductory paragraph of a student essay entitled "A Bit of Bad Luck":

> It's 9:45, and I'm panicking. As a student, I live a life that is almost free of misfortunes. I don't even think about bad luck. Just last week I won forty dollars in the lottery and two tickets to a concert from a radio station. So this in-class writing assignment to tell about an experience I've had with bad luck has caught me completely off guard. I don't know what to write!

In this opening paragraph, the student introduces the main idea—"I don't even think about bad luck"—and gives background information about the in-class writing assignment that has forced her to think about it.

Body paragraphs are those in the middle of essays. Each body paragraph contains a topic sentence and presents detailed information about one subtopic, stage, or idea that relates directly to the essay's thesis. (See p. 231 for more information on organizing body paragraphs.) Here are the body paragraphs of the same essay:

> I try to think of what I would call an unlucky moment. At about 9:08, we finish discussing the prompt for the assignment. "Okay," I say to myself, "this shouldn't be a problem. All I have to do is come up with a topic . . . a topic." I can feel the class ease into deep thought as I sit and

scratch my head for inspiration. By 9:15, pens are flaring all over the room. The grey shirt in front of me shifts in his chair. The guy to my left has at least a paragraph already in front of him. And the girls in front of him scribble away as if they were born to write.

At 9:37, I realize that I will soon run out of time. The minutes pass like seconds, and I find myself watching the class and wondering, "What's wrong with me?" while everyone else is making it look so easy. I'm thinking of high school, boyfriends, this morning's breakfast, and then I realize what is getting me all worked up—not knowing what to write. This has never happened to me before.

Now I glance at my teacher, and even she's writing. How hard could it be to glide ink across a white open field? Then she gets up and tells us she'll be right back. Jennifer, to my right in blue stripes, looks at me and mouths, "Are you stuck?" I nod and add, "This has never happened to me before," cursing my bad luck. Finally, I decide to write the story of the last forty-five minutes, and it rushes easily from pen to paper.

Notice that each of the three body paragraphs discusses a single stage of her experience with bad luck in the form of writer's block.

Concluding paragraphs are the final paragraphs in essays. They bring the discussion to a close and share the writer's final thoughts on the subject. (See p. 230 for more about concluding paragraphs.) Here is the conclusion of the sample essay:

It's about 10:05. Class is over; the teacher is waiting, and I'm still writing. Jennifer has gone, and the white shirt to my left is on his way out. Someone is rustling papers not caring who's around him. As I turn in my essay, I am disappointed in myself, knowing I could have done more. I will keep thinking about it when I get home. But in this misfortune, I still feel quite lucky knowing that I discovered my bit of bad luck, and the results could have been much, much worse.

In this concluding paragraph, the student finishes her story and shares her unwavering optimism even after her "bit of bad luck."

Sample of a Paragraph Alone

Single-paragraph writing assignments may be given in class or as homework. They test the beginning writer's understanding of the unique structure of a paragraph. They may ask the writer to answer a single question, perhaps following a reading, or to provide details about a limited topic. Look at this student paragraph, the result of a homework assignment asking students to report on a technological development in the news:

I just read that doctors have developed a new way to cure people with certain kinds of cancer. Instead of subjecting the entire weakened patient to powerful chemicals and radiation, doctors remove the organ that contains the cancer, bombard the organ itself with customized treatments, then return the organ to the patient's body. A man in Italy was the first to undergo such a procedure to cure multiple malignant tumors in his liver. Doctors treated the man's liver outside of his body for a quarter of an hour during an operation that took nearly a day to complete. That patient, who had been given only months to live before the operation in 2001, is still free from cancer two years later. This new way to cure some types of cancer seems to make such sense. I'm glad to know that doctors are still making progress in cancer treatments.

Source: Current Science, February 28, 2003

These shorter writing assignments help students practice presenting information within the limited structure of a paragraph.

The assignments in the upcoming Writing Skills section will sometimes ask you to write paragraphs. Remember that you may review the previous pages as often as you wish until you understand the unique structure of the paragraph.

II. The Essay

Like the paragraph, an essay has its own profile, usually including a title and several paragraphs.

Title

While the paragraph is the single building block of text used in almost all forms of writing (in essays, magazine articles, letters, novels, newspaper stories, and so on), an essay is a larger, more complex structure.

The Five-Paragraph Essay and Beyond

The student essay analyzed on pages 215–216 illustrates the different kinds of paragraphs within essays. Many people like to include five paragraphs in an essay: an introductory paragraph, three body paragraphs, and a concluding paragraph. Three is a comfortable number of body paragraphs—it is not two, which makes an essay seem like a comparison even when it isn't; and it is not four, which may be too many subtopics for the beginning writer to organize clearly.

However, an essay can contain any number of paragraphs. As you become more comfortable with the flow of your ideas and gain confidence in your ability to express yourself, you are free to create essays of many different shapes and sizes. As in all things, learning about writing begins with structure and then expands to include all possibilities.

Defining an Essay

There is no such thing as a typical essay. Essays may be serious or humorous, but the best of them are thought-provoking and—of course—informative. Try looking up the word *essay* in a dictionary right now. Some words that are used to define what an essay is might need to be explained themselves:

An essay is *prose* (meaning it is written in the ordinary language of sentences and paragraphs).

An essay is *nonfiction* (meaning it deals with real people, factual information, actual opinions and events).

An essay is a *composition* (meaning it is created in parts that make up the whole, several paragraphs that explore a single topic).

An essay is *personal* (meaning it shares the writer's unique perspective, even if only in the choice of topic, method of analysis, and details).

An essay is *analytical* and *instructive* (meaning it examines the workings of a subject and shares the results with the reader).

A Sample Essay

For an example of a piece of writing that fits the previous definition, read the following excerpt from the book *Kid Stuff: Great Toys from Our Childhood* by David Hoffman, in which he traces the creation of one of the most recognizable toys of the past—Raggedy Ann.

Raggedy Ann

The story has all the makings of a three-hankie movie—a dying child, a doting father, and the simple plaything that bonded them together. While there's a good deal of truth in the retelling, no doubt the dramatic details have been embellished over time. But chances are it happened like this.

In 1906, Johnny Gruelle's daughter Marcella found a worn rag doll in the attic of her grandmother's home. With her parents' help, she patched and restuffed it; then Gruelle—a newspaper cartoonist and illustrator—painted on a new face, distinguishing it with a unique triangular nose. Together, they named their creation Raggedy Ann. . . .

In making up Raggedy Ann stories to entertain Marcella, Gruelle quickly realized the character's potential. . . . He secured a patent and a trademark for his design in 1915, and even began handcrafting a small quantity of dolls . . . to sell. During all this, Marcella became terminally ill, the result of a contaminated smallpox vaccination. It was to cope with her death—and to assure that in some way his daughter lived on—that Gruelle wrote and illustrated the *Raggedy Ann Stories*, a compilation of all the tales he had told to her over the years. . . .

She's been called a doll with a heart, and for good reason: every Raggedy Ann actually has one. Most of these hearts have been silk-screened on, but the Gruelles' homemade Anns supposedly had a heart-shaped candy (imprinted with "I Love You") sewn inside, while the first mass-produced . . . version contained a die-cut cardboard heart. It couldn't be seen, but it could be felt, if you ran your fingers across the chest.

The dolls have had an interesting manufacturing history with no less than a half dozen different companies responsible for their production at various times. . . .

Now that you have learned more about the basic structures of the paragraph and the essay, you are ready to practice the skills necessary to write them.

Writing Skills

III. Writing in Your Own Voice

All writing "speaks" on paper, and the person "listening" is the reader. Some beginning writers forget that writing and reading are two-way methods of communication, just like spoken conversations between two people. When you write, your reader listens; when you read, you also listen.

When speaking, you express a personality in your choice of phrases, your movements, your tone of voice. Family and friends probably recognize your voice messages on their answering machines without your having to identify yourself. Would they also be able to recognize your writing? They would if you extended your "voice" into your writing.

Writing should not sound like talking, necessarily, but it should have a "personality" that comes from the way you decide to approach a topic, to develop it with details, to say it your way.

The beginning of this book discusses the difference between spoken English (following looser patterns of speaking) and Standard Written English (following accepted patterns of writing). Don't think that the only way to add "voice" to your writing is to use the patterns of spoken English. Remember that Standard Written English does not have to be dull or sound "academic." Look at this example of Standard Written English that has a distinct voice, part of the book *How Babies Talk*, by Dr. Roberta Michnick Golinkoff and Dr. Kathy Hirsh-Pasek.

Finding a word in the language stream is much harder than you would think. Imagine yourself in a foreign country with people speaking all around you. The analogy between a language and a fast-moving body of water is quite apt. You are awash in this new language, unable to make heads or tails of it, feeling as though the new language is flooding over you and offering you no anchor point. So it is with babies. Speech is not punctuated with commas, periods, and question marks. Instead, like a continuous flow of stream water, language seems to move along quickly with no breaks in the flow.

Six-month-old Sylvia is lying in her crib, having just awakened from a nap. Delighted to see Sylvia awake, Mom notices her looking intently at the stuffed animals. She says, "HelloSylvie!DidSylviehaveanicenap?"

There are no spaces between the words when they are spoken. Someone invented the convention of spaces between words for written material. When we talk, however, words run into each other, and even the familiar words can sound somewhat different depending on how they are said. How does a baby find words in the quick-flowing stream that is speech? Perhaps he doesn't start out looking for words at all.

This excerpt illustrates Standard Written English at its best—from its solid sentence structures to its precise use of words. But more important, the writers' clear voice speaks to us and involves us in their world, in their amazement at the magic of language. Students can involve us in their writing too, when they let their own voices through. Writing does not need to be about something personal to have a voice. Here is an example of a student writing about computer hackers:

Some mischievous hackers are only out to play a joke. One of the first examples was a group who created the famous "Cookie Monster" program at Massachusetts Institute of Technology. Several hackers programmed MIT's computer to display the word "cookie" all over the screens of its users. In order for users to clear this problem, they had to "feed" the Cookie Monster by entering the word "cookie" or lose all the data on their screens.

Notice that both the professional and the student writer tell stories (narration) and paint pictures (description) in their writing. Narration and description require practice, but once you master them, you will gain a stronger voice and will be able to add interest and clarity to even the most challenging academic writing assignments.

Narration

Narrative writing tells the reader a story, and since most of us like to tell stories, it is a good place to begin writing in your own voice. An effective narration allows readers to experience an event with the writer. Since we all see the world differently and feel unique emotions, the purpose of narration is to take readers with us through our experiences. As a result, the writer gains a better understanding of what happened, and readers get to live other lives momentarily. Listen to the "voice" of this student writer telling the story of an important moment in his life:

Learning How to Drive

Learning how to drive has been one of the best experiences of my life so far. I suddenly had all the freedom in the world. I didn't have to beg my mom or dad to take me somewhere or ask one of my friends to pick me up. I was out on my own, and I felt a lot older. I think that it was better that I learned how to drive from my dad before an instructor because Dad took the time to teach me right.

When I was just fourteen, my dad used to say to me on the weekends, "If you wash the car, I'll let you go driving." He only had to say it once, and I was out there scrubbing those bumpers. Then we would drive down to the same long open street, and I would take over. During those lessons, my dad taught me the little things, like how to look at the tires of parked cars to watch for children running out and how to look ahead on the freeway to allow time for the unexpected to happen. Most importantly, he taught me how to drive defensively and how to be aware of my surroundings. As a passenger, Dad was never on edge. If I braked too suddenly or pushed the throttle too hard, he would calmly tell me what I did wrong so that I could do it right the next time.

When it was time for formal lessons, my driving instructor was impressed with what I had already learned. As soon as I sat down in the car and pulled away from the curb, I could tell that he had confidence in my driving ability. I think that, knowing I had prior experience, he eased off a bit and just let me drive. I remember when we first went out, he asked me to pull into a gas station and park the car. I was trying to think of what I had done wrong when he asked, "Do you want anything to drink? I'm thirsty." From then on, it was like a walk in the park.

> Learning how to drive from my dad has played a big
> role in my life. His methods and calm encouragement
> helped me to become the safe and observant driver that
> I am now.

Description

Descriptive writing paints word pictures with details that appeal to the reader's five senses—sight, sound, touch, taste, and smell. The writer of description often uses comparisons to help readers picture one thing by imagining something else, just as the writer of "Learning How to Drive" compares taking driving lessons to "a walk in the park." In the following paragraph, a student uses vivid details to bring the place she loves best to life:

> Fort Baker is located across the bay from San Francisco, almost under the Golden Gate Bridge. When I lived there as a child, nature was all I saw. Deer came onto our porch and nibbled the plants; raccoons dumped the trash cans over; skunks sprayed my brother because he poked them with a stick, and little field mice jumped out of the bread drawer at my sister when she opened it. Behind the house was a small forest of strong green trees; the dirt actually felt soft, and tall grassy plants with bright yellow flowers grew all around. I don't know the plants' real name, but my friend and I called it "sour grass." When we chewed the stems, we got a mouth full of sour juice that made our faces crinkle and our eyes water.

Here is another example, the description of the first meeting of Coretta Scott and her future husband Martin Luther King, Jr. The following is an excerpt from the book *Marry Me! Courtship and Proposals of Legendary Couples*, by Wendy Goldberg and Betty Goodwin. It all started on a blind date arranged by mutual friends. As we read Goldberg and Goodwin's description, we can see, hear, and feel along with these two famous people.

> As soon as Martin picked up Coretta for their first date, lunch at Sharaf's Restaurant, he liked what he saw. She was a pretty woman with long hair and bangs. The first thing Coretta noticed about Martin was that he was short and not terribly handsome. However, when he started talking, she began to find him extremely appealing and magnetic. Coretta liked his focus and self-confidence, but nothing could have prepared her for what came next.
> After lunch, Martin drove her back to [the New England Conservatory of Music, where Coretta was a student] and said, "Do you know something?"

"What is that?"

"You have everything I have ever wanted in a wife. There are four things, and you have them all."

"I don't see how you can say that. You don't even know me."

"Yes, I can tell," he said. "The four things that I look for in a wife are character, intelligence, personality and beauty. And you have them all. I want to see you again. When can I?"

"I don't know," said Coretta. "I'll have to check my schedule. You may call me later."

This was all happening much too quickly. Coretta was intent on pursuing her career and wasn't even thinking about getting married now. Besides, as genuine as Martin seemed, his sudden proposal aroused her suspicions. . . .

Soon, Coretta learned that Martin was thoughtful and polite. They continued to see each other that winter, frequently discussing philosophy, religion and the condition of black Americans. . . .

On June 18, 1953, Daddy King [Martin's father] married Martin and Coretta in the garden of her parents' home in Marion. . . . Daddy King agreed to delete the section of the bride's vows about promising to obey.

You may have noticed that all of the examples in this section use both narration and description. In fact, most effective writing—even a good résumé or biology lab report—calls for clear storytelling and the creation of vivid word pictures for the reader.

Writing Assignments

The following two assignments will help you develop your voice as a writer. For now, don't worry about topic sentences or thesis statements or any of the things we'll consider later. Narration and description have their own logical structures. A story has a beginning, a middle, and an end. And we describe things from top to bottom, side to side, and so on.

Assignment 1

NARRATION: FAMOUS SAYINGS

The following is a list of well-known expressions. No doubt you have had an experience that proves at least one of these to be true. Write a short essay that tells a story from your own life that relates to one of these sayings. You might want to identify the expression you have chosen in your introductory paragraph. Then tell the beginning, middle, and end of the story. Be sure to use vivid details to bring the story to life. Finish with a brief concluding paragraph in which you share your final thoughts on the experience.

When in Rome, do as the Romans do.

Good things come to those who wait.

While the cat's away, the mice will play.

Actions speak louder than words.

Enough is as good as a feast.

Assignment 2

DESCRIPTION: TOY CHOICES

On pages 219–220, you read about the creation of the character doll Raggedy Ann. Children, of course, have varied taste in toys. Some play with character dolls, action figures, and electronic games, while others go for the more generic building blocks and craft supplies. Think back to your childhood and write a description of a few of your favorite toys. Did your choice of toys have any impact on your goals as an adult? Try to use details and comparisons that appeal to the reader's senses in some way. Your goal is to make the reader visualize your toys of choice and understand their effect on you.

IV. Finding a Topic

You will most often be given a topic to write about, perhaps based on a reading assignment. However, when the assignment of a paper calls for you to choose your own topic without any further assistance, try to go immediately to your interests.

Look to Your Interests

If the topic of your paper is something you know about and—more important—something you *care* about, then the whole process of writing will be smoother and more enjoyable for you. If you ski, if you are a musician, or even if you just enjoy watching a lot of television, bring that knowledge and enthusiasm into your papers.

Take a moment to think about and jot down a few of your interests now (no matter how unrelated to school they may seem), and then save the list for use later when deciding what to write about. One student's list of interests might look like this:

buying and selling on eBay
playing video games with friends
boogie boarding in summer
collecting baseball cards

Another student's list might be very different:

playing the violin

going to concerts
watching old musicals on video
drawing pictures of my friends

While still another student might list the following interests:

going to the horse races
reading for my book club
traveling in the summer
buying lottery tickets

These students have listed several worthy topics for papers. And because they are personal interests, the students have the details needed to support them. With a general topic to start with, you can use several ways to gather the details you will need to support it in a paragraph or an essay.

Focused Free Writing (or Brainstorming)

Free writing is a good way to begin. When you are assigned a paper, try writing for ten minutes putting down all your thoughts on one subject—drawing pictures of my friends, for example. Don't stop to think about organization, sentence structures, capitalization, or spelling—just let details flow onto the page. Free writing will help you see what material you have and will help you figure out what aspects of the subject to write about.

Here is an example:

I like to draw pictures of my friends but sometimes they don't like it when I draw them. The nose is to big they think or the hair isn't just right. Once in awhile I get it perfect, but not that often. I like to style my drawings like cartoons kind of. Its almost like you'll see little baloons like in a cartoon strip with little sayings in them. I'm not a big talker myself, so I can express myself with my friends thru my drawings of them. Again, some of them like it and some of them don't.

Now the result of this free writing session is certainly not ready to be typed and turned in as a paragraph. But what did become clear in it was that the student could probably compare the two types of friends—those who like to be drawn and those who don't.

Clustering

Clustering is another way of thinking a topic through on paper before you begin to write. A cluster is more visual than free writing. You could cluster the topic of "book clubs," for instance, by putting it in a circle in the center of a piece of paper and then drawing lines to new circles as ideas or details occur to you. The idea is to free your mind from the limits of sentences and paragraphs to generate pure details and ideas. When you are finished clustering, you can see where you want to go with a topic.

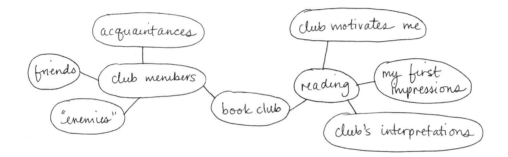

This cluster shows that the student has found two main categories of merchandise at flea markets. This cluster might lead to another where the student chooses one subcategory—early collectibles, for instance—and thinks of more details about them.

Talking with Other Students

It may help to talk to others when deciding on a topic. Many teachers break their classes up into groups at the beginning of an assignment. Talking with other students helps you realize that you see things just a little differently. Value the difference—it will help your written voice that we discussed earlier emerge.

Assignment 3

LIST YOUR INTERESTS

Make a list of four or five of your own interests. Be sure that they are as specific as the examples listed on pp. 225–226. Keep the list for later assignments.

Assignment 4

DO SOME FREE WRITING

Choose one of your interests, and do some focused free writing about it. Write for ten minutes with that topic in mind but without stopping. Don't worry about anything such as spelling or sentence structures while you are free writing. The results are meant to help you find out what you have to say about the topic *before* you start to write a paper about it. Save the results for a later assignment.

Assignment 5

TRY CLUSTERING IDEAS

Choose another of your interests. Put it in the center of a piece of paper, and draw a cluster of details and ideas relating to it following the sample shown earlier. Take the cluster as far as it will go. Then choose one aspect to cluster again on its own. This way you will arrive at specific, interesting details and ideas—not just the first ones that come to mind. Save the results of all your efforts.

V. Organizing Ideas

The most important thing to keep in mind, no matter what you are writing, is the idea you want to get across to your reader. Whether you are writing a paragraph or an essay, you must have in mind a single idea that you want to express. In a paragraph, such an idea is called a topic sentence; in an essay it's called a thesis statement, but they mean the same thing—an idea you want to get across. We will begin with a discussion of thesis statements.

Thesis Statements

Let's choose one of the students' interests listed on pp. 225–226 as a general topic. "Buying and selling on eBay" by itself doesn't make any point. What about it? What does it do for you? What point about buying and selling on eBay would you like to present to your reader? You might write

Buying and selling on eBay is fun and educational.

But this is a vague statement, not worth developing. You might move into more specific territory and write

I have learned about business and geography by buying and selling items on eBay.

Now you have said something specific. *When you write in one sentence the point you want to present to your reader, you have written a thesis statement.*

All good writers have a thesis in mind when they begin to write, or the thesis may well evolve as they write. Whether they are writing essays, novels, poems, or plays, they eventually have in mind an idea they want to present to the reader. They may develop it in various ways, but behind whatever they write is their ruling thought, their reason for writing, their thesis.

For any writing assignment, after you have done some free writing or clustering to explore your topic, the next step is to write a thesis statement. As you write your thesis statement, keep two things in mind:

1. A thesis statement must be a sentence *with a subject and a verb* (not merely a topic).

2. A thesis statement must be *an idea that you can explain or defend* (not simply a statement of fact).

Exercise 1

THESIS OR FACT?

Which of the following are merely topics or facts, and which are thesis statements that you could explain or defend? In front of each one that could be a thesis statement, write THESIS. In front of each one that is just a fact, write FACT. Check your answers with those at the back of the book.

1. _____ Gasoline prices are rising again.

2. _____ Some animals seem to be able to predict earthquakes.

3. _____ On July 20, 1969, Neil Armstrong planted an American flag on the moon.

4. _____ After I became a music major, many job opportunities opened up for me.

5. _____ Computer-generated movie characters can affect us in the same ways as "real-life" characters.

6. _____ Voice-recognition software is improving all the time.

7. _____ Home schooling has both advantages and disadvantages.

8. _____ Tiger Woods is an amazing golfer.

9. _____ Traveling to different countries makes people more open-minded.

10. _____ Vegetarians can suffer from health problems related to their diets.

Assignment 6

WRITE A THESIS STATEMENT

Use your free-writing or clustering results from Assignments 4 and 5 (p. 228) and write at least one thesis statement based on one of your interests. Be sure that the thesis you write is phrased as a complete thought that can be defended or explained in an essay.

Organizing an Essay

Once you have written a good thesis and explored your topic through discussion with others or by free writing and clustering, you are ready to organize your essay.

First you need an introductory paragraph. It should catch your reader's interest, provide necessary background information, and either include or suggest your thesis statement. (See p. 215 and p. 222 for two examples of student writers' introductory paragraphs.) In your introductory paragraph, you may also list supporting points, but a more effective way is to let them unfold paragraph by paragraph rather than to give them all away in the beginning of the essay. Even if your supporting points don't appear in your introduction, your reader will easily spot them later if your paper is clearly organized.

Your second paragraph will present your first supporting point—everything about it and nothing more.

Your next paragraph will be about your second supporting point—all about it and nothing more.

Each additional paragraph will develop another supporting point.

Finally, you'll need a concluding paragraph. In a short paper, it isn't necessary to restate all your points. Your conclusion may be brief; even a single sentence to round out the paper may do the job. Remember that the main purpose of a concluding paragraph is to bring the paper to a close by sharing your final thoughts on the subject. (See p. 216 and p. 223 for two examples of concluding paragraphs.)

Learning to write a brief organized essay of this kind will help you to distinguish between the parts of an essay. Then when you're ready to write a longer paper, you'll be able to organize it clearly and elaborate on its design and content.

Topic Sentences

A topic sentence does for a paragraph what a thesis statement does for an essay—it states the main idea. Like thesis statements, topic sentences must be phrased as complete thoughts to be proven or developed through the presentation of details. But the topic sentence introduces an idea or subtopic that is the right size to cover in a paragraph. The topic sentence doesn't have to be the first sentence in a paragraph. It may come at the end or even in the middle, but putting it first is most common.

Each body paragraph should contain only one main idea, and no detail or example should be in a paragraph if it doesn't support the topic sentence or help to transition from one paragraph to another. (See pp. 215–216, p. 221, and p. 222 for more examples of effective body paragraphs within essays and of paragraphs alone.)

Organizing Body Paragraphs (or Single Paragraphs)

A single paragraph or a body paragraph within an essay is organized in the same way as an entire essay only on a smaller scale. Here's the way you learned to organize an essay:

> Thesis: stated or suggested in introductory paragraph
> First supporting paragraph
> Second supporting paragraph
> Additional supporting paragraphs
> Concluding paragraph

And here's the way to organize a paragraph:

> Topic sentence
> First supporting detail or example
> Second supporting detail or example
> Additional supporting details or examples
> Concluding or transitional sentence

You should have several details to support each topic sentence. If you find that you have little to say after writing the topic sentence, ask yourself what details or examples will make your reader believe that the topic sentence is true for you.

Transitional Expressions

Transitional expressions within a paragraph and between paragraphs in an essay help the reader move from one detail or example to the next and from one supporting point to the next. When first learning to organize an essay, you might start each supporting paragraph in a paper with a transitional expression. Later, if they sound too repetitious, take these individual words out and replace them with more detailed prepositional phrases or dependent clauses, thereby improving your sentence variety.

There are transitions to show addition:

> Also
> Furthermore
> Another (example, point, step, etc. . . .)
> In addition

There are transitions to show sequence:

First	One reason	One example
Second	Another reason	Another example
Finally	Most important	In conclusion

There are transitions to show comparison or contrast:

Similarly	In the same way	In comparison
However	On the other hand	In contrast

Exercise 2

ADDING TRANSITIONAL EXPRESSIONS

Place the appropriate transitional expressions into the blanks in the following paragraph to make it read smoothly. Check your answers with those in the back of the book.

    however   first   then   finally   previously   in addition

This year, my family and I decided to celebrate the Fourth of July in a whole new way. _____, we always attended a fireworks show at the sports stadium near our house. The firework shows got better every year; _____, we were getting tired of the crowds and the noise. _____, we were starting to feel bad about our own lack of creativity. The goal this time was to have each family member think of a craft project, recipe, or game related to the Fourth. The result was a day full of fun activities and good things to eat—all created by us! _____, my sister Helen taught us to make seltzer rockets from an idea she found on the Internet. We used the fireless "firecrackers" as table decorations until late afternoon when we set them off. _____, we ate dinner. Mom and Dad's contribution was "Fourth of July Franks," which were hot dogs topped with ketchup, onions, and a sprinkling of blue-corn chips. For dessert, my brother Leon assembled tall parfaits made with layers of red and blue Jell-O cubes divided by ridges of whipped cream. _____, we played a game of charades in which all of the answers had something to do with the American flag, the Declaration of Independence, Paul Revere's ride, and other such topics. We all enjoyed the Fourth so much that the events will probably become our new tradition.

Assignment 7

A CHIP ON THE OLD BLOCK?

Animal-care professionals are using a computer chip to keep track of dogs, cats, and other animals. The chip is surgically placed under the skin and can hold all sorts of information about the animal, as well as help authorities find the pet in case it gets lost. What do you think about this new way of identifying and tracking animals? Write a long paragraph or a short essay in which you answer this question. Your answer will be your main idea, and the reasons and details that support it should be your own opinions. Be sure to say whether any of your own animals have the chip or not. Try free writing, clustering, or discussing the subject with others to find out how you feel about the topic before you begin to write.

VI. Supporting with Details

Now you're ready to support your main ideas with subtopics and specific details. That is, you'll think of ways to convince your reader that what you say in your thesis is true. How could you convince your reader that buying and selling on eBay has taught you about business and geography? You might write

> I have learned a great deal about business and geography by buying and selling items on eBay. (because)

1. I must be honest in my dealings with other buyers and sellers.
2. I have to keep good records and be very organized.
3. I learn about places I have never heard of before by shipping packages all over the world.

> **Note** - Sometimes if you imagine a *because* at the end of your thesis statement, it will help you write your reasons or subtopics clearly and in parallel form.

Types of Support

The subtopics developing a thesis and the details presented in a paragraph are not always *reasons.* Supporting points may take many forms based on the purpose of the essay or paragraph. They may be

> *examples* (in an illustration)
>
> *steps* (in a how-to or process paper)
>
> *types or kinds* (in a classification)

meanings (in a definition)

similarities and/or differences (in a comparison/contrast)

causes or effects (in a cause-and-effect analysis).

Whatever they are, supporting points should develop the main idea expressed in the thesis or topic sentence and prove it to be true.

Here is the final draft of a student essay about an embarrassing experience. Notice how the body paragraphs follow the stages of the experience. And all of the details within the body paragraphs bring the experience to life.

Super Salad?

About a year ago, I had a really embarrassing experience. It happened at a restaurant in Arcadia. I had moved to California three days before, so everything was new to me. Since I didn't have any relatives or friends in California, I had to move, unpack, and explore the neighborhood on my own. That day, I decided to treat myself to dinner as a reward, but I needed some courage because I had never dined out alone before.

As I opened the door of the restaurant, everybody looked at me, and the attention made me nervous. The manager greeted me with several menus in his hands and asked how many people were in my party. I said, "Just me." He led me over to a square table right in the middle of the restaurant. It had four chairs around it and was set with four sets of napkins and silverware. The manager pulled out one of the chairs for me, and a busboy cleared away the three extra place settings.

A waitress arrived to take my order, and I tried to keep it simple. I asked for steak and a baked potato. Truthfully speaking, before I went to the restaurant, I had practiced ordering, but as she was speaking to me, I got flustered. She said, "Super salad?" as if it were a specialty of the house, so I said, "Okay, that sounds good." Suddenly, her eyebrows went up, and she asked again, "Super salad?" And again I answered, "Yes." Her face turned the color of a red leaf in fall. "You wanna a super salad?" she asked in a louder voice this time, and I answered with certainty, "Yes, that will be fine." From her reaction, I knew that something was wrong.

When the waitress returned, she had the manager with her. He asked, "Do you want soup or a salad? You can't have both." I finally realized the stupid mistake I had been making. But the way the waitress had said "Soup or salad?" sounded just like "Super salad?" to my flustered ears. I clarified that I wanted a salad and eventually finished my meal without incident. I don't remember how the steak tasted or whether I had sour cream on my potato. I just kept going over my moment of confusion in my head while trying to look like a normal person eating dinner.

At the time, I felt embarrassed and ashamed. Going out for a meal isn't usually such a traumatic experience. Of course, whenever I tell the story, instead of sympathy, I get uncontrollable laughter as a response. I guess it is pretty funny. Now whenever I order a meal alone, I use a drive-thru. That way I can blame any misunderstandings on the microphones in the drive-thru lane.

(*Note:* See pp. 236–238 for a rough draft of the preceding essay, before its final revisions.)

Learning to support your main ideas with vivid details is perhaps the most important thing you can accomplish in this course. Many writing problems are not really *writing* problems but *thinking* problems. Whether you're writing a term paper or merely an answer to a test question, if you take enough time to think, you'll be able to write a clear thesis statement and support it with paragraphs loaded with meaningful details.

Assignment 8

WRITE AN ESSAY ON ONE OF YOUR INTERESTS

Return to the thesis statement you wrote about one of your interests for Assignment 6 on p. 230. Now write a short essay to support it. You can explain the allure of your interest, its drawbacks, or its benefits (such as the one about the

Internet improving the student's reading and writing skills). Don't forget to use any free writing or clustering you may have done on the topic beforehand.

Assignment 9

AN EMBARRASSING EXPERIENCE

Like the student writer of "Super Salad?" (pp. 234–235), we have all had embarrassing moments in our lives. Write an essay about a mildly embarrassing experience that you have had or one that you witnessed someone else have. Be sure to include the details that contributed to the embarrassment. For instance, the student writer showed how being in the restaurant alone made it worse. Had he been there with friends or family members, misunderstanding the waitress might have just been humorous, not embarrassing.

VII. Revising Your Papers

Great writers don't just sit down and write a final draft. They write and revise. You may have heard the expression, "Easy writing makes hard reading." True, it is *easier* to turn in a piece of writing the first time it lands on paper. But you and your reader will be disappointed by the results. Try to think of revision as an opportunity instead of a chore, as a necessity instead of a choice.

Whenever possible, write the paper several days before the first draft is due. Let it sit for a while. When you reread it, you'll see ways to improve the organization or to add more details to a weak paragraph. After revising the paper, put it away for another day and try again to improve it. Save all of your drafts along the way to see the progress that you've made or possibly to return to an area left out in later drafts but that fits in again after revision.

Don't call any paper finished until you have worked it through several times. Revising is one of the best ways to improve your writing.

Take a look at an early draft of the student essay you read on pages 234–235. Notice that the student has revised his rough draft by crossing out some parts, correcting word forms, and adding new phrasing or reminders for later improvement.

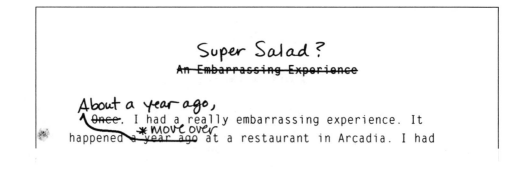

Super Salad?

~~An Embarrassing Experience~~

About a year ago,

~~Once~~. I had a really embarrassing experience. It

＊move over

happened ~~a year ago~~ at a restaurant in Arcadia. I had

moved to California three days before ~~that day~~. so [Since]
everything was new to me. ~~As~~ I didn't have any ~~relations~~ [relatives]
or friends in California. I had to (take care of *add details
everything by myself.) That day, I decided to ~~go out to~~ [treat myself]
dinner ~~by myself~~ as a ~~treat~~. [reward] but I needed some courage
because I had never ~~been in a restaurant all~~ [dined out] alone
before.

[As] ~~When~~ I opened the door of the restaurant, I (gathered
everybody's attention, and it made me a little nervous.) * clarify and correct
~~Eating in a restaurant alone was very new to me~~. The * add details
manager asked me how many people were in my party, ~~and I~~
said, "Just me." He ~~walked~~ [led] me over to a square table in [right]
the middle ~~part~~ of the restaurant. (It had four chairs
pulled up to it, and he pulled out one for me to sit
down.) * add details

A ~~The~~ waitress ~~came~~ [arrived] to take my order, and I tried to
keep it simple. I asked for steak and a baked potato.
~~Frankly~~ [Truthfully] speaking, before I went to the restaurant, I had
practiced ordering, but ~~by the time~~ [as] she was speaking to
me, I got ~~all~~ flustered ~~and embarrassed. I thought~~ She
[as if that were a specialty of the restaurant,]
said, "Super salad?" so I said, "Okay, that sounds good."
Suddenly, her eyebrows went up, and she asked again,
"Super salad?" and again I answered, "Yes." Her face
turned the color of a red leaf in fall. "You wanna a
super salad?" she asked in a louder voice this time, and
[with certainty,] I answered, "Yes, that will be fine." From her reaction,
I ~~thought~~ [knew that] something was wrong.
~~The next time~~ [when] the waitress returned, she had the
manager ~~of the restaurant~~ with her. He asked, "Do you want
soup or a salad? You can't have both." I finally realized
[the] ~~what~~ a stupid mistake I had been making. But I swear the
way the waitress had said "Soup or salad?" sounded just
like "Super salad?" [to my flustered ears] ~~as if that were a specialty of the~~
~~restaurant.~~ * add end of meal details * move up

At the time, I was ~~really~~ embarrassed and ashamed ~~of~~
~~myself~~. * add more But whenever I tell ~~anybody~~ the story, (they laugh
* clarify and correct
so hard that I can't get anyone to feel sorry for me.) I [Now]

> hardly ever eat alone at restaurants after my first
> disaster. I if do, I make it a drive-thru. That way I can
> always blame a misunderstanding on the microphones in the
> drive-thru lane.
>
> → *combine and clarify*

Can you see why each change was made? Analyzing the reasons for the changes will help you improve your own revision skills.

Assignment 10

FIRST IMPRESSIONS

On pages 223–224, you read about Coretta Scott and Martin Luther King's first date and the different first impressions that they made on each other. Note that these impressions went *far* beyond the way they looked. Write about meeting someone that you know now for the first time. What were your first impressions of that person? Did they turn out to be accurate? Discuss the effect that your first impressions had on the relationship.

Write a rough draft of the paper and then set it aside. When you finish writing, reread your paper to see what improvements you can make to your rough draft. Use the checklist on the next page to help guide you through this or any other revision.

Exchanging Papers

The revision checklist could also be used when you exchange papers with another student in your class. Since you both have written a response to the same assignment, you will understand what the other writer went through and learn from the differences between the two papers.

Proofreading Aloud

Finally, read your finished paper *aloud.* If you read it silently, you will see what you *think* is there, but you are sure to miss some errors. Read your paper aloud slowly, pointing to each word as you read it to catch omissions and errors in spelling and punctuation. Reading a paper to yourself this way may take fifteen minutes to half an hour, but it will be time well spent. There are even word processing programs that will "speak" your text in a computer's voice. Using your computer to read your paper

Revision Checklist

Here's a checklist of revision questions. If the answer to any of these questions is no, revise that part of your paper until you're satisfied that the answer is yes.

1. Does the introductory paragraph introduce the topic clearly and suggest or include a thesis statement that the paper will explain or defend?

2. Does each of the other paragraphs support the thesis statement?

3. Does each body paragraph contain a clear topic sentence and focus on only one supporting point?

4. Do the body paragraphs contain enough details, and are transitional expressions well used?

5. Do the final thoughts expressed in the concluding paragraph bring the paper to a smooth close?

6. Does your (the writer's) voice come through?

7. Do the sentences read smoothly and appear to be correct?

8. Are words well-chosen, and are spelling and punctuation consistent and correct?

to you can be fun as well as helpful. If you don't like the way something sounds, don't be afraid to change it! Make it a rule to read each of your papers *aloud* before handing it in.

Here are four additional writing assignments to help you practice the skills of writing and revising.

Assignment 11

ARE YOU AN OPTIMIST OR A PESSIMIST?

The old test of optimism and pessimism is to look at a glass filled with water to the midpoint. An optimist, or positive thinker, would say it was "half *full*." But a pessimist, or negative thinker, would say it was "half *empty*." Which are you—an optimist or a pessimist? Organize your thoughts into the structure of a brief essay.

Assignment 12

ARE THERE DIFFERENT WAYS TO BE SMART?

No word has just one meaning. Take, for example, the word *smart*. The common definition usually involves retaining a lot of knowledge and taking tests well. If that were the only meaning, then why do we call someone "street smart"? Think about the different ways a person can be "smart," and write a long paragraph or short essay about the ways in which people in general and you in particular are smart. For further prompting before you write, read the sample reaction paragraph on p. 242 about Isaac Asimov's essay "What Is Intelligence?"

Assignment 13

THE BEST (OR WORST) DECISION

What was one of the best (or worst) decisions you ever made? Choose one that you feel comfortable sharing with others. When and why did you make the decision, and what effects has it had on your life? Organize the answers to these questions into the structure of a brief essay.

Assignment 14

I WOULD IF I COULD

If you could travel anywhere right now, where would you go? Write a short essay about a trip that you would take if you suddenly had the time, money, and ability necessary to do it. Be sure to state what your destination would be, and use plenty of details for the reader to understand your reasons and what's involved in getting there.

VIII. Presenting Your Work

Part of the success of a paper could depend on how it looks. The same paper written sloppily or typed neatly might even receive different grades. It is human nature to respond positively when a paper has been presented with care. Here are some general guidelines to follow.

Paper Formats

Your paper should be typed or written on a computer, double-spaced, or copied neatly in ink on 8 1/2-by-11-inch paper on one side only. A one-inch margin should be left around the text on all sides for your instructor's comments. The beginning of each paragraph should be indented five spaces.

Most instructors have a particular format for presenting your name and the course material on your papers. Always follow such instructions carefully.

Titles

Finally, spend some time thinking of a good title. Just as you're more likely to read a magazine article with an interesting title, so your readers will be more eager to read your paper if you give it a good title. Which of these titles from student papers would make you want to read further?

A Sad Experience	Of Mice and Me
Falling into "The Gap"	Buying Clothes Can Be Depressing
Hunting: The Best Sport of All?	Got Elk?

Remember these three rules about titles:

1. Only the first letter of the important words in a title should be capitalized.

   A Night at the Races

2. Don't put quotation marks around your own titles unless they include a quotation or title of an article, short story, or poem within them.

   "To Be or Not to Be" Is Not for Me

3. Don't underline (or *italicize*) your own titles unless they include the title of a book, play, movie, or magazine within them.

   Still Stuck on *Titanic*

A wise person once said, "Haste is the assassin of elegance." Instead of rushing to finish a paper and turn it in, take the time to give your writing the polish it deserves.

IX. Writing about What You Read

Reading and writing are related skills. The more you read, the better you will write. When you are asked to prepare for a writing assignment by reading a newspaper story, a magazine article, a professional essay, or part of a book, there are many ways to respond in writing. Among them, you may be asked to write your reaction to a reading assignment or a summary of a reading assignment.

Writing a Reaction

Reading assignments become writing assignments when your teacher asks you to share your opinion about the subject matter or to relate the topic to your own experiences. In a paragraph, you would have enough space to offer only the most immediate impressions about the topic. However, in an essay you could share your personal reactions, as well as your opinions on the value of the writer's ideas and support. Of course, the first step is always to read the selection carefully, looking up unfamiliar words in a dictionary.

Sample Reaction Paragraph

Here is a sample paragraph-length response following the class's reading of an essay called "What Is Intelligence?" by Isaac Asimov. In the essay, Asimov explains that there are other kinds of intelligence besides just knowledge of theories and facts. This student shares Asimov's ideas about intelligence, and she uses her own experiences to support her statements.

> I totally agree with Isaac Asimov. Intelligence doesn't only belong to Nobel Prize winners. I define "intelligence" as being able to value that special skill that a person has been born with. Not everyone is a math genius or a brain surgeon. For example, ask a brain surgeon to rotate the engine in your car. It isn't going to happen. To be able to take that certain skill that you've inherited and push it to its farthest limits I would call "intelligence." Isaac Asimov's definition is similar to mine. He believes that academic questions are only correctly answered by academicians. He gives the example of a farmer. A farming test would only be correctly answered by a farmer. Not everyone has the same talent; we are all different. When I attend my math classes, I must always pay attention. If I don't, I end up struggling with what I missed. On the other hand, when I'm in my singing class, I really do not have to struggle because the musical notes come to me with ease. This is just one example of how skills and talents differ from each other. I would rather sing a song than do math any day. We are all made differently. Some people are athletic, and some people are brainy. Some people can sing, and some can cook. It really doesn't matter what other people can do. If they have a talent—that's a form of intelligence.

If this had been an essay-length response, the student would have included more details about her own and other people's types of intelligence. And she may have wanted to quote and discuss Asimov's most important points.

Assignment 15

WRITE A REACTION PARAGRAPH

The following is an excerpt from *I'm Afraid, You're Afraid: 448 Things to Fear and Why* by Melinda Muse, in which she discusses the surprising effects our initials might have on our lives. Write a paragraph in which you respond thoughtfully to Muse's information, discuss the details she uses to support it, and perhaps share your thoughts about your own initials.

Bad Initials

BUMs and RATs don't live as long as VIPs and GODs, according to a University of California study that examined twenty-seven years worth of men's death certificates. Dr. Nicholas Christenfeld categorized the names of 5 million dead guys according to their initials. He then assigned the words that the initials spelled with the qualities of "good," "bad," or "neutral." The psychologist determined that people with good monograms like JOY, WOW, and LOV lived more than 4.5 years longer than those in the neutral-monogram (WDW and JAY) category. Gents with bad tags, the DUDs and ASSes, died an average of almost 3 years earlier than the more neutrally initialed. SAD also is that people in the bad group—the APEs and PIGs—were more apt to commit suicide or die in an accident.

Dr. Christenfeld asserts that having "bad initials" is a lifelong negative psychological factor. It's a bummer to be called PIG but an ego boost to be recognized as ACE or WOW. The doctor says if a person holds the notion that "accidents aren't really accidents," then the lack of self-esteem might lead to self-destructive behavior.

He could be DED right.

Before starting your reaction paragraph, *read the selection again carefully.* Be sure to use a dictionary to look up any words you don't know. You can also use the free writing and clustering techniques explained on page 226. Or your instructor may want you to discuss the reading in groups.

Coming to Your Own Conclusions

Often you will be asked to come to your own conclusions based on a reading that simply reports information. In other words, you have to think about and write about what it all means. Read the following article, in which writer Mary Roach asks, "If I can't be on a stamp, can I at least put in my 37 cents' worth?":

Going Postal

Last week I asked my husband to pick up some stamps, and he returned with the Duke Kahanamoku commemorative, because they were out of American Bats. I'd never heard of Duke Kahanamoku, and now I am licking the man's back. Who is this man, and how did he get on my stamps? Can I be on a stamp too?

I called the number for the U.S. Stamp Program and wound up talking to a spokesperson named Cathy Yarosky. Yarosky said that Duke Kahanamoku was a Hawaiian surfer and Olympic swimmer in the early 1900s "known for his humility, grace and good sportsmanship."

"So he invented surfing?" I asked her.

He did not. Surfing was invented sometime in Polynesian prehistory. "He was considered the father of it," said Yarosky. I wasn't buying. Everyone knows you cannot give birth to a sport, particularly one that involves a finned, 12-foot board. Really, how did he get on a stamp? While Yarosky read from a press release about the Postal Service's 12 official criteria for Stamp Subject Selection (for starters, you must be dead for ten years), I got on the Internet and looked up Duke Kahanamoku. I found a resolution adopted by the councilpeople of the city and county of Honolulu, "urging the U.S. Postal Service to issue a Duke Kahanamoku commemorative postage stamp." Resolution 99–163 had been introduced by councilman Duke Bainum. It began to appear that the stamp was the fruit of one man's obsession—a plot to put men with the first name Duke onto U.S. postage stamps. No doubt Bainum was behind the 1990 *Stagecoach* stamp that starred John Wayne. The surfing thing was a red herring. In urgent tones, I told Yarosky my theory.

Yarosky sighed. It was the sigh of someone who has dealt with a lot of, as they say, American Bats. She referred me to the Citizens' Stamp Advisory Committee, the 14 men and women who decide which of the 50,000 different individuals and subjects proposed in writing each year by Americans with way too much time on their hands will end up on a postage stamp. She called the committee by its acronym, CSAC, which she pronounced "Sea Sack," bringing to mind those little waxed bags they hand out on boats in rough weather. No doubt there is a stamp for these too.

I no longer wanted to be on a postage stamp. I wanted to be on CSAC.

I asked Yarosky for the CSAC chairperson's phone number, but she could not give it to me. "You can write to her," she offered. Spoken like a true Postal Service representative. While she was reading out the address, I went on the Internet, found Chairperson Virginia Noelke's e-mail address and sent off a note to her. Yarosky was reciting the four-digit zip code addendum when Noelke's reply, complete with phone number, arrived in my in box.

I thanked Yarosky for her humility, grace and good sportsmanship, and dialed Noelke's number.

Noelke is a lovely woman, and CSAC is to be commended. They have kept Colonel Sanders and the Golden Arches off our mail, and they are not swayed by bribery: the sack of onions shipped to Noelke courtesy of the Colorado Onion Association did *not* result in an Edible Bulbs of America series. Who gets to be on the committee? People with "useful skill sets": historians such as Noelke, graphic designers, philatelic experts. Plus Karl Malden, whose skill set is "being someone in Hollywood." When a member with a particular skill passes away or resigns, the Postmaster General appoints someone to replace him or her. Karl Malden, for instance, replaced the similarly skilled Ernest Borgnine, who served on CSAC from 1975–1984.

Is there a writer on the committee whom I might one day replace? There is. His name is David L. Eynon, and I found his bibliography on the Web. It lists ten works of short fiction, all published between 1951 and 1954, leaving him, one might think, plenty of time for philatelic pursuits. So is there a chance for me, a tiny, postage stamp–size chance? Noelke suggested I get to know the Postmaster General. I have now left Postmaster General John E. Potter three phone messages and an e-mail. Perhaps I'll try writing a letter.

Source: Originally appeared in *Smithsonian,* February 2003. Reprinted by permission of the author.

Assignment 16

WHAT ARE YOUR CONCLUSIONS?

In "Going Postal" (above), Mary Roach lightheartedly questions the U.S. Postal Service's stamp-selecting process. Why do you think Roach chose to present her essay as a narration—a personal story complete with names, dates, quotes, and opinions? In what ways does she use the story-telling format to get her ideas across? What people and things does Roach believe should and should not be on stamps? What person or object would you nominate to be on a postage stamp, and what are your reasons? Consider these questions, and write an essay in which you share your conclusions and support them with references to Roach's article.

Writing 100-Word Summaries

One of the best ways to learn to read carefully and to write concisely is to write 100-word summaries. Writing 100 words sounds easy, but actually it isn't. Writing 200- or 300- or 500-word summaries isn't too difficult, but condensing all the main ideas of an essay or article into 100 words is a time-consuming task—not to be undertaken in the last hour before class.

A summary presents only the main ideas of a reading, *without including any reactions to it.* A summary tests your ability to read, understand, and *rephrase* the ideas contained in an essay, article, or book.

If you work at writing summaries conscientiously, you'll improve both your reading and your writing. You'll improve your reading by learning to spot main ideas and your writing by learning to construct a concise, clear, smooth paragraph. Furthermore, your skills will carry over into your reading and writing for other courses.

Sample 100-Word Summary

First, read the following excerpt from the book *The True History of Chocolate,* by Sophie D. Coe and Michael D. Coe. It is followed by a student's 100-word summary.

Milton Hershey and the "Good Old Hershey Bar"

Milton Snavely Hershey (1857–1945) has been aptly characterized as "the Henry Ford of Chocolate Makers." . . . [B]y the time he was 19, he had established his own candy business, . . . producing mainly caramel confections. . . . But after a trip to the chocolate centers of Europe, he sold the caramel business for one million dollars (a huge sum in those days), bought a farm in Derry Township, Pennsylvania, and built his chocolate factory on it. . . .

"Hershey, The Chocolate Town" . . . was dominated by Milton Hershey's imposing private mansion . . . [from which] the great man would sally forth each day to survey the vast domain he had built: the milk chocolate and cocoa factory, . . . the industrial school for orphan boys, . . . The Hershey Department Store, the Hershey Bank, men's and women's clubs, five churches, the free library, the Volunteer Fire Department, two schools, Hershey Park with its fine gardens, zoo, and rollercoaster, the Hershey Hotel, and a golf course. . . . [Y]et this triumph of paternalistic capitalism was a town in name only: it had no mayor nor any form of elected municipal government—it existed only at the whim of its benevolent dictator, Milton S. Hershey. . . .

There is no doubt that Hershey was a marketing genius. . . . Hershey and his chocolate bars soon commanded the American market. Everything was mechanized, with machines and conveyor belts organized into a true assembly-line operation. Hershey's best-selling bar contained almonds imported from southern Europe. . . . But even more popular than these were "Hershey's Kisses." . . . Small wonder that the streetlights of "The Chocolate Town" are the shape of Kisses.

Milton Hershey died peacefully at the age of 85, in his own hospital. His paternalistic empire lives on. . . . So many tourists flock to the wonders of Hershey, Pennsylvania, that the company no longer offers tours of its chocolate factory.

Here is a student's 100-word summary of the article:

Milton Hershey is a big name in the history of chocolate. He was an early achiever, but he wasn't satisfied with just making money selling caramels. Once he saw the way chocolate was made overseas, he decided to become the best chocolate maker in America. The result of his passion for chocolate was a community that he designed himself and named after himself: Hershey, Pennsylvania. It was a complete community, but it wasn't a democracy. Hershey made all the decisions there. Hershey's chocolate was and still is extremely popular due to Milton Hershey's technological advances and devoted interest in chocolate.

Assignment 17

WRITE A 100-WORD SUMMARY

Your aim in writing your summary should be to give someone who has not read a piece of writing a clear idea of its content. First, read the following excerpt from the introduction to the book *Catwatching,* by Desmond Morris. Then follow the instructions given after it.

Cat Lovers vs. Dog Lovers

Because of this difference between domestic cats and domestic dogs, cat lovers tend to be rather different from dog lovers. As a rule they have a stronger personality bias toward independent thought and action. Artists like cats; soldiers like dogs. The much-lauded "group loyalty" phenomenon is alien to both cats and cat lovers. . . . The ambitious Yuppie, the aspiring politician, the professional athlete, these are not typical cat owners. It is hard to picture a football player with a cat in his lap—much easier to envisage him taking his dog for a walk.

Those who have studied cat owners and dog owners as two distinct groups report that there is also a gender bias. Cat lovers show a greater tendency to be female. This is not surprising in view of the division of labor that developed during human evolution. Prehistoric males became specialized as group hunters, while the females concentrated on food-gathering and childrearing. This difference led to a human male "pack mentality" that is far less marked in females. . . . [S]o the modern dog has much more in common with the human male than with the human female. . . .

The argument will always go on—feline self-sufficiency and individualism versus canine camaraderie and good-fellowship. But it is important to stress that in making a valid point I have caricatured the two positions. In reality there are many people who enjoy equally the company of both cats and dogs. All of us, or nearly all of us, have both feline and canine elements in our personalities. We have moods when we want to be alone and thoughtful, and other times when we wish to be in the center of a crowded, noisy room.

A good way to begin the summary is to figure out the thesis statement, the main idea the author wants to get across to the reader. Write that idea down now *before reading further.*

How honest are you with yourself? Did you write that thesis statement? If you didn't, *write it now* before you read further.

You probably wrote something like this:

Certain characteristics make people prefer either cats or dogs as pets.

Using that main idea as your first sentence, summarize the article by choosing the most important points. *Be sure to put them in your own words.* Your rough draft may be 150 words or more.

Now cut it down by including only essential points and by getting rid of wordiness. Keep within the 100-word limit. You may have a few words less but not one word more. (And every word counts—even *a, and,* and *the.*) By forcing yourself to keep within 100 words, you'll get to the kernel of the author's thought and understand the article better.

When you have written the best summary you can, then and only then compare it with the summary on page 331. If you look at the model sooner, you'll cheat yourself of the opportunity to learn to write summaries because, once you read the model, it will be almost impossible not to make yours similar. So do your own thinking and writing, and then compare.

Summary Checklist

Even though your summary is different from the model, it may be just as good. If you're not sure how yours compares, answer these questions:

1. Did you include the same main ideas?
2. Did you leave out all unnecessary words and examples?
3. Did you rephrase the writer's ideas, not just recopy them?
4. Does the summary read smoothly?
5. Would someone who had not read the article get a clear idea of it from your summary?

Assignment 18

WRITE A REACTION OR A 100-WORD SUMMARY

Respond to Steve Mirsky's "Sheer Lunacy" in any of the three ways we've discussed—in a reaction paragraph, an essay, or a 100-word summary. If you plan to respond with an essay, briefly summarize Mirsky's main ideas about the moon-landing controversy in your introductory paragraph. Then write about your reactions to his ideas in your body paragraphs. Save your final thoughts for your concluding paragraph.

Sheer Lunacy

Which is nuttier: denying we ever went to the moon or trying to convince the true nonbelievers?

Once upon a time—July 20, 1969, to be specific—two earthlings got out of their little spaceship and wandered around on the moon for a while. Ten more earthlings walked on the moon over the next three and a half years. The end.

Unfortunately, not quite. A fair number of Americans think that this whole business of moon landings really *is* a fairy tale. They believe that the moon landings were a big hoax staged on a set in the Mojave Desert, perpetuated apparently to convince everyone that U.S. technology was the bestest in the whole wide world.

Time to shave with Occam's razor. Which is the harder thing to do: Send men to the moon or make believe we did? The fact is the brute-force physics behind blasting people to the moon is simple. You can do it with slide rules and with computers whose entire memory capacities can now fit on RAM chips the size of postage stamps and that cost about as much as, well, a postage stamp. I know you can because we *did*.

Nevertheless, last fall NASA considered spending $15,000 on what amounted to a public-relations campaign to convince the unimpressed that Americans had in fact gone to the moon. That idea was mostly a reaction to a Fox television program, first aired in February 2001, that claimed to expose the hoax [see "Fox's Flapdoodle," by Michael Shermer; Skeptic, *Scientific American*, June 2001]. The show's creator is a publicity hound who has lived up to the name in more ways than one by hounding Buzz Aldrin. Mr. X (as I will call him, thereby denying him the joyous sight of his name in print) recently followed the second man on the moon around and called him "a thief, liar and coward" until the 72-year-old astronaut finally lost it and—bang, zoom, to the moon, Alice—punched the 37-year-old Mr. X in the face.

Of course, the only Fox show that features good science is *The Simpsons*, on which Stephen J. Gould, Stephen Hawking and, for that matter, Aldrin have all guest-starred, although there's some instructive physics in The World's Most Hilarious Fatal Car Crashes—or whatever they call this week's special in which large objects traveling at high speed smash into one another.

The moon-hoax show claimed that 20 percent of Americans have doubts about whether we ever really went (apparently up from the 6 percent that a 1999 Gallup poll identified). At first glance, that number looks alarming, but I would estimate that 20 percent of Americans think that *Malcolm in the Middle* is a documentary about a family in crisis. (Sonoma State University astronomer Phil Plait supplies the details of the moon-landing polls and many other related items on his excellent Web site, www.badastronomy.com.)

Anyway, NASA's publicity campaign began to retrorocket as conspiracy theorists pointed to the effort as confirmation of something to hide and rational thinkers contended that $15,000 to convince people that the world was round— I mean, that we had gone to the moon—was simply a waste of money. (Actually, the $15,000 was supposed to pay for a rebuttal monograph by James E. Oberg, a serious astronomy writer who, with Aldrin, has contributed to *Scientific American*. As far as I'm concerned, paying a science writer is never a waste of money, but I'm severely prejudiced.)

If NASA's not paying Oberg, perhaps it could put the money to good use by hiring two big guys to drag Neil Armstrong out of the house. Armstrong is an extremely private man, but he is also *the first man on the moon*, so maybe he has an obligation to be a bit more vocal about the experience. Or NASA could just buy Aldrin a nice plaque commemorating his most recent moon shot, in which his fist slipped the surly bonds of decorum and touched the face of Mr. X.

Answers

WORDS OFTEN CONFUSED, SET 1 (PP. 9–14)

Exercise 1

1. hear
2. It's, desserts
3. feel
4. do
5. A, effect
6. chose
7. knew
8. fill
9. an, are
10. advice, desserts

Exercise 2

1. It's, new
2. have, accepted
3. feel, an
4. chose
5. already, fourth
6. fill, except, have
7. hear, an, advice
8. are
9. course, effects
10. complemented

Exercise 3

1. clothes, an
2. Due, a
3. accept
4. course, are, all ready
5. coarse, new
6. conscious
7. an
8. break, feel
9. have, already
10. It's, no

Exercise 4

1. already	6. affected, coarse
2. clothes	7. here, conscious
3. its, brakes	8. It's, feel, our
4. choose, advice	9. know, have
5. desert	10. forth, accept

Exercise 5

1. a	6. brake, it's
2. complement	7. affect
3. fill, desserts, have	8. effect
4. do	9. fourth
5. its	10. here, advise

Proofreading Exercise

During my singing recital last semester, I suddenly became very self-~~con-science~~ *conscious.* My heart started beating faster, and I didn't ~~no~~ *know* what to ~~due~~ *do.* I looked around to see if my show of nerves was having an ~~affect~~ *effect* on the audience. Of ~~coarse~~ *course,* they could ~~here~~ *hear* my voice shaking. I was the ~~forth~~ *fourth* singer in the program, and everyone else had done so well. I felt my face turn red and would ~~of~~ *have* run out the door if it had been closer. After my performance, people tried to give me ~~complements~~ *compliments,* but I ~~new~~ *knew* that they weren't sincere.

WORDS OFTEN CONFUSED, SET 2 (PP. 19–23)

Exercise 1

1. peace, their	6. Whether
2. they're	7. past
3. their	8. than
4. They're	9. There, write
5. through	10. too

Exercise 2

1. lose
2. where
3. quiet, write
4. personnel
5. there, two, right

6. principal
7. who's
8. principal
9. whether, quiet, past
10. than

Exercise 3

1. You're, where
2. Whether, you're, woman, wear
3. too, loose, too
4. They're, quite, right
5. who's, than

6. personal
7. your, you're, who's, wear
8. passed, right
9. whose
10. woman, weather

Exercise 4

1. piece, were, quite
2. whose
3. principal
4. personal
5. to, who's, woman

6. were, wear, their
7. were, right
8. through
9. to
10. led, there, were

Exercise 5

1. your
2. you're, than
3. whether
4. piece, women
5. They're, their

6. principle
7. to, than
8. principal, their
9. to, then
10. they're, through

Proofreading Exercise

Sometimes it's hard to find the ~~write~~ *right* place to study on campus. The library used ~~too~~ *to* be the ~~principle~~ *principal* location for students to do ~~they're~~ *their* difficult course work, ~~weather~~ *whether* it was preparing research papers or writing critical essays. But now most library resources are available online, ~~two~~ *too.* This change has ~~lead~~ *led* students to use campus computer labs and cafés as study halls. There, students can go online, get up-to-date sources, write their reports, and have peace and ~~quite~~ *quiet* without the stuffy atmosphere of the library. The only problem with doing research online is that it's easier to ~~loose~~ *lose* a piece of information on the computer ~~then~~ *than* it is to lose a hard copy in the library.

THE EIGHT PARTS OF SPEECH (PP. 26–29)

Exercise 1

　　 adj 　　 n 　　　 v 　　　 n
1. Good movies entertain people.

　　 pro adv 　 v 　 conj 　 v 　　　 n
2. They also educate and motivate people.

　　　　 adj 　　　　 n 　　 v 　 adj prep 　　 n
3. Well-written characters seem real on the screen.

　　　 adj 　　 n 　 conj 　 n 　　 v 　 adj 　 n 　 prep 　　　 n
4. Their downfalls or successes have lasting effects on the audience.

　　　 n 　 v 　　 n 　 prep 　 adj 　 n 　 prep pro
5. A person sees a movie with a wild character in it.

　　 pro conj pro 　 v 　　 prep 　　 n
6. She or he learns about wildness.

　　 adv 　　　 n 　　 v 　　 prep 　　　 n
7. Often, the story revolves around a secret.

　　　 pro 　　　 v 　　　　 n 　 conj 　 v 　 pro prep 　 n
8. Someone discovers the secret and reveals it in the end.

　　　 n 　 adv 　 v 　 adv 　 conj 　 adj 　　 n 　　　 v
9. The story usually moves ahead when the main character changes.

　　 adj 　　 n 　 v 　 adv 　 adv 　 adj
10. Such changes are not always positive.

Exercise 2

　 prep n 　　　　 n 　 prep adj 　　 n 　　 v 　 prep 　 n 　 prep 　　 adj 　 n
1. In 1992, a boatload of rubber ducks sailed from China to the west coast

　 prep 　 n
　　 of America.

　　　 n 　 prep pro 　 v 　　 adv 　 prep 　　 n 　 prep 　　　　 n
2. Thousands of them washed overboard in the middle of the Pacific Ocean.

        n   v   prep n prep n
3. The ducks floated from sea to sea.

     pro   v   adj   n   conj   adj   n   v prep adj   n
4. They traveled the same route that the infamous *Titanic* did at one point.

     adj   n   v   n   prep   adj   n
5. Ocean experts used the "duck-slick" as a study tool.

   prep n   adj   adj   n   adv   v   prep   n
6. In 2003, the bleached bath toys finally arrived in America.

       adv   pro   v   prep   adj   n
7. However, they landed on the Atlantic coast.

          n   v   adj   n
8. The journey took a long time.

      adj   n   v   prep adj   n
9. The rubber ducks floated for eleven years.

    adj   adj   n   v   prep   adj   conj   adj   n
10. Some stray ducks landed on European and Hawaiian shores.

Exercise 3

    interj   adj   n   v   adj   n
1. Wow, mechanical pencils are delicate instruments.

   pro v adj   n   prep   pro
2. I see other students with them.

     adv pro v   pro
3. Then I buy one.

   pro   v   n
4. I open the package.

   pro   v   n   prep   adj   n prep n
5. I load the pencil with the tiny shaft of lead.

  conj pro v   adj   n   adv prep   n   n   v   adv
6. As I put the pencil tip down on the paper, the lead snaps off.

     v pro   adj   n
7. Am I an unrefined clod?

   pro   v   conj pro v
8. I believe that I am.

    adv pro v   adj   n
9. Now I know my limitations.

         adj   n   conj adj   n   v   adj   adj   n prep pro

10. Ballpoint pens and wooden pencils are the only writing tools for me.

Exercise 4

         adj   adj   n   adv v   n   adv

1. The following old sayings still have meaning today.

       n   adj v   n   adj

2. A penny saved is a penny earned.

      n prep n   v   n   adj   n

3. A stitch in time saves nine (or nine stitches).

        n   v   n

4. Haste makes waste.

       v   pro   v   adj   n

5. Love me, love my dog.

       n   v adj   adj   n

6. A picture is worth a thousand words.

     pro conj pro pro   v   v adj

7. He or she who hesitates is lost.

      n   v   conj pro v   v   n

8. Time flies when you are having fun.

      n   v adv   adj prep   adj   n prep   n

9. The grass is always greener on the other side of the fence.

        n prep adj   adj   n   v   prep   adj   n

10. The truth of many old sayings lies beneath their surfaces.

Exercise 5

        adj   n   prep   n   v   adj   n

1. Most children in schools take standardized tests.

        adj   n   v   n prep   adj   adj   n

2. The test results become part of the children's permanent records.

        adj   n   v   adj   n prep adj   n

3. School districts want high scores from their students.

       n   conj   n   v prep adj   n   prep pro adv

4. Parents and children hope for good scores from them, too.

     n   v   v   adj   adj   n

5. Sugar may raise the children's test scores.

        n   v   n   prep   adj   n   conj adj   adj   n

6. A researcher discovered a link between high calories and higher test scores.

     n   adv   v adj   n   adj   n   prep   adj   n

7. Schools sometimes feed their students more calories during testing time.

    adj   n   v   n   prep adj   adj   n

8. Test results show increases of several percentage points.

    adj   n   v   prep adj   n   adv

9. Some parents know about this link now.

     n   prep   n   prep adj   n   v   v   adj   n

10. Cookies for breakfast on test days may be a good idea!

PARAGRAPH EXERCISE

     adj   n   v   adj   n   prep n   pro   v   adj   n

Some materials are excellent conductors of heat. Some are poor conductors.

pro   v   adj   n   v adj   n   v   n   prep adj   n prep

Each does a different job. Try this experiment: hold a match against low heat on

     n   n   prep   n   v   adj adv conj   n   v   conj

the stove. The wood of the match remains cool even when the match ignites and

v   prep   n   conj   n v   adj   n   prep n   adv   v

burns toward the fingers because wood is a poor conductor of heat. Now place

    adj   n prep adj adj   n   conj   v   n   adv   prep   n   prep

an empty pan on that low heat and hold a hand flat against the bottom for a

    n   adj   n   adj   n   v adj   adv   adv

moment. The metal pan, an excellent conductor, gets hot almost immediately. . . .

adj   n   v   n   prep pro prep   adj   n prep n   conj

This experiment indicates the reason for many of the common uses of wood and

   n

metal.

CONTRACTIONS (PP. 31–35)

Exercise 1

1. you've, hadn't
2. that's
3. It's
4. no contractions
5. no contractions

6. couldn't
7. no contractions
8. There's
9. It's
10. Lets, don't

Exercise 2

1. who's
2. It's
3. isn't
4. That's
5. she'd

6. She'd
7. What's
8. hadn't
9. could've
10. didn't

Exercise 3

1. There's, that's
2. wasn't
3. don't, it's
4. hasn't
5. don't

6. aren't
7. They're
8. haven't
9. They've
10. they're, don't

Exercise 4

1. should've
2. didn't, I'd
3. didn't, could've, didn't
4. wasn't, don't
5. It's, I've

6. I'm, it'd
7. wouldn't, they'd
8. who's, he'd
9. might've
10. there's

Exercise 5

1. I'm, she's
2. We've, we've

3. aren't
4. they're

5. they're

6. that's

7. We've, can't, doesn't

8. we'd

9. that's, it's, they're

10. can't

Proofreading Exercise

If ~~youve~~ *you've* ever driven through Lancaster County, Pennsylvania, you ~~mightve~~ *might've* encountered one of the horse-drawn buggies that the Amish use as their main method of transportation. In the daytime, the black buggies stand out against the vivid landscape. But it ~~isnt~~ *isn't* as easy to see them when ~~its~~ *it's* dark. You ~~wouldnt~~ *wouldn't* expect to see an Amish buggy driving down the road with its headlights on. In fact, when it comes to headlights and taillights on Amish buggies, ~~theyre~~ *they're* usually not there. As a result, the buggies ~~arent~~ *aren't* as safe as they could be. Due to their beliefs, the Amish ~~dont~~ *don't* use electricity. However, a new kind of LED headlight technology ~~doesnt~~ *doesn't* rely on electricity. It works with solar energy, a form of power accepted by some members of the Amish community. These new headlights and taillights ~~havent~~ *haven't* been universally embraced, partly because of their cost.

POSSESSIVES (PP. 37–42)

Exercise 4

1. bat's, animal's

2. patient's

3. person's

4. condition's

5. bat's

6. no possessives

7. patients', bat's

8. enzyme's

9. DSPA's

10. bat's

Exercise 5

1. Beethoven's

2. symphony's

3. Beethoven's

4. composer's

5. copyist's

6. Symphony's, Beethoven's

7. copyists'

8. master's, manuscript's

9. symphony's

10. Ninth's

Proofreading Exercise

I've been surprised by ~~peoples'~~ *people's* reactions to my recent haircut. My ~~hairs~~ *hair's* new length is very short, and ~~it's~~ *its* style is kind of a controlled mess. When I first got the haircut, I thought that everyone would hate it, but I was wrong. My previous ~~hairstyles'~~ *hairstyle's* problem was that it was boring—too long and too straight. Now that it's got some spikiness to it, my hair can reveal my personality's natural ~~quirks'~~ *quirks*.

REVIEW OF CONTRACTIONS AND POSSESSIVES (PP. 42–44)

1. People's
2. money's
3. I've
4. I'd, month's
5. don't

6. can't
7. doesn't
8. statement's
9. wouldn't, company's
10. person's

A Journal of My Own

I've been keeping a journal ever since I was in high school. I *don't* write it for my *teachers'* sake. I *wouldn't* turn it in even if they asked me to. *It's* mine, and it helps me remember all of the changes *I've* gone through so far in my life. The way I see it, a *diary's* purpose *isn't* just to record the facts; *it's* to capture my true feelings.

When I record the *day's* events in my journal, they *aren't* written in minute-by-minute details. Instead, if *I've* been staying at a *friend's* house for the weekend, *I'll* write something like this: "*Sharon's* the only friend I have who listens to my whole sentence before starting hers. *She's* never in a hurry to end a good conversation. Today we talked for an hour or so about the pets *we'd* had when we were kids. We agreed that *we're* both 'dog people.' We *can't* imagine our lives without dogs. Her favorites are Pomeranians, and mine are golden retrievers." *That's* the kind of an entry *I'd* make in my journal. It *doesn't* mean much to anyone but me, and *that's* the way it should be.

I know that another *person's* diary would be different from mine and that most people *don't* even keep one. *I'm* glad that writing comes easily to me. I *don't* think *I'll* ever stop writing in my journal because it helps me believe in myself and value *others'* beliefs as well.

RULE FOR DOUBLING A FINAL LETTER (PP. 46–47)

Exercise 1

1. betting
2. milking
3. waiting
4. parking
5. skimming
6. admitting
7. slapping
8. thinking
9. tapping
10. hitting

Exercise 2

1. wrapping
2. ripping
3. peeling
4. referring
5. investing
6. ordering
7. profiting
8. screaming
9. slipping
10. predicting

Exercise 3

1. boxing
2. munching
3. rolling
4. mopping
5. flavoring
6. cashing
7. beeping
8. talking
9. traveling
10. playing

Exercise 4

1. painting
2. rowing
3. shivering
4. defending
5. trimming
6. pressing
7. dealing
8. knitting
9. blundering
10. chugging

Exercise 5

1. shouting
2. deploying
3. referring
4. equaling

5. digging

6. mixing

7. dripping

8. sending

9. hemming

10. taxing

PROGRESS TEST (P. 48)

1. A. complimented

2. B. where

3. A. could have

4. A. traveled

5. A. conscience

6. A. children's

7. B. already

8. B. effects

9. A. principle

10. A. You're

SENTENCE STRUCTURE

FINDING SUBJECTS AND VERBS (PP. 59–62)

Exercise 1

1. The summer <u>heat</u> <u>causes</u> many problems for people.

2. <u>Food</u> <u>spoils</u> more quickly in the summer.

3. <u>Insects</u> and other <u>pests</u> <u>seek</u> shelter inside.

4. There <u>are</u> power <u>outages</u> due to excessive use of air conditioners and fans.

5. In some areas, smog <u>levels</u> <u>increase</u> dramatically in the summer.

6. <u>Schoolchildren</u> <u>suffer</u> in overheated classrooms.

7. On the worst days, <u>everyone</u> <u>searches</u> for a swimming pool or <u>drives</u> to the beach.

8. <u>Sleeping</u> comfortably <u>becomes</u> impossible.

9. No <u>activity</u> <u>seems</u> worth the effort.

10. But the <u>heat</u> of summer <u>fades</u> in our minds at the first real break in the weather.

Exercise 2

1. In 1992, <u>Jacquelyn Barrett</u> <u>became</u> the sheriff of Fulton County, Georgia.

2. <u>She</u> <u>was</u> the first African-American woman sheriff in U.S. history.

3. As sheriff of Fulton County, <u>Barrett</u> <u>managed</u> the biggest system of jails in the state of Georgia.

4. Her <u>department</u> <u>had</u> a yearly budget of sixty-five million dollars.

5. Over a thousand <u>people</u> <u>worked</u> for the Fulton County Sheriff's office.

6. <u>Barrett</u> definitely <u>broke</u> the stereotype of southern sheriffs in TV and movies.

7. By 1999, there <u>were</u> over eleven hundred <u>sheriffs</u> in the South.

8. African-American <u>men</u> and <u>women</u> <u>represented</u> just five percent of the total.

9. Only one <u>percent</u> of them <u>were</u> women.

10. However, of the twenty-four female sheriffs in the country, <u>nine</u> <u>were</u> from the South.

Exercise 3

1. <u>Katharine M. Rogers</u> recently <u>published</u> her biography of L. Frank Baum.

2. Most <u>people</u> <u>know</u> Baum's work but not his name.

3. <u>L. Frank Baum</u> <u>wrote</u> *The Wonderful Wizard of Oz* and many other children's books and stories.

4. Of course, <u>filmmakers</u> <u>used</u> Baum's tale of the Wizard of Oz in the classic movie of the same name.

5. Baum's memorable <u>character</u> of the Scarecrow <u>has</u> an interesting story behind him.

6. During Baum's childhood, his <u>father</u> <u>bought</u> some farmland.

7. <u>Baum</u> <u>saw</u> scarecrows in the fields and <u>found</u> them fascinating.

8. Unfortunately, his keen <u>imagination</u> <u>led</u> to bad dreams about a scarecrow.

9. The <u>scarecrow</u> in his dreams <u>ran</u> after him but <u>fell</u> into a heap of straw just in time.

10. As a writer, <u>Baum</u> <u>brought</u> the Scarecrow to life in his Oz stories and <u>made</u> him less of a nightmare and more of a friend.

Exercise 4

1. In 2000, the <u>American Film Institute</u> <u>made</u> a list of "America's Funniest Movies."

2. AFI called the list "100 Years . . . 100 Laughs."

3. Many of the movies had their stars or their directors in common.

4. For instance, Katherine Hepburn and Cary Grant were leading actors in both *Bringing Up Baby* and *The Philadelphia Story*.

5. The films of director Woody Allen appeared five times on the list.

6. Some decades produced more of the best comedies than others.

7. Filmmakers in the 1980s, for example, created twenty-two of the funniest.

8. But there were only two films from the 1990s.

9. Perhaps millennium mania resulted in an increase in scary movies instead of comedies.

10. AFI's list of great comedies offered a resource for people in search of a good movie.

Exercise 5

1. There was another cloning breakthrough in the news in 2003.

2. Scientists in Italy cloned a horse.

3. The foal's name was Prometea.

4. Unusually, her mother was also her twin.

5. Prometea's DNA came from a mare.

6. Then that mare carried the cloned filly to term.

7. Upon Prometea's arrival, the two horses were unique in the world.

8. Prometea was the first cloned horse.

9. And her mother was first to carry her own clone to term. [*To carry* is a verbal.]

10. Not surprisingly, the success of a Prometea's cloning interested horseracing fans.

Paragraph Exercise

I was on the volleyball team in high school, so my high school gym was a special place for me. It was an ordinary gym with bleachers on both sides. There were basketball court <u>lines</u> on the floors and the school's mascot in the center. <u>We</u>

<u>stretched</u> a net across the middle for our volleyball games. The pale wooden <u>floors</u>

<u>sparkled</u>, sometimes with sweat and sometimes with tears. The <u>gym</u> <u>had</u> a distinct

stuffy smell of grimy socks, stale potato chips, and sticky sodas. <u>I</u> <u>liked</u> the smell

and <u>remember</u> it fondly. <u>Songs</u> from dances and <u>screams</u> and <u>cheers</u> from games

<u>echoed</u> throughout the big old building. In the gym during those high school

years, <u>I</u> <u>felt</u> a sense of privacy and community.

LOCATING PREPOSITIONAL PHRASES (PP. 65–69)

Exercise 1

1. (For nearly thirty years), a phone <u>booth</u> <u>stood</u> (in the middle) (of the Mojave Desert) (with absolutely nothing) (around it).

2. <u>It</u> <u>was</u> far (from any sign) (of civilization) but originally <u>served</u> miners (in camps) far away.

3. The <u>number</u> (for this pay phone) <u>became</u> well-known (over time): 760-733-9969.

4. <u>People</u> <u>called</u> it (from around the world) and <u>traveled</u> (to it) (for fun and adventure).

5. <u>Sites</u> (on the Internet) <u>posted</u> the isolated phone's number and <u>offered</u> maps (to its remote location) (near Baker, California).

6. <u>Individuals</u> <u>camped</u> (outside the booth) and <u>waited</u> (for random calls) (from strangers).

7. <u>Callers</u> never <u>expected</u> an answer (from a phone) (in the middle) (of nowhere).

8. (On many occasions), <u>callers</u> <u>panicked</u> and <u>said</u> nothing (for a minute or two).

9. (In addition), <u>some</u> (of its visitors) <u>vandalized</u> the booth and the phone itself.

10. So phone-company <u>workers</u> <u>removed</u> the infamous Mojave phone booth (in May 2000).

Exercise 2

1. (At some point) (at a restaurant), most <u>people</u> <u>ask</u> (for a box or a bag) (for leftovers).
2. (At home), such <u>containers</u> <u>go</u> (into the refrigerator) and <u>sit</u> (for a few days).
3. Sometimes <u>they</u> <u>sit</u> (for too many days).
4. Unaware (of the age) (of those leftovers), a <u>person</u> <u>eats</u> them and <u>gets</u> sick.
5. A <u>chain</u> (of restaurants) (in Chicago) now <u>labels</u> "doggie bags" (with freshness information).
6. (Like the dates and warnings) (on products) (at supermarkets), these <u>labels</u> (for leftovers) <u>inform</u> people (about food-safety issues).
7. Leftovers <u>need</u> almost immediate refrigeration (for safety's sake).
8. Such <u>food</u> <u>stays</u> fresh (in the fridge) (for only a few days).
9. Leftover <u>food</u> also <u>needs</u> special reheating (to a specific temperature).
10. (With this information), food-safety <u>associations</u> <u>hope</u> to save many people (from unnecessary illness). [*To save many people* is a verbal phrase.]

Exercise 3

1. <u>Twiggy the Squirrel</u> <u>is</u> a star (in the world) (of trained animals).
2. <u>Twiggy</u> <u>performs</u> (on a pair) (of tiny water skis) and <u>delights</u> crowds (at boat shows and other events).
3. (Like many other famous animal entertainers), the current <u>Twiggy</u> <u>is</u> not the original.
4. The <u>Twiggy</u> (of today) <u>is</u> fifth (in the line) (of Twiggys).
5. <u>Lou Ann Best</u> <u>is</u> Twiggy's trainer and <u>continues</u> the work begun (by her husband Chuck) (during the 1970s). [*Begun* is a verbal.]
6. (In his time), <u>Chuck Best</u> <u>convinced</u> many types (of animals) to ride (on water skis). [*To ride* is a verbal.]

7. <u>He</u> <u><u>had</u></u> success (with everything) (from a dog) (to a frog).

8. But <u>Twiggy the Squirrel</u> <u><u>was</u></u> a hit (with crowds) (from the beginning).

9. <u>All</u> (of the Twiggys) <u><u>seemed</u></u> happy (with their show-biz lifestyles).

10. (In fact), the <u>Bests</u> <u><u>received</u></u> four (of the Twiggys) (from the Humane Society).

Exercise 4

1. (At 2 A.M.) (on the first Sunday) (in April), <u>something</u> <u><u>happens</u></u> (to nearly everyone) (in America): Daylight Saving Time.

2. But few <u>people</u> <u><u>are</u></u> awake (at two) (in the morning).

3. So <u>we</u> <u><u>set</u></u> the hands or digits (of our clocks) ahead one hour (on Saturday night) (in preparation) (for it).

4. And (before bed) (on the last Saturday) (in October), <u>we</u> <u><u>turn</u></u> them back again.

5. (For days) (after both events), <u>I</u> <u><u>have</u></u> trouble (with my sleep patterns and my mood).

6. (In spring), the <u>feeling</u> <u><u>is</u></u> one (of loss).

7. That Saturday-night <u>sleep</u> (into Sunday) <u><u>is</u></u> one hour shorter than usual.

8. But (in fall), <u>I</u> <u><u>gain</u></u> a false sense (of security) (about time).

9. That endless Sunday <u>morning</u> quickly <u><u>melts</u></u> (into the start) (of a hectic week) (like the other fifty-one) (in the year).

10. <u>All</u> (of this upheaval) <u><u>is</u></u> due (to the Uniform Time Act) (of 1966).

Exercise 5

1. <u>I</u> <u><u>saw</u></u> a news story (about an art exhibit) (with a unique focus and message).

2. <u>All</u> (of the pieces) (in the art show) <u><u>started</u></u> (with the same basic materials).

3. The <u>materials</u> <u><u>were</u></u> all (of the parts) (of a huge English oak tree).

4. <u>Most</u> (of a tree) usually <u><u>becomes</u></u> waste (except the large trunk section).

5. But (in the case) (of this tree), <u>artists</u> <u><u>took</u></u> every last bit and <u><u>made</u></u> "art" (with it) (as a tribute) (to the tree).

6. One <u>artist</u> even <u><u>made</u></u> clothes (from some) (of the smallest pieces)—tiny branches, sawdust, and leaves.

7. Another <u>artist</u> <u><u>used</u></u> thousands (of bits) (of the tree) (in a kind) (of mosaic painting).

8. Still <u>another</u> <u><u>turned</u></u> one hunk (of the tree's timber) (into a pig sculpture).

9. Other <u>chunks</u>, <u>branches</u>, and even the <u>roots</u> <u><u>became</u></u> abstract pieces (of art).

10. The <u>tree</u> <u><u>lives</u></u> on (as art) and (as a new tree) (with the sprouting) (of an acorn) (in its old location).

Paragraph Exercise

Water Storage

Lakes and ponds obviously store a great deal (of water). Not so obvious is the immense reservoir (of water) stored (in the polar ice caps), (in glaciers), and (in snow) (on mountains) and (on the cold northern plains) (during winter). Winter snows (in the mountains) determine the water supply (for irrigation) and (for power use). This snow melts (with the spring thaw) and fills the rivers.

UNDERSTANDING DEPENDENT CLAUSES (PP. 72–76)

Exercise 1

1. When <u>I</u> <u><u>was</u></u> on vacation in New York City, <u>I</u> <u><u>loved</u></u> the look of the Empire State Building at night.

2. <u>I</u> <u><u>thought</u></u> that the colored <u>lights</u> at the top of this landmark <u><u>were</u></u> just decorative.

3. <u>I</u> <u>did</u> not <u><u>know</u></u> that their <u>patterns</u> also <u><u>have</u></u> meaning.

4. While <u>I</u> <u><u>waited</u></u> at the airport, <u>I</u> <u><u>read</u></u> a pamphlet that <u><u>explained</u></u> what the <u>patterns</u> <u><u>mean</u></u>.

5. <u>Some</u> of the light combinations <u><u>reveal</u></u> connections that <u>are</u> obvious.

6. For instance, if the <u>occasion</u> <u><u>is</u></u> St. Patrick's Day, the <u>top</u> of the building <u><u>glows</u></u> with green lights.

7. Whenever the holiday involves a celebration of America, the three levels of lights shine red, white, and blue.

8. There are other combinations that are less well-known.

9. Red-black-green is a pattern that signals Martin Luther King, Jr. Day.

10. Whenever I visit the city again and see pink and white lights at the top of that famous building, I'll know that they are there for breast-cancer awareness.

Exercise 2

1. When Barbara Mitchell ate lunch at a California restaurant in late 1997, she thought that the service was terrible.

2. The lunch that Mitchell ordered consisted of salad, soup, pasta, and iced tea.

3. She received the bill, which came to twenty-four dollars, and charged it to her credit card.

4. Because the service was so bad, Mitchell wrote in a one-cent tip.

5. But when Mitchell saw her credit-card statement, she nearly fainted.

6. The tip that was a penny turned into a charge of ten thousand dollars, in addition to the twenty-four dollars for her food.

7. The waiter told authorities that he entered the huge tip amount by mistake.

8. When the restaurant's manager learned of the error, she suspended the waiter for seven days.

9. Mitchell received a full refund, an apology, and a gift certificate from the restaurant.

10. Mitchell wishes that she paid the bill with cash.

Exercise 3

1. In June of 2000, there was another incident of mistaken tipping at a bar in Chicago.

2. This time, a male customer left a real ten-thousand-dollar tip for a waitress who was especially nice to him.

3. At least everyone thought that he gave her that amount until the man later denied his generosity.

4. The customer, who was a London resident on a trip to the United States, did everything to convince the people in the bar that he was serious.

5. Melanie Uczen was the waitress who served the man his drinks, which added up to nine dollars.

6. He told her that he was a doctor and wanted to help with her college plans.

7. When the bar's owner questioned the tip, the customer allowed the owner to make a copy of his passport.

8. He even signed a note that verified the tip's amount.

9. Back in London, the man said that he was not a doctor and claimed that he was drunk when he signed the note.

10. Because the big tip brought the bar so much publicity, the owners paid Melanie Uczen the ten thousand dollars themselves.

Exercise 4

1. The happiest ending to a big-tipper story came in July of 2000.

2. It began when Karen Steinmetz, who dispatches cars for Continental Limo company, received a call for a driver and limo at two-thirty in the morning.

3. The most unusual part of the customer's request was that he wanted the driver to take him over nine hundred miles, from Southern California to Oregon.

4. When Steinmetz contacted the first driver to see if he wanted the job, he told her that he wanted only sleep at that hour.

5. So Steinmetz called Major Cephas, another driver who worked for Continental.

6. Cephas took the job and picked the customer up in the city of Garden Grove.

7. The two men drove through the night but stopped in Sacramento and other spots along the way for exercise and refreshments.

8. Overall, the trip took nearly eighteen hours, which resulted in a twenty-two-hundred-dollar fare.

9. The passenger paid the fare and gave Cephas a twenty-thousand-dollar tip because Cephas was so patient with him.

10. This time the tip was as real as the disappointment of the first driver who turned down the job.

Exercise 5

1. My coworker told me about a news story that he saw on television.

2. It involved those baby turtles that hatch in the sand at night.

3. Normally, once they hatch, they run as fast as they can toward the comforting waves.

4. As soon as they reach the water, they begin their lives as sea turtles.

5. The story that my friend saw told of a potential danger to these motivated little animals.

6. It seems that the turtles instinctively know which direction leads to the sea.

7. The bright white <u>foam</u> of the waves <u>is</u> the trigger <u>that</u> <u>lures</u> them across the sand to their proper destination.

8. Unfortunately, on some beaches where this <u>phenomenon</u> <u>occurs</u>, the tourist <u>business</u> <u>causes</u> a big problem for the turtles.

9. <u>Tourists</u> <u>who</u> <u>want</u> to see the turtles <u>gather</u> at shoreline restaurants and dance pavilions whose <u>lights</u> <u>are</u> so bright that <u>they</u> <u>prompt</u> the turtles to run in the wrong direction—up the beach away from the water.

10. <u>Stories</u> like these <u>remind</u> us of how delicate the <u>balance</u> of nature <u>is</u>.

Paragraph Exercise

Today <u>experts</u> <u>disagree</u> over the impact of television on our lives. <u>Some</u> <u>argue</u> that increased <u>crime</u> <u>is</u> a direct outcome of television since <u>programs</u> <u>show</u> crime as an everyday event and [since] <u>advertisements</u> <u>make</u> people aware of what <u>they</u> <u>don't</u> <u>have</u>. <u>Critics</u> also <u>maintain</u> that television <u>stimulates</u> aggressive behavior, <u>reinforces</u> ethnic stereotyping, and <u>leads</u> to a decrease in activity and creativity. <u>Proponents</u> of television <u>counter</u> [when <u>they</u> <u>cite</u>] increased awareness in world events, improved verbal abilities, and greater curiosity as benefits of television viewing.

CORRECTING FRAGMENTS (PP. 80–83)

Exercise 1

Answers may vary, but here are some possible revisions.

1. I read an article about bananas for my health class in high school. (sentence)

2. *The article said that* bananas are in danger of extinction in the near future. (fragment)

3. *The danger comes from* a crop disease that infects the banana plants' leaves. (fragment)

4. The disease makes the bananas get ripe too fast. (sentence)

5. All of the kinds of bananas that people eat are at risk. (sentence)

6. Some banana experts *are warning* about no more bananas to eat. (fragment)

7. *That would mean* no banana cream pies, banana splits, banana muffins, or banana bread. (fragment)

8. Such an idea is new to a lot of us. (sentence)

9. Most people never think about plant extinction. (sentence)

10. Chocolate and coffee *have been threatened by* similar scares in the past. (fragment)

Exercise 2

Changes used to make the fragments into sentences are *italicized*.

1. In my psychology class, we talk about gender a lot. (sentence)

2. *We discuss* ways of raising children without gender bias. (fragment)

3. *Gender bias means having* different expectations about boys' abilities and girls' abilities. (fragment)

4. Experts have several suggestions for parents and teachers. (sentence)

5. Ask girls to work in the yard and boys to do dishes sometimes. (sentence) (In numbers 5–10, the subject is an understood *You*.)

6. *Do not make* a big deal out of it. (fragment)

7. Give both girls and boys affection as well as helpful criticism. (sentence)

8. *Encourage* physically challenging activities for both genders. (fragment)

9. Give girls access to tools, and praise boys for kindness. (sentence)

10. Most of all, value their different approaches to math and computers. (sentence)

Exercise 3

Answers may vary, but here are some possible revisions.

1. The oceanliner *Titanic* sank in April of 1912, affecting thousands of families and inspiring books and movies around the world.

2. With three close relatives on the *Titanic* that April night, the Belman family re-members details of the disaster.

3. Two of the Belmans were lost after the sinking. One *survived* by swimming along next to a lifeboat and eventually climbing aboard.

4. The survivor, Grandfather Belman, returned to his family in Lebanon and told them about the terrifying events of that night.

5. He recalled the efforts of the crew, the courage of the passengers, the icy cold water, and the reassuring sight of the *Carpathia*.

6. Anthony Belman is Grandfather Belman's descendent, now living in the United States and working as a bartender.

7. Inspired by the stories of his grandfather's survival and the loss of his other two relatives, Belman has created a cocktail in honor of all those touched by the Titanic disaster.

8. It's called the Titanic Iceberg, *and it's* made with rum, crème de menthe, and blue Curaçao.

9. After blending the mixture with ice and transferring it to a margarita glass, Belman adds two wedges of vanilla ice cream to the sea-blue drink for icebergs.

10. And as a final touch to remind everyone of the human toll of the disaster, the cocktail calls for two white Lifesaver candies floating on top of the icy blue slush.

Exercise 4

Answers may vary, but here are some possible revisions.

1. When Nathan King turned twelve, he had a heart-stopping experience.

2. Nathan was tossing a football against his bedroom wall, which made the ball ricochet and land on his bed.

3. In a diving motion, Nathan fell on his bed to catch the ball as it landed.

4. After he caught the ball, Nathan felt a strange sensation in his chest.

5. To his surprise, he looked down and saw the eraser end of a no. 2 pencil that had pierced his chest and entered his heart.

6. Nathan immediately shouted for his mother, who luckily was in the house at the time.

7. Because Nathan's mom is a nurse, she knew not to remove the pencil.

8. If she had pulled the pencil out of her son's chest, he would have died.

9. After Nathan was taken to a hospital equipped for open-heart surgery, he had the pencil carefully removed.

10. Fate may be partly responsible for Nathan's happy birthday story since it turned out to be his heart surgeon's birthday too.

Exercise 5

Answers may vary, but here are some possible revisions. (Changes and additions are in *italics*.)

1. One of the people sitting next to me on the train sneezed four times in a row.

2. Before intermission, the movie seemed endless.

3. Before the paint was dry in the classrooms, *the new semester began.*

4. The judge's question rattled the nerves of the contestants.

5. Because there were fewer students in the program this year, *it ran smoothly.*

6. *His speech lasted* for over an hour.

7. Whenever the teacher reminds us about the midterm exam, *we get nervous.*

8. Then we moved to Kentucky and stayed for two years.

9. *Please notify us* as soon as the order form reaches the warehouse.

10. Buildings with odd shapes always interest me.

Proofreading Exercise

Answers may vary, but here are some possible revisions. (Changes are in *italics*.)

I love fireworks shows. *They can be* backyard displays or huge Fourth of July events. *The whole sky lights up* with color and booms with noise. In fact, I have a dream to become a fireworks expert. If I could take a class in pyrotechnics right now, I would. Instead, I have to take general education *classes like English, math, and psychology.* Maybe an appointment with a career counselor would be a good idea. *The counselor could* help me find the right *school—one with a training program* in fireworks preparation.

CORRECTING RUN-ON SENTENCES (PP. 86–90)

Exercise 1

Your answers may differ depending on how you chose to separate the two clauses.

1. I just read an article about prehistoric rodents, and I was surprised by their size.

2. Scientists recently discovered the remains of a rat-like creature called *Phoberomys*; it was as big as a buffalo.

3. *Phoberomys* sat back on its large rear feet and fed itself with its smaller front feet in just the way rats and mice do now.

4. This supersized rodent lived in South America, but luckily that was nearly ten million years ago.

5. At that time, South America was a separate continent; it had no cows or horses to graze on its open land.

6. South America and North America were separated by the sea, so there were also no large cats around to hunt and kill other large animals.

7. Scientists believe that *Phoberomys* thrived and grew large because of the lack of predators and competitors for food.

8. The *Phoberomys'* carefree lifestyle eventually disappeared, for the watery separation between North and South America slowly became a land route.

9. The big carnivores of North America could travel down the new land route, and the big rodents were defenseless against them.

10. The rodents who survived were the smaller ones who could escape underground, and that is the reason we have no buffalo-sized rats today.

Exercise 2

Your answers may differ depending on how you chose to separate the two clauses.

1. One day is hard for me every year. That day is my birthday.

2. I don't mind getting older; I just never enjoy the day of my birth.

3. For one thing, I was born in August, but summer is my least favorite season.

4. I hate the heat and the sun, so even traditional warm-weather activities get me down.

5. Sunblock spoils swimming; smog spoils biking; and crowds spoil the national parks.

6. To most people, the beach is a summer haven. To me, the beach in the summer is bright, busy, and boring.

7. I love to walk on the beach on the cold, misty days of winter or early spring. I wear a big sweater and have the whole place to myself.

8. August also brings fire season to most parts of the country; therefore, even television is depressing.

9. There are no holidays to brighten up August. In fact, it's like a black hole in the yearly holiday calendar—after the Fourth of July but before Halloween and the other holidays.

10. I have considered moving my birthday to February. Even being close to Groundhog Day would cheer me up.

Exercise 3

Your answers may differ since various words can be used to begin dependent clauses.

1. You may have seen one of the funniest *Simpsons* episodes in which dolphins rise from the sea and take over Springfield.

2. The Simpsons and the other residents of Springfield are defenseless against the dolphins because the dolphins are smarter than the humans.

3. Of course, dolphins do have amazing abilities that allow them to perform mental and physical feats beyond those of other animals.

4. For this reason, the U.S. government has trained dolphins for certain tasks that cannot be performed as well by machines or humans.

5. The sentence is correct.

6. Since then, dolphins have been put on patrol around ships and piers that were in danger of attack in many locations throughout the world.

7. The sentence is correct.

8. Dolphins have special sonar skills that allow them to tell the difference between natural objects and manmade objects as small as pearls.

9. Finding these underwater mines is not dangerous for the dolphins because they can use their sonar skills from far away and alert divers who then disarm the explosives.

10. The *Simpsons* episode is funny because dolphins do seem to be better equipped in many ways than we are.

Exercise 4

Your answers may differ since various words can be used to begin dependent clauses.

1. Our town has recently installed a new rapid transit system that uses trains instead of only buses.

2. The new metro train tracks follow the same old route that freight trains used to run on behind the buildings in town.

3. I might try this new transportation method since the parking on campus has been getting worse every semester.

4. Because the stations are near my house and school, I would have to walk only a few blocks each day.

5. Students who don't live near the train stations would have to take a bus to the train.

6. Whereas the old buses are bulky and ugly, the new trains are sleek and attractive.

7. Although the new trains seem to be inspiring many people to be more conscious of their driving habits, some people will never change.

8. I would gladly give up my car if the convenience matched the benefits.

9. The city has plans for additional routes that will bring more commuters in from out of town.

10. I am glad that my town is making progress.

Exercise 5

Your answers may differ depending on how you chose to separate the clauses.

1. If it's summer time, there will be bugs.

2. People at picnics and backyard barbecues see bees and wasps as pests, but they're just being themselves.

3. Since these creatures build their nests earlier in the year, late summer is their vacation time too.

4. They leave their homes and look for sweets that are easy to find at picnics and barbecues.

5. The smell of a soda, for instance, attracts these insects, so such drinks should be covered.

6. Also, people who wear perfume are more likely to attract insects.

7. The sentence is correct.

8. The picnic location may be near a hive, but the hive might not be obvious.

9. Because it is so dangerous to upset or threaten any hive of insects, people must be aware of their surroundings.

10. Insects can pose a threat to the peace and safety of summer activities; therefore, the best defense is understanding.

REVIEW OF FRAGMENTS AND RUN-ON SENTENCES (PP. 90–92)

Your revisions may differ depending on how you chose to correct the errors.

People and animals require different amounts of sleep. People have to balance on two legs all day; therefore, we need to get off our feet and sleep for about eight hours each night. Horses, however, are able to rest better standing up because their four legs support their bodies without a strain on any one area. When horses lie down, their large bodies press uncomfortably against the earth. This pressure makes their hearts and lungs work harder than they do in standing position. Generally speaking, horses lie on the ground for about two hours a day, and they spend only a little of the remaining time drowsy or lightly sleeping while still on their feet.

IDENTIFYING VERB PHRASES (PP. 93–97)

Exercise 1

1. Have you ever felt a craving (for art)?

2. Have you said (to yourself), "I need a new painting, or I am going to go crazy"?

3. If you ever find yourself (in this situation), you can get instant satisfaction.

4. I am referring to Art-o-Mat machines, (of course).

5. These vending machines dispense small pieces (of modern art).

6. You insert five dollars, pull a knob (on a refurbished cigarette dispenser), and out comes an original art piece.

7. The artists themselves get fifty percent (of the selling price).

8. Art-o-Mat machines can be found (at locations) (across the country).

9. Art-o-Mats are currently dispensing tiny paintings, photographs, and sculptures (in twelve states).

10. The machines have sold the works (of hundreds) (of contemporary artists).

Exercise 2

1. My <u>daughter</u> and <u>I</u> <u>had been seeing</u> commercials (for the latest Cirque du Soleil tour) (on television).

2. The <u>name</u> (of the show) <u>was</u> *Varekai*, and the <u>commercials</u> <u>promised</u> creative costumes, evocative music, and breathtaking feats (of physical skill).

3. <u>We</u> <u>bought</u> our tickets (over the Internet) and <u>could</u> not <u>wait</u> (for the date) (of our show) to arrive.

4. As <u>we</u> <u>were approaching</u> the arena, <u>we</u> <u>caught</u> a glimpse (of the company's trademark blue and yellow circus tent) (in the parking lot).

5. The <u>audience</u> <u>was arriving</u> outside while the <u>performers</u> <u>were warming</u> up inside.

6. (From outside the tent), <u>we</u> <u>could hear</u> music and the commotion (of pre-show preparations).

7. Once the <u>doors</u>—or <u>should</u> <u>I</u> <u>say</u> flaps—(of the tent) <u>were opened</u>, the audience <u>members</u> <u>were ushered</u> (to their seats).

8. <u>We</u> <u>could</u> not <u>believe</u> how incredible the *Varekai* <u>show</u> <u>was</u>.

9. The <u>acrobats</u>, <u>contortionists</u>, and flying <u>acts</u> <u>dazzled</u> and <u>amazed</u> the whole crowd.

10. The appreciative <u>audience</u> <u>brought</u> the performers out (for three standing-ovation curtain calls), and <u>they</u> <u>waved</u> and <u>blew</u> kisses out (to everyone).

Exercise 3

1. The largest <u>meteorite</u> <u>that</u> <u>has</u> ever <u>been found</u> (on Earth) <u>was</u> recently (at the center) (of a custody battle).

2. <u>The American Museum of Natural History</u> (in New York) <u>has owned</u> the Willamette meteorite (since the early 1900s), and <u>it</u> <u>was displayed</u> (at the Hayden Planetarium).

3. <u>Scientists</u> <u>believe</u> that the car-sized <u>meteor</u> <u>landed</u> (between eight thousand and ten thousand years ago) (in <u>what</u> <u>is</u> now <u>called</u> Oregon). (The last prepositional phrase includes a subject and verb because it has a dependent clause as its object.)

4. The Willamette <u>meteorite</u> <u>may</u> actually <u>be</u> the central part (of an exploded planet).

5. But (to one group) (of Native Americans), the huge <u>meteor</u> <u>has</u> always <u>been</u> <u>known</u> (as "Tomanowos," or "Sky Person").

6. (In a lawsuit) (against the museum), Grand Ronde tribe <u>members</u> <u>claimed</u> that their <u>ancestors</u> <u>had worshipped</u> Tomanowos (for thousands of years) before <u>it</u> <u>was sold</u> (to the museum).

7. <u>They</u> <u>could support</u> their claims (with tribal songs and dances) <u>that</u> <u>revealed</u> a close relationship (between the Grand Ronde people and the meteorite).

8. The <u>museum</u> and the Grand Ronde <u>tribes</u> <u>did settle</u> the dispute (in August) (of 2000).

9. The two <u>sides</u> <u>agreed</u> that the Willamette <u>meteorite</u> <u>would remain</u> (on display) (at the Hayden Planetarium) but <u>would be accompanied</u> (by a plaque) <u>that</u> <u>described</u> the Grand Ronde tribes' connection (to the meteor).

10. The <u>museum</u> also <u>agreed</u> to give the Grand Ronde people special access (to the Willamette meteorite) so that <u>they</u> <u>may continue</u> their relationship (with Tomanowos).

Exercise 4

1. <u>Bill</u> and <u>Melinda Gates</u> <u>have been</u> two (of the wealthiest people) (in the world) (for a while) now.

2. (In 2003), the <u>Gateses</u> <u>donated</u> fifty million dollars (to the New York City public school system).

3. The <u>couple</u> <u>is hoping</u> that the <u>gift</u> <u>will be used</u> (for the creation) (of hundreds) (of smaller schools) (within the system).

4. The <u>curricula</u> (at the downsized schools) <u>would focus</u> (on single themes), such as law or medicine.

5. <u>Teachers</u> and <u>administrators</u> <u>can cope</u> better (with fewer students) and <u>can have</u> a greater impact (on their pupils).

6. The <u>people</u> (of New York City) <u>are</u> not <u>complaining</u> (about the Gates donation), but <u>some</u> <u>do worry</u> (about the results).

7. <u>Changing</u> large academic institutions <u>can be</u> difficult.

8. Some <u>educators</u> <u>question</u> the concept (of throwing money) (at the problem).

9. <u>Others</u> <u>see</u> such donations (as good investments) (in the future).

10. If the Gates <u>gamble</u> <u>pays</u> off, <u>students</u> (in New York City) <u>will be</u> the winners.

Exercise 5

1. Prehistoric musical <u>instruments</u> <u>have been found</u> before.

2. But the ancient <u>flutes</u> <u>that</u> <u>were</u> <u>discovered</u> (in China's Henan Province) <u>included</u> the oldest playable instrument (on record).

3. The nine-thousand-year-old <u>flute</u> <u>was made</u> (from the wing bone) (of a bird).

4. The <u>bone</u> <u>was hollowed</u> out and <u>pierced</u> (with seven holes) <u>that</u> <u>produce</u> the notes (of an ancient Chinese musical scale).

5. Because <u>one</u> (of the holes' pitches) <u>missed</u> the mark, an additional tiny <u>hole</u> <u>was added</u> (by the flute's maker).

6. The <u>flute</u> <u>is played</u> (in the vertical position).

7. <u>People</u> <u>who</u> <u>have studied</u> ancient instruments <u>are hoping</u> to learn more (about the culture) <u>that</u> <u>produced</u> this ancient flute.

8. Other bone <u>flutes</u> <u>were found</u> (at the same time) and (in the same location), but <u>they</u> <u>were</u> not intact or strong enough (for playing).

9. <u>Visitors</u> (to the Brookhaven National Laboratory's Web site) <u>can listen</u> (to music) (from the world's oldest working flute).

10. <u>Listeners</u> <u>will be taken</u> back (to 7,000 years B.C.)

REVIEW EXERCISE (P. 98)

My <u>brain</u> <u>feels</u> (like a computer's central processing unit). <u>Information</u> <u>is</u> continually <u>pumping</u> (into its circuits). <u>I</u> <u>organize</u> the data, <u>format</u> it (to my individual preferences), and <u>lay</u> it out (in my own style). As <u>I</u> endlessly <u>sculpt</u> existing for-

mulas, <u>they</u> <u>become</u> something (of my own). When <u>I</u> <u>need</u> a solution (to a prob-

lem), <u>I</u> <u>access</u> the data that <u>I</u> <u>have gathered</u> (from my whole existence), even my

preprogrammed DNA.

Since <u>I</u> <u>am</u> a student, <u>teachers</u> <u>require</u> that <u>I</u> <u>supply</u> them (with specific in-

formation) (in various formats). When <u>they</u> <u>assign</u> an essay, <u>I</u> <u>produce</u> several

paragraphs. If <u>they</u> <u>need</u> a summary, <u>I</u> <u>scan</u> the text, <u>find</u> its main ideas, and <u>put</u>

them briefly (into my own words). <u>I</u> <u>know</u> that <u>I</u> <u>can accomplish</u> whatever the

<u>teachers</u> <u>ask</u> so that <u>I</u> <u>can obtain</u> a bachelor's degree and <u>continue</u> processing

ideas to make a living.

<u>I</u> <u>compare</u> my brain (to a processor) because right now <u>I</u> <u>feel</u> that <u>I</u> <u>must</u>

<u>work</u> (like one). As <u>I</u> <u>go</u> further (into my education), my <u>processor</u> <u>will be</u> contin-

ually <u>updated</u>—just (like a Pentium)! And (with any luck), <u>I</u> <u>will end</u> up (with real,

not artificial, intelligence).

USING STANDARD ENGLISH VERBS (PP. 100–104)

Exercise 1

1. has, had
2. does, did
3. am, was
4. votes, voted
5. have, had

6. shops, shopped
7. are, was
8. pick, picked
9. do, did
10. ends, ended

Exercise 2

1. are, were
2. does, did

3. has, had
4. tags, tagged

5. have, had

6. stuffs, stuffed

7. are, were

8. do, did

9. dance, danced

10. are, were

Exercise 3

1. changed, want

2. had

3. enrolled, were, expected

4. were, were

5. did, were, does

6. observed, had

7. watched, cared, followed

8. had

9. imagined, had

10. needs, are, am

Exercise 4

1. have

2. play

3. plays

4. play

5. practices, do

6. is

7. am, is, am

8. reminds

9. follows

10. have, am, is

Exercise 5

1. Last semester my drawing teacher *handed* us an assignment.

2. The sentence is correct.

3. We *had* to draw in the other half of the picture.

4. My picture *showed* a woman sitting against the bottom of a tree trunk.

5. Her shoulders, hat, and umbrella *were* only partly there.

6. I tried to imagine what the missing parts *looked* like.

7. The sentence is correct.

8. Therefore, I *started* with the tree, the sky, and the ground.

9. The sentence is correct.

10. I *received* an "A" grade for my drawing.

Proofreading Exercise

I like family parties, especially when we *invite* all of our favorite relatives and friends. My dad usually *does* all of the shopping for food and supplies. If the party is a potluck, the meat dishes *are* the most popular. We *have* sliced beef, baked ham, and roast turkey. I *look* forward to trying new salads. I remember that I love the ones that *have* the glazed walnuts in them. All I have to do is think about the food at our parties, and I *start* to get hungry.

USING REGULAR AND IRREGULAR VERBS (PP. 109–113)

Exercise 1

1. live
2. lived
3. live
4. living
5. lived

6. lives
7. live
8. living
9. live
10. living

Exercise 2

1. got, gets
2. gave, given
3. am, is
4. thought, think
5. grown, grow

6. leave, left
7. wave, waves
8. knows, know
9. does, do
10. was, be, am

Exercise 3

1. took, supposed
2. was, go
3. called, left, feel
4. imagined, was
5. buying, drove, saw

6. felt, knew, be
7. tried, went (or got)
8. been, undo
9. wish, take
10. did, was

Exercise 4

1. use, have
2. do, speak, dials
3. are, are
4. is, like, started
5. does, wants

6. trusts, is
7. imagine, dialing
8. asking, told, is
9. looked, smiled
10. has

Exercise 5

1. sitting, saw
2. was, appeared
3. flipped, turned, looked
4. was, wore, thought, was
5. passed, seemed

6. waiting, cut
7. called, watched, recognize
8. look, figured, was
9. got, chatted, was
10. come, left

PROGRESS TEST (P. 114)

1. B. run-on sentence (. . . a night of decorating, so I was disappointed.)
2. B. fragment (*It leaves us only a little time . . .*)
3. B. incorrect verb form (He *used* to work . . .)
4. B. incorrect verb form (They were *lying* on the floor . . .)
5. A. fragment (Attach this phrase to the next sentence.)
6. A. incorrect verb form (have *taken*)
7. B. fragment (Attach the dependent clause to the previous sentence.)
8. B. run-on sentence (Their teacher was driving; he knew the road well.)
9. B. fragment (*We have learned that they can be fragments if they are used alone.*)
10. A. incorrect verb form (was *supposed*)

MAINTAINING SUBJECT/VERB AGREEMENT (PP. 117–122)

Exercise 1

1. have
2. were
3. was
4. is
5. allows

6. travels
7. breaks, melts
8. are
9. realize
10. is, are

Exercise 2

1. is, rates, portray
2. is

3. include, spark, explode, are
4. give

5. rank

6. get, are, make

7. is, are

8. were

9. was

10. were, were

Exercise 3

1. explains, seem, happen

2. feels, don't

3. begin, react

4. are, have

5. is, sense

6. don't, get

7. isn't

8. do

9. have, do, is

10. look, run, has, do

Exercise 4

1. sound

2. was, explains

3. were

4. was, were

5. was

6. were, was

7. were, was

8. was, was

9. were

10. shows, have, was

Exercise 5

1. gives

2. sounds, is

3. connects

4. says, means

5. forecasts

6. are, mean

7. are, foretell

8. means

9. are

10. seem

Proofreading Exercise

With today's high food prices, you should choose your produce wisely. However, buying ripe fruits and vegetables *is* a tricky process. How can you tell if an apple or a bunch of bananas *is* ready to buy or eat? A good rule of thumb for apples, oranges, and lemons is to judge the weight of the fruit. If the fruit *is* heavy, then it will probably be juicy and tasty. Lightweight fruits *tend* to lack juice and be tasteless. A melon, on the other hand, *is* almost always heavy, but a good one sloshes when you *shake* it. And the stem end of a ripe cantaloupe will give slightly when you *press* on it. Vegetables *need* to be chosen carefully, too. If there *are* sprouted eyes on a potato, you should pass that one by. The sprouted eyes *show* a change in the chemical structure of the potato, and it is not a good idea to eat them. When in doubt, you can ask the produce clerk, who should know a lot about the merchandise.

AVOIDING SHIFTS IN TIME (PP. 123–124)

1. The last time I took my car in for a scheduled service, I noticed a few problems when I *picked* it up. I *checked* the oil dipstick, and it *had* really dark oil still on it. Also, there was a screwdriver balancing on my air-filter cover. I *couldn't* believe it when I *saw* it, but as soon as I showed the tool to the service manager, he *called* the mechanic over to take my car back to the service area. After another hour, my car *was* ready, the dipstick *had* clean oil on it, and the service manager cleared the bill so that I didn't have to pay anything.

2. Back in the early 1900s, Sears Roebuck sold houses through the mail. The houses *were* listed along with the rest of the products in Sears' famous catalog. The house kits arrived in thousands of pieces, and people *would* put them together themselves. Or they *got* a builder to help them. In 1919, one company, Standard Oil, *placed* an order for an entire town's worth of houses as shelter for their employees. The house kits even included the paint that the homeowners *used* to paint the houses when they *were* finished. The ability to order a whole house from the Sears catalog ended in 1940, but thousands of them are still being lived in by people across America.

3. The paragraph is correct.

RECOGNIZING VERBAL PHRASES (PP. 126-130)

Exercise 1

1. I <u>love</u> [to drive my new car on the freeway and on [winding] country roads].

2. Its convertible roof <u>folds</u> back into the trunk [to allow for a [feeling] of complete freedom].

3. At high speeds, I <u>hear</u> the rush of wind and <u>feel</u> it [whipping my hair around].

4. Wind-[blown] hair <u>is</u> the only drawback to [owning a convertible].

5. Sometimes I <u>wear</u> a hat or a bandana [to keep my hair from [looking too crazy]] when I <u>get</u> home.

6. One time, after [taking a long drive around the lake], I <u>couldn't</u> even <u>comb</u> my hair out without [using a [detangling] shampoo].

7. In fact, humid weather [combined with wind] <u>seems</u> [to make matters worse].

8. I <u>am</u> still happy [to have my new car].

9. I <u>will accept</u> a little inconvenience in exchange for [owning such a great automobile].

10. And now I <u>know</u> all of the best places [to buy hats and bandanas].

Exercise 2

1. [To paraphrase Mark Twain], [golfing] <u>is</u> just a way [to ruin a good walk].

2. In fact, [becoming a golfer] <u>can be</u> dangerous.

3. Golf professionals commonly <u>suffer</u> a couple of injuries per year [resulting from long hours] of [practicing their swings].

4. Amateur golfers <u>tend</u> [to injure themselves] much more often.

5. Most injuries <u>come</u> from the [twisting], [squatting], and [bending] [involved in [golfing]].

6. And [moving the heavy bags of clubs] from cars to carts <u>can wrench</u> the backs of potential golfers before they even <u>begin</u> [to play].

7. Of course, there <u>are</u> the unfortunate incidents of people on golf courses [being struck by lightning].

8. But some of the sources of golfers' ailments <u>may be</u> [surprising].

9. [Cleaning the dirt and debris off the golf balls] by [licking them], for instance, <u>may have</u> serious repercussions.

10. After [swallowing the chemicals] [sprayed on the turf] of the golf course, players <u>can develop</u> liver problems.

Exercise 3

1. <u>Do</u> you <u>remember</u> [receiving your first [greeting] card] that <u>played</u> a song when you <u>opened</u> it?

2. You <u>have</u> probably also <u>seen</u> characters in recent movies [looking through the pages of [enchanted] books].

3. The magical books <u>contain</u> [moving] pictures, similar to video.

4. [Thinking logically], you <u>might have said</u> to yourself, "Books <u>don't have</u> pictures that <u>move</u>, but I <u>wish</u> that they <u>did</u>."

5. Actually, the technology necessary [to include bits of video in magazines, newspapers, and books] <u>may</u> not <u>be</u> too far away.

6. In simple terms, the e-ink <u>will display</u> [moving] images after [being jolted with electricity].

7. Such technology <u>is</u> already <u>used</u> [to change black letters on a white background].

8. It <u>may be</u> hard [to imagine this], but the video-on-paper <u>will appear</u> in full color.

9. Many companies <u>are competing</u> [to perfect the video e-paper process].

10. Someday soon you <u>will be</u> able [to watch clips from sports or world events in your newspaper]—as if by magic.

Exercise 4

1. Why <u>do</u> [plumbing] emergencies always <u>happen</u> on the weekends?

2. Toilets, sinks, and tubs <u>seem</u> [to know when plumbers' rates go up].

3. Some emergencies—a slow-[draining] sink, for instance—<u>can be tolerated</u> for a couple of days.

4. And a [dripping] shower faucet <u>may cause</u> annoyance, but not panic.

5. However, a [backed]-up sewer pipe definitely <u>can't wait</u> until Monday.

6. No one <u>wants</u> [to see that water [rising] and [overflowing] the rim of the bowl].

7. At that point, the only question <u>is</u> which "rooter" service [to call].

8. [Finding the main drainage line] often <u>takes</u> more time than [clearing it].

9. Once the plumber <u>has finished</u> [fixing the problem], he or she usually <u>eyes</u> future potential disasters and <u>offers</u> [to prevent them with even more work].

10. After [getting the final bill], I <u>hope</u> that my children <u>will grow</u> up [to be not doctors but plumbers].

Exercise 5

1. In the past, the library <u>was</u> the perfect place [to study] or [to do research or homework].

2. But lately it <u>has become</u> a place [to meet friends].

3. Things <u>changed</u> when students <u>began</u> [to access the Internet].

4. Now two or three students <u>gather</u> near each terminal and <u>show</u> each other the best sites [to visit on the Web].

5. Library officials <u>have designated</u> certain rooms as ["talking areas"].

6. However, such territories <u>are</u> hard [to enforce].

7. The old image of the librarian [telling everyone [to be quiet]] <u>is</u> just that—an old image.

8. So people <u>talk</u> to each other and <u>giggle</u> right there in the [reading] room.

9. One of the librarians <u>told</u> me about a plan [to take the Internet-access computers out of the main study room] and [to put them into the "[talking] areas"].

10. I <u>hate</u> [to read in a noisy room], so I <u>hope</u> that he <u>was</u> right.

Paragraph Exercise

The Wright brothers <u>would have applauded</u> truckdriver Larry Walters's inventiveness. From readily available and inexpensive materials, he <u>built</u> an aircraft, of sorts, <u>flew</u> it to an altitude of 16,000 feet near Long Beach, California, then <u>landed</u> safely. The ninety-minute maiden voyage <u>took</u> place on the sunny morning of July 2, 1982, [fulfilling Walters's twenty-year dream] of a free-[floating] airborne adventure.

The amateur's [flying] machine <u>could</u> scarcely <u>have been</u> simpler. It <u>consisted</u> of an aluminum lawn chair [buoyed by forty-odd helium weather balloons] [arranged in four tiers]. When Walters <u>took</u> off from his girlfriend's backyard in San Pedro, his equipment <u>included</u> a portable CB radio and a BB pistol, with which he

planned [to pop balloons for his descent]. Sensibly cautious, Walters <u>wore</u> a parachute and, of course, <u>buckled</u> his seat belt before the chair's tether cables <u>were</u>
finally <u>cast</u> off.

Although Walters <u>had</u> no experience [flying any kind of aircraft], he <u>felt</u> reasonably confident that the wind <u>would waft</u> him to the Mojave Desert, [located
some fifty miles northeast of San Pedro]. He <u>was</u> mistaken. His chair <u>zipped</u> upward at a [startling] rate and <u>headed</u> southeast toward Long Beach.

It <u>was</u> chilly up there and dangerous besides, for Walters soon <u>found</u> himself
[bobbing amid commercial jets] [approaching the Long Beach airport]. He
<u>radioed</u> air-traffic controllers, <u>shot</u> ten weather balloons with his BB pistol, and
<u>began</u> his descent, [praying earnestly]. [Floating low over a Long Beach neigh-
borhood], Walters <u>ran</u> into a power line, but the police <u>had seen</u> him [coming]
and <u>had shut</u> off the electricity. He <u>disembarked</u> [unscathed] fifteen miles from his
liftoff point.

Sentence Writing

Your sentences may vary, but make sure that your verbals are not actually the
main verbs of your clauses. You should be able to double underline your real
verbs, as we have done here.

1. [Thinking of a good title] <u>takes</u> time.

2. We <u>spent</u> the morning [folding laundry].

3. I <u>enjoy</u> [skiing in spring] even though the snow <u>is</u> better in winter.

4. I <u>was taught</u> that [marking up a book] <u>is</u> wrong.

5. I <u>would love</u> [to take you to school].

6. I <u>need</u> [to get a good grade on the next quiz].

7. Yesterday, I <u>started</u> [to paste my old photos in a scrapbook].

8. He <u>doesn't have</u> the desire [to exercise regularly].

9. The school <u>canceled</u> the [planned] parking lot next to the library.

10. [Given the opportunity], my dog <u>will escape</u> from our yard.

CORRECTING MISPLACED OR DANGLING MODIFIERS (PP. 132–135)

Exercise 1

1. Digital cameras produce beautiful pictures, *even when taken by amateurs.*

2. *Walking past a bench in the park,* they noticed a wallet.

3. The sentence is correct.

4. *Sitting on a little chair in front of the preschoolers,* the teacher read a story about a scary troll character.

5. *Because I watched television all weekend,* my homework never got done.

6. The sentence is correct.

7. *Although we made it to the movie on time,* our popcorn was stale.

8. The sentence is correct but could be clearer: Geology students *read their textbooks to find out about different kinds of rock formations.*

9. Two shoppers were almost hurt by falling boxes *loaded with potatoes.*

10. *When we went home for the weekend,* our parents took us to all of our favorite places again.

Exercise 2

1. Everyone enjoys eating corndogs *smeared with mustard or ketchup.*

2. *Before we asked for an extension,* the teacher told us that we had a few extra days to finish our papers.

3. *Looking through their binoculars,* they spotted a hawk and its babies.

4. The sentence is correct.

5. I called the doctor *while I was on the roof.*

6. The sentence is correct.

7. *After it screeched to a stop,* I got on the bus and took my seat among the rest of the passengers.

8. I can't eat a hamburger *without onions.*

9. The sentence is correct.

10. We had to write a paragraph *in our notebooks, and the topic was the weather.*

Exercise 3

1. The kids at the party still enjoyed the cake *even though it was baked in an odd-shaped pan.*

2. The sentence is correct.

3. I looked at the baked potato, *loaded with butter and sour cream,* and wondered how I would eat it because I am allergic to dairy products.

4. The sentence is correct.

5. *Unless someone has natural talent,* the violin is almost impossible to learn.

6. *As I was riding on a bus into town,* the sunshine felt warm on my arm.

7. The sentence is correct.

8. I have given up on that comedian *who tells one bad joke after another.*

9. The sentence is correct.

10. I loved *my friends' presents tied with pretty bows.*

Exercise 4

1. *Because I took an aspirin before my nap,* my headache was gone.

2. *I filled my new car's gas tank and drove home.*

3. After thirteen months of planning, *we had a successful reunion.*

4. She wrapped all the gifts *while she was still in her pajamas.*

5. The sentence is correct.

6. The sentence is correct.

7. The children gave *the bunch of daisies* to their teacher.

8. I watched the stone *as it skipped across the water and reached the middle of the lake.*

9. *As he tried to look happy,* his heart was breaking.

10. We saw *weeds all along the sidewalk.*

Exercise 5

1. *Because I felt the thrill of a day at the amusement park,* my blisters didn't bother me.

2. My friends and I saw the new tearjerker, *which is full of touching scenes.*

3. The sentence is correct.

4. Practicing for an hour a day, *she improved her piano playing.*

5. The sentence is correct.

6. *While she was sitting on a bench all day,* an idea came to her.

7. They discovered a new outlet mall *on the road to their cousins' house.*

8. *From his parents,* he felt the pressure of trying to get a good job.

9. The sentence is correct.

10. The sentence is correct.

Proofreading Exercise

Corrections are italicized. Yours may differ slightly.

As I walked into my neighborhood polling place during the last election, a volunteer greeted me and checked my name and address. *Because it was misspelled slightly on their printout, the volunteer couldn't find my name* at first. I pointed to what I thought was my name. At least upside down, *it looked like mine.* But actually, it was another person's name. *Once the printout was turned toward me,* I could see *it* more clearly. My name was there, but it had an extra letter stuck on the end of it. *With a polite smile,* the volunteer handed me a change-of-name form. I filled it out and punched my ballot. Stuck on my wall at home, *my voting receipt reminds me* to check my name carefully when the next election comes around.

FOLLOWING SENTENCE PATTERNS (PP. 138–141)

Exercise 1

1. Wendy Hasnip (S) lives (AV) (in England).

2. She (S) does not speak (AV) French (Obj).

3. (At the age) (of forty-seven), Hasnip (S) had (AV) a stroke (Obj).

4. (For two weeks) (after the stroke), she (S) could not talk (AV).

5. Eventually, Hasnip (S) regained (AV) her speaking ability (Obj).

6. But suddenly, she (S) spoke (AV) (with a distinct French accent).

               S   LV

7. Strangely, this <u>condition</u> <u>is</u> a known—but extremely rare—post-brain-injury

   Desc

symptom.

        S   AV Obj

8. <u>Doctors</u> <u>call</u> it the Foreign Accent Syndrome.

        S   AV

9. One <u>man</u> (in Russia) <u>recovered</u> (from a brain injury).

      S   AV   AV   Obj

10. Now <u>he</u> can <u>speak</u> and <u>understand</u> ninety-three languages.

Exercise 2

               S   LV   Desc

1. Local news <u>programs</u> <u>are</u> all alike.

      S   AV

2. <u>They</u> <u>begin</u> (with the top stories) (of the day).

          S   LV   Desc   Desc   Desc

3. These <u>stories</u> <u>may be</u> local, national, or international.

      S   AV   Obj   Obj   Obj

4. <u>They</u> <u>might include</u> violent crimes, traffic jams, natural disasters, and political

   Obj

upheavals.

                     S   AV   Obj

5. (After the top stories), <u>one</u> (of the anchors) <u>offers</u> a quick weather update.

               S   AV   Obj   Obj

6. Then a <u>sportscaster</u> <u>covers</u> the latest scores and team standings.

                             S   AV   Obj

7. (At some point), a "human interest" <u>story</u> <u>lightens</u> the mood (of the broadcast).

              S   AV   Obj

8. And then <u>we</u> <u>hear</u> the latest entertainment news.

                             S   AV

9. (Near the end) (of the half hour), the <u>weatherperson</u> <u>gives</u> the full weather

   Obj

forecast.

       S   AV   Obj

10. News <u>programs</u> <u>could use</u> an update (of their own).

Exercise 3

       S   S   AV

1. My <u>friend</u> and <u>I</u> <u>studied</u> (in the library) yesterday.

    S   AV

2. <u>We</u> <u>stopped</u> (at the "New Books" shelf).

   S AV   Obj

3. <u>I</u> <u>found</u> so many books (of interest) there.

    S   AV   Obj

4. <u>One</u> (of them) <u>traced</u> the history (of tools).

        S   LV   Desc

5. Another <u>book</u> <u>was</u> a collection (of essays) (about children and sports).

       S   LV   Desc

6. <u>Biographies</u> <u>are</u> always interesting (to me).

   S   AV Obj

7. <u>I</u> especially <u>love</u> books (about art and artists).

        S   S   AV Obj

8. The <u>pictures</u> and <u>stories</u> <u>take</u> me away (from my daily problems).

  S AV   Obj

9. <u>I</u> <u>chose</u> a book (about the life) (of Frida Kahlo).

  S AV   Obj   AV Obj

10. <u>I</u> <u>saw</u> the movie (about her) and <u>liked</u> it a lot.

Exercise 4

        S   AV   Obj

1. Some <u>facts</u> (about coins) (in America) <u>might surprise</u> you.

           S   AV   Obj

2. An average <u>American</u> <u>handles</u> six hundred dollars (in coins) every year.

          S   AV   Obj

3. Most <u>Americans</u> <u>keep</u> small stashes (of pennies, nickels, dimes, quarters, half-

dollars, and dollar coins) (at home).

           S   LV   Desc

4. The total (of these unused coins) may be ten billion dollars (at any one time).

           S   AV   Obj

5. Researchers have asked people (about their coin use).

                 S   AV   Obj

6. Some people use coins (in place) (of small tools).

          S   AV   Obj

7. Others perform magic (with them).

                 S   LV   Desc

8. Younger people are more careless (with their coins).

         S   AV   Obj

9. They might toss a penny (in the trash).

               S   AV   Obj

10. Older Americans would save the penny instead.

Exercise 5

            S   LV   Desc   Desc   Desc   Desc

1. Charles Osgood is a writer, editor, TV host, and radio personality.

     S   AV   Obj

2. He has edited a new book.

               S LV   Desc

3. The book's title is *Funny Letters (from Famous People).*

                 S   AV   Obj

4. (In his book), Osgood shares hilarious letters (from history).

         S   AV

5. Thomas Jefferson wrote (to an acquaintance) (about rodents) [eating his wallet].

         S   AV   Obj

6. Benjamin Franklin penned the perfect recommendation letter.

        S   AV   Obj

7. Franklin did not know the recommended fellow (at all).

        S   AV   Obj

8. Beethoven cursed his friend bitterly (in a letter) one day.

                                    S   AV   Obj

9. (In a letter) the following day, Beethoven praised the same friend excessively

           AV   Obj

    and asked him (for a visit).

```
           S      AV      Obj                                      AV        Obj
```
10. <u>Osgood</u> <u>ends</u> the <u>book</u> (with a letter) (by Julia Child) and <u>includes</u> her secrets

(for a long life).

Paragraph Exercise

```
                                    S     AV   Obj
```
Slow (in school) and poor (at math), <u>Edison</u> <u>quit</u> school (at twelve) [to work
```
                    S    AV        Obj                              S    AV
```
as a newsboy (on a train)]. <u>He</u> <u>used</u> his wages [to buy chemicals], for <u>he</u> <u>loved</u>
```
      Obj         S      AV      Obj
```
[experimenting]. <u>He</u> even <u>built</u> a little lab (in the baggage car) (on the train). Later
```
  S    AV                                  AV                              S
```
<u>he</u> <u>worked</u> (as a telegraph operator) and <u>learned</u> (about electricity). (By 1876), <u>he</u>
```
  AV        Obj                       Obj
```
<u>had</u> his own lab and . . . a staggering series (of inventions): a phonograph, a

practical light bulb, a strip (of motion picture film), and many others. (By trial and
```
                                           S       LV
```
error, sleepless nights, and tireless work), <u>Edison</u> <u>became</u> the most productive
```
  Desc                            S          AV   S   LV
```
inventor (of practical devices) that <u>America</u> <u>has</u> ever <u>seen</u>. <u>He</u> <u>was</u> also probably
```
        Desc    S   LV      Desc
```
the only inventor <u>who</u> <u>was</u> as well-known (to every American) as the most famous

movie star. (The word *as* in the last sentence does not begin a prepositional

phrase either time it's used.)

AVOIDING CLICHÉS, AWKWARD PHRASING, AND WORDINESS (PP. 145–151)

Your answers may differ from these possible revisions.

Exercise 1

1. I have a strong will and determination.

2. (Sentence 2 was combined with the previous sentence.)

3. So I knew that I could learn how to juggle.

4. Passing two beanbags from hand to hand was easy.

5. But introducing a third bag was more difficult.

6. I would improve and then fail again.

7. Then a juggler friend gave me some advice.

8. He suggested that I practice the circular movement without catching the bags before I continued.

9. Soon I was juggling three bags without any difficulty.

10. I learned how to juggle with some helpful advice.

Exercise 2

1. I was reading a book the other day about inventions of the 1800s.

2. (Sentence 2 was combined with the previous sentence.)

3. I learned that inventors always have to apply for legal documents called patents.

4. The book described the patents for many useful inventions, such as automobiles, can openers, safety pins, and vending machines.

5. However, other patents were for strange inventions.

6. One example from 1872 described a leather device to cover a man's moustache and keep food out of it at mealtime.

7. Another odd example patented a big stiff fabric parachute for the head and thick spongy pads for the feet in case of emergencies in high places.

8. That inventor made three miscalculations: parachutes should attach to people's bodies; such equipment would be too bulky to carry around, and people wouldn't always land on their feet.

9. As silly as the man's moustache cover was a veil with some pink shading at the cheek areas so that a woman appeared to have rosy cheeks even from outside her black veil.

10. The drawings used to illustrate these old inventions were the best part of the book.

Exercise 3

1. Many supermarket shoppers want organic meats and vegetables.

2. They will buy fresh, canned, or packaged organic foods.

3. I've learned about shoppers' preferences by working at a busy supermarket.

4. Most shoppers prefer foods grown without pesticides and hormones.

5. (Sentence 5 was combined with the previous sentence.)

6. People care about what they eat and what their children eat.

7. I enjoy the taste of organic eggs.

8. I also feel good that the eggs come from happy, free-ranging chickens.

9. Price will always affect some people's choices.

10. These people will not buy organic foods if they cost more than traditionally grown foods.

Exercise 4

1. I just saw a news story about an unusual animal.

2. It resembles a teddy bear, a little monkey, and a miniature dog.

3. I found out that this animal is a celebrity with his own Web site.

4. His name is Mr. Winkle, and even his owner doesn't know what he is.

5. Questions flash across his loading Web page: Is it an "alien?" a "stuffed animal?" a "hamster with a permanent?"

6. Certainly, he is cute.

7. I can understand why his owner took him home after finding him by the side of the road one day.

8. Since then, she has photographed him wearing quirky costumes and even running in a hamster wheel.

9. Of course, pictures of Mr. Winkle fill posters and calendars, which can be purchased at reasonable prices.

10. His Web address is simply mrwinkle.com.

Exercise 5

1. As with any widely used service, network television must respond to its viewers.

2. Nearly everyone watches some network television.

3. Such a broad audience demands a wide range of programming.

4. To satisfy everyone, TV would have to offer a separate channel for each person.

5. Products that do let people customize their viewing are expensive.

6. Network TV is free, so it is difficult to criticize.

7. Watching a "typical" person have a life-altering experience with paper towels is the price we pay for free TV.

8. In truth, the commercials are often more educational and entertaining than the regular programs.

9. And Americans can watch TV whenever they want.

10. The American people need diverse programming to satisfy most of the people most of the time.

Proofreading Exercise

Your revisions may vary, but here is one possibility:

I have a friend who used to be a struggling actor, but now she has become a professional house sitter. First, she joined a house sitters' organization that advertises house-sitting opportunities. My friend's first house-sitting job was in Malibu. Unbelievably, she was paid to live in a house on the beach, eat free food, and watch free movies. All she had to do was stay at the house and feed the owners' indoor cat. Now my friend is house-sitting in Sedona for friends of the owners of the Malibu house. I am thinking seriously of becoming a house sitter myself.

CORRECTING FOR PARALLEL STRUCTURE (PP. 153–158)

Your revisions may vary.

Exercise 1

1. I started preparations for my winter vacation last week and realized that my luggage and cold-weather coat are completely inadequate for a trip to Chicago.

2. The sentence is correct but could be shortened: My brother lives in "The Windy City" and says that it gets very cold there.

3. Temperatures in San Francisco hardly ever dip below the thirties or forties.

4. The jacket I normally use is lightweight and unlined.

5. I'll need to buy a coat made of down or fleece, like the ones that skiers wear.

6. My soft-bodied, duffel-bag style suitcases are inadequate as well; they have several outer compartments closed by zippers.

7. These cases may be appropriate for car trips but not for plane travel.

8. The sentence is correct.

9. I don't want to worry about things being stolen or a pocket ripping.

10. As a result of these deficiencies, I'm currently looking for new luggage and a proper winter coat.

Exercise 2

1. The sentence is correct.

2. The sentence is correct. (Or: McNally won the title and a prize of over fifteen thousand dollars.)

3. Before winning the national title, McNally and forty-seven fellow contestants traveled on a special train.

4. The chartered train, called the "Reading Railroad," ran from Chicago to Atlantic City.

5. The outside of the train was decorated with images from the Monopoly board: the property cards, the playing pieces, the "Chance" and "Community Chest" cards.

6. Contestants played Monopoly on the train: those who lost became spectators; those who won went on to compete in the championship games in Atlantic City.

7. The prize money included $1,000 for fourth place, $2,500 for third place, $5,000 for second place, and $15,140 for first place. The first-place prize equals the amount of fake money in a Monopoly game.

8. To participate in the Monopoly Championship, contestants had to visit the Monopoly site online and take a quiz or be previous competitors in Monopoly championships.

9. Matt turns out to be a lucky name and a lucky spelling for would-be Monopoly champions.

10. The sentence is correct.

Exercise 3

1. The sentence is correct.

2. It has a plush lounge that offers free coffee, cookies, and even pretzels for those who don't like sweets.

3. The sentence is correct.

4. Full plate-glass windows line the front wall of the lounge so that people can see their vehicles being dried and check out the cars of the people around them.

5. For those who don't like to sit down, a full assortment of greeting cards and car accessories lines the back wall of the lounge.

6. To keep things interesting, every hour there is a drawing for a free car wash, but I have never won one.

7. The sentence is correct.

8. Why do people talk on cell phones when they could be resting, and why do some people stand up when they could be sitting on a nice leather sofa?

9. The sentence is correct.

10. It's the modern equivalent of going to the barbershop or getting a new hairdo at the beauty parlor.

Exercise 4

1. The sentence is correct.

2. Joining the scientists were car-sized robots and massive computers that worked continuously to analyze the most basic structures of human tissues.

3. The genome project has already cost nearly four billion dollars and has taken ten years to complete.

4. The sentence is correct.

5. The code is made up of billions of combinations of letters standing for four different chemicals: "A" for adenine, "C" for cystosine, "G" for guanine, and "T" for thymine.

6. The sentence is correct.

7. Within DNA, genes are the smaller groupings of chemicals that instruct the different cells of the body, but the genome includes fifty thousand genes.

8. The sentence is correct.

9. The future of human life, disease, and longevity may all be affected once the experts begin to identify the individual genes.

10. Some people look forward to that day optimistically, but others fear it.

Exercise 5

1. The U.S. Surgeon General makes the following recommendations for living a healthy and happy life.

2. Eating well is one way to enhance your life, especially if your daily intake includes the right amount of fruits and vegetables and the right amount of meat and dairy products (or their vegetarian equivalents).

3. Seeing a doctor regularly and getting all the usual tests and check-ups can lead to a better life as well.

4. Of course, knowing about any illnesses or conditions that run in your family is also very important.

5. Getting enough rest and sleep will obviously help improve your overall health.

6. Along with relaxing, communicating with your friends and family is another recommendation that the Surgeon General makes.

7. Wearing seatbelts and other safety devices such as helmets will help prevent harm that can be avoided.

8. Using drugs and consuming alcohol can have either beneficial or extremely harmful results.

9. Not smoking or breathing in second-hand smoke is the Surgeon General's strongest recommendation.

10. The Surgeon General's recommendations and warnings make very good sense.

Proofreading Exercise

Every year in late spring, a long caravan of vehicles arrives at the park in my neighborhood. The caravan consists of a combination of trucks, campers, vans, and trailers full of folded-up kiddy rides. Everyone who lives by or drives by the park can tell that the fair has come to town. It isn't a big fair, but a small, child-friendly one. Most people remember these fairs from when they were growing up. In childhood, the rides seemed huge and scary; in adulthood, they seem small and almost silly. As the fair is being set up in the park for a few days, the kids in the neighborhood look forward to getting on one of those "wild" rides. Their parents look forward to eating the "fair food": the sweet popcorn, the salty popcorn, the mouth-watering corndogs, the deep-fried candy bars, and the juicy snow cones. I can't wait until next year's fair; I'm getting hungry just thinking about it.

USING PRONOUNS (PP. 163–167)

Exercise 1

1. I	6. I
2. I	7. I, I
3. he and I	8. you and me
4. I	9. him and me
5. he and I, me	10. me

Exercise 2

1. *Good parents* give *their* children advice.

2. their

3. it's

4. *Children* often *look* to *their* parents for guidance in difficult times.

5. For instance, a child might have encountered a bully *in elementary school.*

6. The other schoolchildren might tell the child to keep *quiet* about it.

7. A parent would probably offer *the* child very different advice—to speak to the principal about the problem right away.

8. *Bullies* can only get away with *their* activities if everyone else is too scared or too uninformed to stop *them.*

9. their

10. their, themselves

Exercise 3

1. he

2. us

3. He and she

4. I

5. The ushers wore badges on their jackets.

6. its

7. Members of the club have special duties to perform at the fund-raiser.

8. its

9. she

10. him and me

Exercise 4

1. The sentence is correct.

2. I finished my painting, put my supplies in my art box, and waited for the painting to dry.

3. Kelly told her friend, "There is a backpack on top of your car."

4. Working at the car wash this weekend made us all sore.

5. Trent drove his car to the prom with his father's permission.

6. When I placed my key in the lock, my key broke.

7. Janel didn't like my sister and told her so.

8. As we were spreading the blanket on the grass, the blanket ripped.

wired the pitchers' joints with s
vealed that the energy or force of
on, flows from there to the leg tha
and out the end of the arm that th

2. I was reading about superstitions
   lot of these beliefs concern broo
   whenever *people* change *their* res
   should not take their old brooms
   bad luck that was swept up at the
   people sweep dirt out an open doo
   bad luck will depart forever. If *th*
   luck will come right back in aga
   fallen broomstick unless *they* nev
   anyone who steps over a brooms
   how many things can go wrong w

3. The paragraph is correct.

REVIEW OF SENTENCE STRU

1. A. cliché (I've been working cont
2. B. pro ref (I received a message o
   message.)
3. A. frag (The total, including air f
4. B. dm (*She sneezed so softly that h*
5. B. s/v agr (Neither she nor I *was*
6. A. ro (I had an idea for an invent
7. B. pro agr (*True friends are* not a
8. B. wordy (*The building was extr*
9. A. mm (*When my brother was tw*
10. A. pro (Just between you and *me*
11. B. frag and cliché (*The growth cy*
12. A. shift in time (The porter escor
    basket of goodies waiting for
13. A. ro (Some people like wall cale
14. B. pro (However, we have more
15. A. wordy (I received *a unique gif*

---

ossibility:

volved

siness can be both right and wrong,
tuations. For example, if one friend is
ned, it may be time for the concerned
shows real friendship but might also
ike to be nosey, and they get involved
ople need to know the details of oth-
esting. I have been in situations where
nd problems. All of their discoveries
stakes, I would never get involved in
fit them in some way. People should
ut anyone else's.

LETTERS

**AMATION POINT,
175–179)**

ce that your alarm did not go off.
to your first class: skip your shower,
alk out the door without coffee or
's seat, and turn the key; your car bat-
ur friend Tracy; she has a reliable car.
like you—answers the phone out of a
ready gone to school.
et her message as usual. (or —as usual.)
ailed; there is only one option left.
fast; you sit in front of the TV and

Exercise 2

1. What have spiders done for you lately?

2. In the near future, a spider may save your life. (or !)

3. Researchers in New York have discovered the healing power of one species in particular: the Chilean Rose tarantula.

4. This spider's venom includes a substance that could stop a human's heart attack once it begins.

5. The substance has the ability to restore the rhythm of a heart that has stopped beating.

6. A scientist in Connecticut is experimenting with the killing power of another arachnid; the creature he is studying is the Australian funnel-web spider.

7. Currently, pesticides that destroy insects on crops also end up killing animals accidentally.

8. The funnel-web spider's venom is lethal to unwanted insects; however, it's harmless to animals.

9. Scientists would have to reproduce the funnel-web spider's venom artificially in order to have enough to use in fields.

10. As a result of these studies into the power of spider venom, you may live longer and enjoy pesticide-free foods.

Exercise 3

1. The change from one millennium to another has prompted us to look back over the twentieth century and wonder what its most important elements were.

2. Writers of history books—whose usual topics are influential people—are choosing these days to write about indispensable things.

3. The twentieth century saw the rise of two particularly important objects: the banana and the pointed screw.

4. Virginia Scott Jenkins has written *Bananas: An American History.*

5. And Witold Rybczynski is the author of *One Good Turn: A Natural History of the Screwdriver and the Screw.*

6. Jenkins' book includes facts and stories about the banana's rise in popularity during the twentieth century in America.

7. Before 1900, the banana was an unfamiliar fruit in the United States; now each American consumes about seventy-five bananas per year. (or !)

8. Rybczynski points out that the basic ideas for the screwdriver and the screw have been around since the ancient Greeks; however, screws did not have sharpened points until the twentieth century.

9. So for thousands of years, builders had to drill holes first; only then could they get the screws' threads to take hold.

10. Where would we be without bananas and self-starting screws?

Exercise 4

1. Thunderstorms are spectacular demonstrations of nature's power.

2. Do you know where the safest places are during a thunderstorm?

3. One relatively safe place is inside a building that has plumbing pipes or electrical wires; those channels can absorb the electrical energy unleashed by lightning.

4. Of course, once inside such a building, people should stay away from the end sources of plumbing and wiring: faucets, hoses, phone receivers, and computer terminals.

5. Buildings without pipes or wires are not safe shelters during lightning strikes; these might include pergolas, dugouts, and tents.

6. Outside, lightning can move over the ground; therefore, you should be aware of a position that emergency officials call the "lightning squat."

7. This emergency position involves curling up into the smallest ball you can while balancing on the balls of your feet and covering your ears.

8. That way, there is less of you in contact with the ground if lightning strikes.

9. Lightning is electrical energy; consequently, it can travel far from the actual storm clouds.

10. In fact, lightning has struck as far as twenty miles away from the storm that caused it.

Exercise 5

1. "Daddy, am I going to get old like Grandpa?"

2. This question is typical of the ones children ask their parents about aging; luckily, there are books that help parents answer them.

3. Lynne S. Dumas wrote the book *Talking with Your Children about a Troubled World;* in it, she discusses children's concerns and suggests ways of dealing with them.

4. In response to the question about getting old "like Grandpa," Dumas stresses one main point: be positive. (or —be positive.)

5. Too often, Dumas says, parents pass their own fears on to children; parents who focus on the negative aspects of aging will probably have children who worry about growing old.

6. Other subjects—homelessness, for instance—require special consideration for parents.

7. Dumas explains that children carefully observe how parents deal with a person asking for spare change or offering to wash windshields for money.

8. The unplanned nature of these encounters often catches parents off guard; therefore, they should try to prepare a uniform response to such situations.

9. Dumas also suggests that parents take positive action—involving children in charitable donations and activities, for example—in order to illustrate their compassion for the homeless.

10. The most important aspect in communicating with children is honesty; the second and third most important are patience and understanding.

Proofreading Exercise

The ingredients you will need to make delicious beef stew include beef cubes, potatoes, onions, and carrots; tomatoes are optional. First, at the bottom of a big heavy pot on high heat, you should brown the meat cubes after dusting them with a little flour, salt, and pepper. Once the meat chunks have been browned on all sides; it's time to add the water and seasonings. You can use beef bouillon or beef stew seasoning mix. Or you can add any blend of seasonings to fit your own taste. Next, you put in the vegetables; they should be no larger than bite-sized pieces. Heat the watery stew mixture on medium heat until it begins to boil. Finally, lower the temperature and cook the stew—the longer the better—until a thick and tasty gravy develops. Add a little flour cooked in butter if you need to thicken the broth. Bon appétit!

COMMA RULES 1, 2, AND 3 (PP. 181–186)

Exercise 1

1. Chickens are the subject of riddles, jokes, and sayings.

2. We think of funny ways to respond to the "Why did the chicken cross the road?" question, and we endlessly ponder the answer to "Which came first—the chicken or the egg?"

3. A person who runs around in a hurry is often compared to "a chicken with its head cut off."

4. Although we try not to visualize the image of the last comparison, most people understand the reference to a fowl's final moments of frantic activity.

5. Anyone who has heard the story of Mike "the headless chicken" will consider the popular saying differently from that moment on, for it will come to mean having a strong determination to live in spite of major setbacks.

6. On September 10, 1945, a farmer in Fruita, Colorado, chose one of his chickens to have for dinner that night.

7. But after having his head cut off, the rooster didn't die, didn't seem to be in pain, and continued to act "normally."

8. In fact, Mike went on to become a national celebrity, and his owner took him around the country so that people could see him for themselves.

9. When both *Time* and *Life* magazines ran feature stories complete with photos of Mike in October 1945, the public became fascinated by the details of Mike's ability to eat, drink, hear, and move without a head.

10. Mike lived for eighteen months after his date with a chopping block and would have lived longer, but he died by accidentally choking in 1947.

Exercise 2

1. Whenever I need to borrow some blueberries, an onion, or a teaspoon of ginger, I go next door to my neighbor's apartment.

2. My neighbor's name is Albert, and he is originally from Belgium.

3. Albert always has the season's best fruits, the tastiest vegetables, and the freshest spices.

4. Albert feels comfortable borrowing things from me, too.

5. He doesn't ask for blueberries, onions, or ginger, but he will ask to borrow a hammer, a wrench, or a Phillips-head screwdriver.

6. The sentence is correct.

7. If I buy myself a new dustpan, I buy an extra one for Albert.

8. When he visits the farmer's market on Thursdays, Albert picks up an extra basket of strawberries for me.

9. The sentence is correct.

10. Whatever one of us doesn't buy, the other one will.

Exercise 3

1. As if people didn't have enough to worry about, Melinda Muse has written a book called *I'm Afraid, You're Afraid: 448 Things to Fear and Why.*

2. In her book, Muse points out the dangers of common places, objects, foods, months, days, and activities.

3. One place that the author warns about is Las Vegas casinos, and the reason is that paramedics can't get to ailing gamblers due to the crowds and huge size of the buildings.

4. Another dangerous spot is the beauty parlor, where people suffer strokes caused by leaning their heads back too far into the shampoo sink.

5. New clothes need to be washed before they are worn, or they may transfer dangerous chemicals to the wearers' eyes, skin, and lungs.

6. Grapefruit juice can interfere with certain medications' effectiveness, and nutmeg contains hallucinogenic substances, so these are among the foods to be avoided.

7. The sentence is correct.

8. Mondays have two dangerous distinctions, for more suicides and heart attacks occur on Mondays than on any other day of the week.

9. The sentence is correct.

10. After reading *I'm Afraid, You're Afraid,* it's possible to be afraid of almost everything.

Exercise 4

1. Speaking of worst-case scenarios, there is a book about how to survive them, and it's called *The Worst-Case Scenario Survival Handbook.*

2. The coauthors of this self-help book are aware that most of us will never have to overpower an alligator or make an emergency landing on an airplane, yet they want us to be prepared nonetheless.

3. In the "About the Authors" section of the book, readers learn that Joshua Piven is a first-time writer, but he has survived encounters with robbers, muggers, and stalled subway trains.

4. About Piven's coauthor, we discover that David Borgenicht has written two other books and has had his share of worst-case scenarios, especially while traveling.

5. Although the overall tone of the book is somewhat humorous because it covers such outlandish topics, the information it shares is deadly serious and could save a life.

6. The sentence is correct.

7. One of the best examples illustrates a way to avoid being attacked by a mountain lion, and that is to try to appear as large as possible, so the drawing shows a man holding the sides of his jacket out wide like bat wings to scare the lion away.

8. If readers wonder whether they can trust the advice on escaping from quicksand, they can just flip to the list of sources consulted for each section, in this case an expert on the physics of natural phenomena at the University of Sydney, Australia.

9. Wisely, Piven and Borgenicht begin the book by warning readers to seek professional help whenever possible instead of trying the survival techniques themselves.

10. The authors know that if people go looking for trouble, they'll probably find it.

Exercise 5

1. Fish may be considered "brain food," but I've never liked it.

2. While everyone is saying how delicious a big salmon steak is or how yummy the shrimp tastes, you'll find me grimacing and munching on a piece of bread and butter.

3. Part of the problem with fish is the smell, but my friends who love to eat fish also love the smell of fish cooking.

4. I always thought that was strange, but it makes sense, doesn't it?

5. If someone hates the taste of onions, that person probably also hates the smell of onions cooking.

6. Come to think of it, my husband hates to eat sweets and doesn't like the smell of them either.

7. When we walk into a bakery together, he practically has to hold his nose the way I would in a fish market.

8. To me, that's odd, but my aversion must be just as odd to someone who loves fish.

9. Our daughter loves the taste of bacon, but she hates the smell of bacon frying.

10. The sentence is correct.

Proofreading Exercise

During the last thirty years of the twentieth century, the number of broken arm injuries rose more than forty percent in Rochester, Minnesota. Experts at the Mayo Clinic studied the number of forearm bone fractures during that time, and they found that young people are the most susceptible to these injuries. Between the ages of ten and sixteen, youngsters break their arms while skating, skiing, and participating in team sports. Looking for a reason for the startling rise in the number of broken arm bones, researchers point to the common practice of drinking sodas instead of milk. Young people are getting less calcium, and their bones may be paying the price.

Sentence Writing

Here are some possible revisions. Yours may differ.

The test was long and difficult, but most students completed it on time.

Since the gardeners arrive and start up their leaf blowers at 7:00 in the morning, no one in the neighborhood can sleep in anymore.

When I was a child in the 1960s, people rode in cars without seatbelts, without protective car seats for children, and without air bags.

COMMA RULES 4, 5, AND 6 (PP. 189–194)

For Exercises 1 and 2, correct sentences remain in the answers without commas for the sake of comparison.

Exercise 1

1. This year's office party, I believe, was worse than last year's.

2. I believe this year's office party was worse than last year's.

3. Lee's lasagna, however, was better than ever.

4. However Lee's lasagna was better than ever. (or However, Lee's lasagna was better . . .)

5. The clerk who works in the claims division didn't bring a dessert even though he signed up for one.

6. Justin Banks, who works in the claims division, didn't bring a dessert even though he signed up for one.

7. And Mr. Hopkins, who planned the party, needed to think of a few more party games.

8. And the person who planned the party needed to think of a few more party games.

9. As usual, no one, it seems, had time to decorate beyond a few balloons.

10. As usual, it seems that no one had time to decorate beyond a few balloons.

Exercise 2

1. We hope, of course, that people will honor their summons for jury duty.

2. Of course we hope that people will honor their summons for jury duty.

3. People who serve as jurors every time they're called deserve our appreciation.

4. Thelma and Trevor Martin, who serve as jurors every time they're called, deserve our appreciation.

5. We should therefore be as understanding as we can be about the slow legal process.

6. Therefore, we should be as understanding as we can be about the slow legal process.

7. A legal system that believes people are innocent until proven guilty must offer a trial-by-jury option.

8. The U.S. legal system, which believes people are innocent until proven guilty, offers a trial-by-jury option.

9. With that option, we hope that no one will receive an unfair trial.

10. With that option, no one, we hope, will receive an unfair trial.

Exercise 3

1. Bobble-head dolls, those figurines with heads that bob up and down, have become the souvenir of choice for many modern teams and companies.

2. The sentence is correct.

3. Others say these types of ceramic nodding figures, called "nodder" dolls in Europe, originated there in the 1800s.

4. Much more recently, in the 1960s to be exact, Japan began producing what some call "bobbinheads" as souvenirs to sell at baseball parks in the United States.

5. The sentence is correct.

6. Two of the most famous people of the twentieth century, President Kennedy and Elvis Presley, were immortalized as bobble-head dolls.

7. The sentence is correct.

8. Now some cereal boxes, traditionally the showplaces for athletic triumphs, include tiny bobble-heads as prizes inside.

9. Even William Rehnquist, Chief Justice of the U.S. Supreme Court, has a bobble-head doll in his likeness.

10. The Rehnquist bobble-head, a must-have for any nodding-doll collector, was commissioned by a law journal to encourage people to read about legal issues.

Exercise 4

1. The Ironman competition, one of the most grueling athletic races in the world, takes place in Hawaii every year.

2. The sentence is correct.

3. The sentence is correct.

4. As if that race weren't enough for some fitness fanatics, it is followed soon after by the XTerra World Championship, another attraction for triathletes from around the world.

5. The Xterra, an obstacle course through the extreme Hawaiian landscape, takes participants over ocean waves, blistering sand, dried lava, fallen tree limbs, exposed roots, and huge chunks of coral.

6. The sentence is correct.

7. Some triathletes participate in both races, Ironman and Xterra, in what triathletes refer to as The Double.

8. The sentence is correct.

9. The sentence is correct.

10. However, the male and female athletes with the best times overall in both races are considered winners of the The Double; they earn a thousand dollars and an invaluable title, World's Toughest Athlete.

Exercise 5

1. One of the weirdest competitions on earth, the Wife Carrying World Championships, takes place in Finland once a year.

2. These load-carrying races, which may have begun as training rituals for Finnish soldiers, have become popular in the United States and all over the world.

3. Each pair of participants, made up of one man and one "wife," has to make it through an obstacle course in the shortest time possible.

4. The "wife" half of the team has to weigh at least 49 kilos, 108 pounds.

5. She does not have to be married to the man who carries her; she can, indeed, be someone else's wife or even unmarried.

6. The wife-carrying course includes two sections, a part on land and a part in water.

7. The sentence is correct.

8. The wife-dropping penalty, which is fifteen seconds added to the pair's time, is enough to disqualify most couples.

9. Contest officials allow one piece of equipment, a belt that the man can wear so that the "wife" has something to hold on to during the race.

10. The winning couple wins a prize, but the coveted title, Wife Carrying World Champion, is reward enough for most.

Proofreading Exercise

There are two types of punctuation, internal punctuation and end punctuation. Internal punctuation is used within the sentence, and end punctuation is used at the end of the sentence. There are six main rules for the placement of commas, the most important pieces of internal punctuation. Semicolons, the next most important, have two main functions. Their primary function, separating two independent clauses, is also the most widely known. A lesser-known need for semicolons, to separate items in a list already containing commas, occurs rarely in college writing. Colons and dashes have special uses within sentences. And of the three pieces of end punctuation—periods, question marks, and exclamation points—one is obviously the most common. That piece is the period, which signals the end of the majority of English sentences.

Sentence Writing

Here are some possible combinations. Yours may differ.

I think that restaurant's dress code is old-fashioned and may be bad for business. (or) That restaurant's dress code, I think, is old-fashioned and may be bad for business.

He bought a pack of gum in cinnamon, his favorite flavor. (or) He bought a pack of his favorite cinnamon-flavored gum.

Molly Price, a woman standing on the corner at the time, answered the question correctly and won a thousand dollars in cash. (or) A woman named Molly Price was standing on the corner at the time, answered the question correctly, and won a thousand dollars in cash.

Comma Review Exercise

We're writing you this e-mail, Lena, to give you directions to the reunion this weekend. [4] We know that you will be driving with a few others, but we want to be sure that everyone knows the way. [1] When we contacted some of our classmates over the Internet several of the messages were returned as "undeliverable." [3] We hope, therefore, that this one gets through to you. [5] We can't wait to see everyone again: Michelle, Tom, Olivia, and Brad. [2] Dr. Milford, our favorite professor, will be there to welcome all of the returning students. [6]

QUOTATION MARKS AND UNDERLINING/ITALICS (PP. 197–202)

Exercise 1

1. I am reading a book called <u>Don't: A Manual of Mistakes & Improprieties More or Less Prevalent in Conduct and Speech</u>.

2. The book's contents are divided into chapters with titles such as "At Table," "In Public," and "In General."

3. In the section about table don'ts, the book offers the following warning: "Don't bend over your plate, or drop your head to get each mouthful."

4. The table advice continues by adding, "Don't bite your bread. Break it off."

5. This book offers particularly comforting advice about conducting oneself in public.

6. For instance, it states, "Don't brush against people, or elbow people, or in any way show disregard for others."

7. When meeting others on the street, the book advises, "Don't be in a haste to introduce. Be sure that it is mutually desired before presenting one person to another."

8. In the section titled "In General," there are more tips about how to get along in society, such as "Don't underrate everything that others do, and overstate your own doings."

9. The <u>Don't</u> book has this to say about books, whether borrowed or owned: "Read them, but treat them as friends that must not be abused."

10. And one can never take the following warning too much to heart: "Don't make yourself in any particular way a nuisance to your neighbors or your family."

Exercise 2

1. "Have you been to the bookstore yet?" Monica asked.

2. "No, why?" I answered.

3. "They've rearranged the books," she said, "and now I can't find anything."

4. "Are all of the books for one subject still together?" I wondered.

5. "Yes, they are," Monica told me, "but there are no markers underneath the books to say which teacher's class they're used in, so it's really confusing."

6. "Why don't we just wait until the teachers show us the books and then buy them?" I replied.

7. "That will be too late!" Monica shouted.

8. "Calm down," I told her, "you are worrying for nothing."

9. "I guess so," she said once she took a deep breath.

10. "I sure hope I'm not wrong," I thought to myself, "or Monica will really be mad at me."

Exercise 3

1. "Stopping by Woods on a Snowy Evening" is a poem by Robert Frost.

2. "Once you finish your responses," the teacher said, "bring your test papers up to my desk."

3. I subscribe to several periodicals, including <u>Time</u> and <u>U.S. News & World Report</u>.

4. "Our country is the world," William Lloyd Garrison believed, "our country-men are all mankind."

5. "Do you know," my teacher asked, "that there are only three ways to end a sentence?"

6. Edward Young warned young people to "Be wise with speed. A fool at forty is a fool indeed."

7. In Shakespeare's play <u>Romeo and Juliet</u>, Mercutio accidentally gets stabbed and shouts, "A plague on both your houses!"

8. "There is no such thing as a moral or an immoral book," Oscar Wilde writes in his novel <u>The Picture of Dorian Gray</u>; "Books are either well written, or badly written."

9. Molière felt that "One should eat to live, and not live to eat."

10. Did you say, "I'm sleepy" or "I'm beeping"?

Exercise 4

1. <u>Women's Wit and Wisdom</u> is the title of a book I found in the library.

2. The book includes many great insights that were written or spoken by women throughout history.

3. England's Queen Elizabeth I noted in the sixteenth century that "A clear and innocent conscience fears nothing."

4. "Nothing is so good as it seems beforehand," observed George Eliot, a female author whose real name was Mary Ann Evans.

5. Some of the women's quotations are funny; Alice Roosevelt Longworth, for instance, said, "If you don't have anything good to say about anyone, come and sit by me."

6. "If life is a bowl of cherries," asked Erma Bombeck, "what am I doing in the pits?"

7. Some of the quotations are serious, such as Gloria Steinem's statement, "The future depends on what each of us does every day."

8. Maya Lin, the woman who designed Washington D.C.'s Vietnam Veterans Memorial, reminded us that, as she put it, "War is not just a victory or a loss. . . . People die."

9. Emily Dickinson had this to say about truth: "Truth is such a rare thing, it is delightful to tell it."

10. Finally, columnist Ann Landers advised one of her readers that "The naked truth is always better than the best-dressed lie."

Exercise 5

1. In his book <u>Who's Buried in Grant's Tomb? A Tour of Presidential Gravesites</u>, Brian Lamb records the final words of American presidents who have passed away.

2. Some of their goodbyes were directed at their loved ones; for example, President Zachary Taylor told those around him, "I regret nothing, but I am sorry that I am about to leave my friends."

3. Other presidents, such as William Henry Harrison, who died after only one month in office, addressed more political concerns; Harrison said, "I wish you to understand the true principles of the government. I wish them carried out. I ask for nothing more."

4. John Tyler became president due to Harrison's sudden death; Tyler served his term, lived to be seventy-one, and said, "Perhaps it is best" when his time came.

5. At the age of eighty-three, Thomas Jefferson fought to live long enough to see the fiftieth anniversary of America's independence; on that day in 1826, Jefferson was one of only three (out of fifty-six) signers of the "Declaration of Independence" still living, and he asked repeatedly before he died, "Is it the fourth?"

6. John Adams, one of the other three remaining signers, died later the same day—July 4, 1826—and his last words ironically were "Thomas Jefferson still survives."

7. The third president to die on the Fourth of July (1831) was James Monroe; while he was president, people within the government got along so well that his time in office was known as "the era of good feelings."

8. Doctors attempted to help James Madison live until the Fourth of July, but he put off their assistance; on June 26, 1836, when a member of his family became alarmed at his condition, Madison comforted her by saying, "Nothing more than a change of mind, my dear," and he passed away.

9. Grover Cleveland, who had suffered from many physical problems, was uneasy at his death; before losing consciousness, he said, "I have tried so hard to do right."

10. Finally, George Washington, our first president, also suffered greatly but faced death bravely; "I die hard," he told the people by his bedside, "but I am not afraid to go. 'Tis well."

Proofreading Exercise

We read part of <u>The Autobiography of Benjamin Franklin</u> in class the other day. In the section we read, Franklin spells out the details of his concept of "Order": "Let all your things have their places; let each part of your business have its time." Then a few pages later, he includes a chart of what he calls the twenty-four hours of a natural day. Along with the notations of "Work," "Read," and "Sleep" that Franklin filled in were two questions to consider. At the start of each new day, he would ask himself, "What good shall I do this day?" And at the end of each day, he would ask, "What good have I done to-day?" After reading this brief section of Franklin's <u>Autobiography,</u> I am not surprised that he accomplished so much during his lifetime.

CAPITAL LETTERS (PP. 204–208)

In this section, titles of larger works are italicized rather than underlined.

Exercise 1

1. I have always wanted to learn another language besides English.

2. Right now, I am taking English 410 in addition to my writing class.

3. The course title for English 410 is Basic Grammar.

4. English 410 is a one-unit, short-term class designed to help students with their verb forms, parts of speech, phrases, and clauses.

5. I hope that learning more about English grammar will help me understand the grammar of another language more easily.

6. Now I must decide whether I want to take Spanish, French, Italian, or Chinese.

7. I guess I could even take a class in Greek or Russian.

8. When I was in high school, I did take French for two years, but my clearest memory is of the teacher, Mrs. Gautier.

9. She was one of the best teachers that Hillside High School ever had.

10. Unfortunately, I did not study hard enough and can't remember most of the French that Mrs. Gautier taught me.

Exercise 2

1. When people think of jazz, they think of *Down Beat* magazine.

2. *Down Beat*'s motto may be "Jazz, Blues & Beyond," but some people think that the magazine has gone too far "beyond" by including two guitarists in the *Down Beat* Hall of Fame.

3. The two musicians in question are Jimi Hendrix and Frank Zappa.

4. Jimi Hendrix was inducted into the Hall of Fame in 1970.

5. *Down Beat* added Frank Zappa to the list in 1994.

6. Since then, readers and editors have been debating whether Hendrix and Zappa belong in the same group as Duke Ellington, John Coltrane, and Miles Davis.

7. Those who play jazz guitar have some of the strongest opinions on the subject.

8. Russell Malone, Mark Elf, and John Abercrombie all agree that Hendrix and Zappa were great guitarists but not jazz guitarists.

9. Others like Steve Tibbetts and Bill Frisell don't have any problem putting Hendrix on the list, but Tibbetts isn't so sure about including Zappa.

10. It will be interesting to see who *Down Beat*'s future inductees will be.

Exercise 3

1. I grew up watching *It's a Wonderful Life* once a year on TV in the winter.

2. That was before the colorized version and before every station started showing it fifteen times a week throughout the months of November and December.

3. I especially remember enjoying that holiday classic with my mother and brothers when we lived on Seventh Avenue.

4. "Hurry up!" Mom would yell, "You're going to miss the beginning!"

5. My favorite part has always been when Jimmy Stewart's character, George Bailey, uses his own money to help the people of Bedford Falls and to save his father's Building and Loan.

6. George's disappointment turns to happiness after he and Donna Reed's character, Mary, move into the abandoned house on their honeymoon.

7. Of course, mean old Mr. Potter takes advantage of Uncle Billy's carelessness at the bank, and that starts George's breakdown.

8. In his despair, George places the petals of his daughter Zuzu's flower in his pocket, leaves his house, and wants to commit suicide.

9. Luckily, all of George's good deeds have added up over the years, and he is given a chance to see that thanks to a character named Clarence.

10. When George feels Zuzu's petals in his pocket, he knows that he's really made it home again, and the people of Bedford Falls come to help him.

Exercise 4

1. Most people don't know the name Elzie Crisler Segar.

2. Segar was the creator of the comic character Popeye.

3. Segar based Popeye and many of his fellow characters on residents of the town of Chester, Illinois, where Segar was born.

4. Popeye's inspiration was a Chester bartender named Frank "Rocky" Fiegel.

5. Fiegel was a brawler by nature and might have even been a sailor at some point.

6. Segar learned how to draw by taking a correspondence course.

7. One of Segar's bosses at a Chester movie house, J. William Schuchert, was the prototype for Wimpy.

8. Segar introduced Olive Oyl's character in his *Thimble Theater* comic strip.

9. Olive was based on a Chester store owner, Dora Paskel.

10. The town of Chester celebrates the work of Elzie Crisler Segar with a yearly Popeye picnic, the Popeye Museum, a Popeye statue, and Segar Memorial Park.

Exercise 5

1. Helen Hunt has been acting on TV and in movies since she was nine years old.

2. She portrayed the cyclone-chasing scientist named Jo Harding in *Twister.*

3. She gave an Oscar-winning performance alongside Jack Nicholson in *As Good as It Gets.*

4. Her most recognizable and long-lasting TV character so far has been Jamie Buckman in *Mad about You,* which costarred Paul Reiser.

5. Having wanted to act with Kevin Spacey since she saw *American Beauty,* Hunt took the part of Haley Joel Osment's mom in *Pay It Forward.*

6. She also worked with famous director Robert Altman and actor Richard Gere on the film *Dr. T and the Women.*

7. Hunt played Tom Hanks' love interest in *Cast Away.*

8. She and Mel Gibson starred together in the romantic comedy *What Women Want.*

9. In addition to acting, Hunt loves the Olympics and even worked event tickets into her contract with NBC while she was making *Mad about You.*

10. Hunt has collected souvenir pins like any normal fan at the Olympic games in Atlanta and in Sydney, Australia.

REVIEW OF PUNCTUATION AND CAPITAL LETTERS (P. 209)

1. Tower Bridge is one of the most famous landmarks in London.

2. Have you ever read E. B. White's essay "Goodbye to 48th Street"?

3. Constance and Jennifer drove up the coast from Los Angeles to San Francisco.

4. "How many years of Spanish have you taken?" my counselor asked.

5. We received your application, Ms. Tomkins; we would like you to call us to set up an appointment for an interview.

6. The person who wins the contest will fly to Italy.

7. I am majoring in architecture, and my best friend is in the Nursing Program.

8. Due to the shortage of qualified applicants, the financial aid office has extended its deadline.

9. The drama club needs new costumes, new sets, and new scripts.

10. Neil Armstrong said the famous words, "One small step for man, one giant leap for mankind," at the moment when he first set foot on the moon.

11. My parents gave me the following advice: "Trust your own instincts whenever you face difficult decisions."

12. We need a new car; however, we can't afford one right now.

13. "Because I Could Not Stop for Death" is a famous poem by Emily Dickinson.

14. J. K. Rowling is the author of the <u>Harry Potter</u> books.

15. The overlooked bus passenger ran into the street and yelled, "Come back here!"

COMPREHENSIVE TEST (PP. 210–211)

1. (ww) The scary scenes in the movie really *affected* me; I couldn't sleep that night.

2. (sp) The police asked us what time the theft had *occurred.*

3. (wordy and awk) *We can solve our money problems.*

4. (cap) Last semester, I took art history, *Spanish,* and geography.

5. (pro) The department store hired my friend and *me* as gift wrappers for the holidays.

6. (//) In just six weeks, we learned to find main ideas, to remember details, and *to integrate* new words into our vocabulary.

7. (ro) The chairs should be straightened, and the chalkboard should be erased before the next class.

8. (mm) The students noticed *a tiny frog hopping into the room* from the biology lab.

9. (shift in time) He tells the same joke in every speech, and people *laugh.*

10. (pro ref) I bring pies to potluck parties because *pies* are always appreciated.

11. (p) We don't know if the buses run that late at night.

12. (apos) The *women's* teams have their own trophy case across the hall.

13. (dm) *When I turned twenty-one,* my mom handed me a beer.

14. (ro) Their car wouldn't start; the battery was dead.

15. (cliché) I asked the car salesman about the actual price.

16. (wordy) That restaurant serves terrible food.

17. (pro agr) *All of the people* in the audience raised their *hands.*

18. (frag) *We left* because the lines were long and we couldn't find our friends.

19. (cs) I plan to stay in town for spring break; it's more restful that way.

20. (s/v agr) Each of the kittens *has* white paws. (or *All* of the kittens have white paws.)

WRITING

ORGANIZING IDEAS (P. 229)

Exercise 1   Thesis or Fact?

1. FACT
2. THESIS
3. FACT
4. THESIS
5. THESIS

6. FACT
7. THESIS
8. FACT
9. THESIS
10. THESIS

ADDING TRANSITIONAL EXPRESSIONS (P. 232)

Exercise 2   Adding Transitional Expressions

This year, my family and I decided to celebrate the Fourth of July in a whole new way. *Previously,* we always attended a fireworks show at the sports stadium near our house. The firework shows got better every year; *however,* we were getting tired of the crowds and the noise. *In addition,* we were starting to feel bad about our own lack of creativity. The goal this time was to have each family member think of a craft project, recipe, or game related to the Fourth. The result was a day full of fun activities and good things to eat—all created by us! *First,* my sister Helen taught us to make seltzer rockets from an idea she found on the Internet. We used the fireless "firecrackers" as table decorations until late afternoon when we set them off. *Then,* we ate dinner. Mom and Dad's contribution was "Fourth of July Franks," which were hot dogs topped with ketchup, onions, and a sprinkling of blue-corn chips. For dessert, my brother Leon assembled tall parfaits made with layers of red and blue Jell-O cubes divided by ridges of whipped cream. *Finally,* we played a game of charades in which all of the answers had something to do with the American flag, the Declaration of Independence, Paul Revere's ride, and other such topics. We all enjoyed the Fourth so much that the events will probably become our new tradition.

WRITING ABOUT WHAT YOU READ (PP. 247–248)

Assignment 17   Write a 100-Word Summary

100-Word Summary of "Cat Lovers vs. Dog Lovers"

Certain characteristics make people prefer either cats or dogs as pets. The first is whether people seek solitude or companionship. Cat people like to be alone, and dog people like to be with others. Also, studies show that women prefer cats and men prefer dogs. This division goes back to the cave-dwelling days of our ancestors. Obviously, some people like both animals and have no preference. And most people exhibit catlike and doglike qualities in the ways they behave. So there is really no simple answer to whether a particular person would like a cat or a dog the best.

Index